THE CHILDREN (SCOTLAND) ACT 1995

DEVELOPING POLICY AND LAW FOR SCOTLAND'S CHILDREN

Other Children in Scotland titles:

CHALLENGING RACISM IN THE EARLY YEARS
The role of childcare services in Scotland and Europe
Edited by Annie Gunner

CHILD WELFARE
Reviewing the framework
Edited by E. Kay M. Tisdall

THE CHILDREN ACT REVIEW
A Scottish experience
Edited by Carolyn Martin

CHILDREN'S SERVICES:
SHAPING UP FOR THE MILLENNIUM
Supporting children and families in the UK and Scandinavia
Edited by Bronwen Cohen and Unni Hagen

FATHER FIGURES
Fathers in the families of the 1990s
Edited by Peter Moss

HIV AND CHILDREN
A training manual
Joy Barlow

PROTECTING CHILDREN
Cleveland to Orkney: more lessons to learn?
Edited by Stewart Asquith

A SPECIAL PARTNERSHIP
A practical guide for named persons and parents of children with special educational needs
Linda Kerr, Liz Sutherland and Joyce Wilson

CHILDREN AND HIV
Supporting children and their families
Edited by Sarah Morton amd David Johnson

THE CHILDREN (SCOTLAND) ACT 1995

DEVELOPING POLICY AND LAW FOR SCOTLAND'S CHILDREN

by

E Kay M Tisdall

Foreword by
Maria Fyfe MP

CLANN AN ALBA

working for children and their families

EDINBURGH: THE STATIONERY OFFICE

© The Stationery Office Limited 1997

The Stationery Office Limited
South Gyle Crescent
Edinburgh EH12 9EB

Applications for reproduction should be made to
The Stationery Office Limited

First published 1997

British Library Cataloguing in Publication Data
A catalogue record for this book is available from the British Library

Front cover picture by Patrick McCall, *Highland Dancer*

ISBN 0 11 495788 6

CONTENTS

Acknowledgements vi

Foreword vii

About the author viii

About Children in Scotland viii

Chapter 1 Introduction 1

Chapter 2 Twenty-five years of child care policy 8

Chapter 3 Themes and issues 29

Chapter 4 The Children (Scotland) Bill in Parliament 48

Chapter 5 An analysis of the Act 68

Chapter 6 Comparisons across the UK 98

Chapter 7 Thoughts on the future 129

References 151

Appendix 1 The UN Convention on the Rights of the Child 160

Appendix 2 Summary of the recommendations of the *Review of Scottish Child Care Law* (The Scottish Office 1991) 181

Appendix 3 Orkney Inquiry: Summary 185

Appendix 4 Summary of the provisions of the Children (Scotland) Act 1995 190

Index 193

◆

ACKNOWLEDGEMENTS

Numerous people have been invaluable in the production of this book.

Thanks must go to Children in Scotland and, in particular, to the Information and Publications Manager Annie Gunner, for the organisational support and helpful suggestions throughout the book's development.

Great appreciation is given to the numerous people who provided both detailed and general comments on early drafts of the book: Bronwen Cohen; Rosemary Gallagher, Judge Meier from Milton Keynes County Court; Lorraine Waterhouse; and John Fotheringham. Chris Atkinson, Policy Officer at the NSPCC, provided up-to-date information on the Family Law Act 1996. Members of the Centre for the Child & Society, at the University of Glasgow, patiently waded through various chapters; particular mention must be made of Malcolm Hill, Kathleen Marshall, and Kathleen Murray for their assistance. Irene Bloomfield's suggestions in relation to the child protection diagram in Chapter Five were very useful. The expertise of these people greatly helped in ensuring the accuracy and comprehensibility of the various chapters.

The Centre for Child Care Research at Queen's University Belfast provided valuable information on implementation in Northern Ireland.

This book emerged from the practical work on children's legislation that I undertook as Policy and Research Officer at Children in Scotland and later at the Centre for the Child & Society. It thus brings together discussion, debates and inputs from a wide range of people: from parents, young people, services providers and politicians. The issues raised and ideas put forward in analysing the legislation are in large part the result of this collective and often arduous work, and the contributions of all those who worked for and on the Children (Scotland) Act 1995 should be recognised.

FOREWORD

I got to know Kay Tisdall when she was working as Policy and Research Officer at Children in Scotland. This was a time of hard work and optimism all round.

Hard work because there was a lot to do, both for Government and Opposition and all concerned had to master a great deal of detail and seek advice on the whole range of issues addressed in the Bill. It was the Opposition's job to look critically at the Government's proposals, and bring forward ideas of our own.

Optimism, because at long last, after much delay, numerous reports and reviews, culminating in the White Paper *Scotland's Children*, were being acted on, and there had been no substantial legislation affecting our children since 1968.

Throughout this lengthy process Kay Tisdall showed a comprehensive knowledge and understanding of every aspect, and gave invaluable service to all those organisations who sought to come under the umbrella of Children in Scotland, in making representations to the members of the Standing Committee. I know that, as my job at that time was to lead for the Opposition on the Bill, I relied on her heavily for her expertise.

I am delighted that she has chosen to write what I am sure will be the definitive work on the Children (Scotland) Act 1995, and offer what I can confidently say will be a reliable guide for the many bodies and individuals who will seek information in its pages.

Maria Fyfe MP
Convenor of the Scottish All Party
Parliamentary Group for Children

About the Author

Dr. Kay Tisdall is presently a lecturer in Social Policy at the University of Glasgow, and a member of the Centre for the Child & Society. She undertook her undergraduate degree at Harvard University, and obtained her Ph.D. in Social Policy and Education from the University of Edinburgh. While Policy and Research Officer for Children in Scotland, she worked to establish the Scottish All Party Parliamentary Group for Children and then facilitated (with the Scottish Child Law Centre) the Consortium for the Children (Scotland) Bill.

Her present research and writing interests include UK children's legislation, girls and violent behaviour, and issues for disabled young people. Recent and forthcoming publications include: Hill, M. and Tisdall, K. (Oct. 1997) *Children and Society*. Essex: Longmans and Tisdall, E. K. M. and Plumtree, A. (Autumn 1997) 'A Comparative Look—the Children Act 1989 and the Children (Scotland) Act 1995' *Adoption & Fostering*.

About Children in Scotland

Children in Scotland is the national agency for voluntary, statutory and professional organisations and individuals working with children and their families in Scotland.

It exists to identify and promote the interests of children and their families in Scotland and to ensure that relevant policies, services and other provisions are of the highest possible quality and able to meet the needs of a diverse society. It does this with, through and for its members.

Children in Scotland works in partnership with the National Children's Bureau and Children in Wales.

◆

INTRODUCTION

> The Act is a major new piece of legislation, covering matters of private and public law. At the core of the Act are the rights of children and the responsibilities of adults and public organisations to care for and protect them. (Lord James Douglas-Hamilton, Minister of State: Foreword to *Scotland's Children: A Brief Guide to The Children (Scotland) Act 1995* (Scottish Office 1995a: 4))

An Act for Scotland's children

The Children (Scotland) Act was given Royal Assent on 19 July 1995. It represents the first comprehensive revision of Scottish child care law since the Social Work (Scotland) Act 1968, although important changes in specific areas had been made by legislation such as the Children Act 1975.

The 1995 Act's new terminology and concepts—including parental responsibilities, children's rights, and 'children in need'—have the potential to provide the impetus for substantial changes in practice and to influence more positive attitudes towards children. But the Act is not only about social work services for children. It brings together different areas of law affecting children—family, child care and adoption law—and attempts to rationalise and co-ordinate them. Basic principles are introduced across the three areas of law (although not always comprehensively):

- a child's welfare is paramount
- attention must be given to a child's views subject to the child's age and maturity
- state intervention should be limited unless in the child's best interests
- attention must be given to a child's religious persuasion, racial origin and cultural and linguistic background.

These principles take Scotland a considerable way towards meeting the standards set out in the United Nations Convention on the Rights of the Child, ratified by the UK in 1991.

The Act was introduced at the end of a lengthy review period during which law, policy and practice in relation to children were put under the microscope. It is the culmination of a process of policy consultation and review conducted throughout the 1990s which included the *Review of Scottish Child Care Law* (Scottish Office 1991), the Scottish Law Commission's Family Law Report (1992a), and the White Paper *Scotland's Children* (Social Work Services Group (SWSG 1993a). The numerous child care scandals and critical incidents of the late 1980s and early 1990s created a demand for substantial change, including Lord Clyde's Orkney report (1992), Sheriff Kearney's report on Fife Regional Council's child care policy (1992) and the Social Work Services Inspectorate report on residential child care (1992). Decisions made by the European Court on Human Rights also rang alarm bells among Scotland's policy makers, particularly in relation to the legal assailability of the children's hearing system. As the 1990s progressed, there were strong calls from many quarters that revised children's legislation for Scotland was required.

Scotland was also influenced by revisions in children's legislation elsewhere in the UK. England and Wales came first, with the Children Act passed in 1989 and implemented in 1991. Northern Ireland and Scotland had to wait several years for parallel legislation, and it was not until 1995 that the Children (Northern Ireland (NI)) Order and the Children (Scotland) Act completed the parliamentary process. Their implementation has been swift: Northern Ireland implemented its Order on 4 November 1996 and Scotland has had a phased period of implementation, completed on 1 April 1997.

The three pieces of legislation have many similarities. They all bring together aspects of family, child care and adoption law affecting children: they all attempt to set out basic principles, common to the different settings in which children find themselves; all three have been claimed by the government to enshrine children's rights in law. Common terminology can be found in all the relevant documents, although exact meanings and interpretations may differ. The similarities are such that the experience of each can inform the implementation process of the others.

At the same time, the three pieces of legislation are not exact replicas of each other. The Children Act 1989 and the Children (NI) Order 1995 are perhaps the closest relatives, as many sections of the 1989 Act are repeated verbatim in the NI Order. Nevertheless, Northern Ireland has a different structure for children's services to England and Wales, with amalgamated Health and Social Services Boards and Trusts (discussed below) responsible for child care.

The Children (Scotland) Act 1995, however, is quite distinct from other UK legislation, in part because of Scotland's substantially different laws, procedures and traditions. Since the Act of Union in 1707, Scotland has maintained its separate judicial system, and most public services affecting children—for example, health, education and social work[1]—have been the subject of separate Scottish legislation. In 1968, a children's hearing system was introduced to deal both with children in need of care

---

[1] Services in different areas of the UK can have different names—e.g. 'social work' in Scotland versus 'social services' elsewhere. These differences can be more than terminology: they can exemplify important differences in approaches and practice. While not wanting to diminish the possible implications of these differences, this book will generally use the Scottish terminology unless specifically referring to elsewhere in the UK.

or protection and with children who offend (see Chapter Two), which remains unique in the UK.

A new Act in a time of change

The Children (Scotland) Act 1995 is being implemented at a time of considerable change. Local government reorganisation, undertaken in 1996, has radically altered both the map and the areas of competence of Scotland's local authorities; public awareness of children's rights (the concept itself as well as individual illustrations) has been raised, and a children's rights discourse is beginning to emerge within children's services; and the economic and social circumstances in which children live and grow up have altered dramatically in recent years.

Implementation of the Act at this time represents both a challenge (in that resources are precious and under threat) and an opportunity (for example, to set up new ways of working that better meet the needs of children). Those who are charged with implementing the Act shoulder the responsibility of translating this opportunity into meaningful changes to services.

Local authorities remain central to Scotland's services to children—but they are functioning in a different environment to that of twenty or even ten years ago. Since 1979, policies promoting the rights of consumers, the primacy of the market and importance of competition in public services have been vigorously promoted, and services used by children have been no exception.

For example, the Education (Scotland) Act 1980, as amended, allows parents to choose which school their children will attend (albeit with several limitations). State schools have been encouraged to 'opt out' of local authority control. The Citizen's Charter initiative encompassed, among other 'mini-charters', a Parents' Charter for Scottish education, laying out parents' rights and the standards they can expect (Scottish Office 1995b). While the trend towards 'parent power' has been slower in Scotland than in England and Wales, particularly in relation to self-governing schools, individual schools and parents have been gaining power within the education system while local authorities have been losing it.

Competition has arrived in the National Health Service in the guise of the 'purchaser–provider' split. Scotland's Health Boards are now responsible for assessing community need and, on that basis, planning and purchasing services, while a range of providers (from NHS Trusts to the private sector) compete to provide those services. This separation is intended to ensure that service provision is needs-led, rather than service-led.

A similar concept has been applied to local authorities, through the promotion of 'enabling authorities'. Rather than provide services themselves, local authorities have been encouraged to become 'enablers' and contract out their statutory services. Compulsory competitive tendering (CCT) has been applied to many areas of local authority services, forcing local authorities to consider bids from a diversity of providers. Although CCT has been limited in relation to the majority of children's services, many authorities, either from choice or necessity, contract out at least part of their range of children's services to providers from the private and voluntary sectors. Government policy refers to this as the 'mixed economy of welfare' (Scottish Office 1994a). In children's services, this mixed economy has particularly flourished in the provision of early years services (Scottish Office 1995c).

A major role of health service purchasers and enabling authorities is planning. Housing legislation requires local authorities to review the housing needs of local residents; community care legislation specifically requires local authorities to assess need and construct plans; Health Boards are required to plan services, again on the basis of assessed need and according to targets determined nationally. Faith has increasingly been put into the planning process as a way to ensure effective and co-ordinated services, and the Children (Scotland) Act 1995 applies this process in the shape of children's services plans, required from all local authorities by 1998.

Another concept which has gained favour among policy makers in recent years is decentralisation. The Local Government etc. (Scotland) Act 1994 required all local authorities to prepare decentralisation schemes for their areas, which were to be drafted for consultation by 1 April 1997. The benefits of decentralisation are listed by the Scottish Office in its guidance on decentralisation (1995d), including 'a more flexible, accessible and accountable performance by managers and other employees' and 'enhancing local democracy and accountability'. Further, the 1994 Act firmly supports the continuation of community councils. In terms of specific services, the picture is similar: education budgets have been devolved to individual state schools; GPs have the (financially attractive) option of becoming fundholders, thus controlling their own budget allocation; and local government reorganisation in Wales and in Scotland has resulted in radically smaller local authorities, itself a form of decentralisation.

At the same time, however, many of the responsibilities of local authorities have been moved to the centre (the diminution of local fiscal control for example, through rate-capping and other measures has been clearly evident since the early 1980s) and children's services have not been immune from this trend. For example, responsibility for Reporters to the children's panel was removed by the 1994 Act from local authorities to an independent national service (the Scottish Children's Reporter Administration), under the aegis of a Principal Reporter for Scotland.

The Local Government etc. (Scotland) Act 1994 did far more than require decentralisation plans and nationalise the Children's Reporter system. It changed the two-tier system of Scottish local government (districts and regions) to a system of all-purpose unitary authorities, ending the separation between, for example, housing and recreation services on the one hand and social work and education on the other. Twenty-nine councils were created on mainland Scotland, with the three Island Councils remaining for Orkney, Shetland and the Western Isles. Mainland social work and education services, previously delivered by nine regional authorities, are now the responsibility of considerably smaller units. Powers are provided by the 1994 Act for local authorities to work together in either Joint Boards or Joint Committees.

Welsh local government has gone through a similar process of reorganisation, with the creation of 22 unitary authorities from the previous eight county councils and 37 district councils. England did not have such widespread change, but after a review process single-tier authorities were created in certain areas while others continued with two tiers.

No guidance was provided, either from the Scottish Office or from the Welsh Office, on how children's services should be delivered after local government reorganisation. Williams (1995) reported that, for the most part, traditional structures were generally maintained. Rather than a deliberate choice, many of the Welsh unitary authorities felt so pressurised by the need to ensure service continuity that they did not have the time to prepare well-thought out alternatives. In Scotland, the familiar structure of separate housing, social work and education departments and committees was maintained in many local authorities. Nevertheless, the 1994 Act removed the statutory requirement for all local authorities to have a social work and an education committee and director (although they are required to engage a 'chief social work officer'). With this new structural flexibility, some unitary local authorities combined departments, with several of the new authorities joining together social work and housing. Fife Council has been quite unusual in organising itself around strategies rather than traditional departments. Thus the 'Social Strategy' will largely take on responsibilities created by the Children (Scotland) Act 1995 for local authorities. Councils such as Stirling have established a children's committee amongst their elected members. Further amalgamations and restructuring may occur in other councils as they continue to evolve after local government reorganisation.

Local authorities are now generally much smaller in Wales and Scotland than the Health Boards with which they work, with Health Boards often covering more than one local authority area. Similarly, police boundaries are not coterminous with local authorities, with implications for co-ordination of services.

Northern Ireland has a very different structure for children's services to other parts of UK. The Health and Personal Social Services (Northern Ireland) Order 1972 removed social services from local government and placed them under the control of the NHS. Thus, when health services were reorganised in the late 1980s into a purchaser–provider split, in Northern Ireland it meant that the personal social services were also affected. Health and Social Service Boards are primarily responsible for assessing the health and social care needs in their area and for commissioning services; Health and Social Services Trusts compete with independent and voluntary service providers, and sometimes other Trusts, to provide such services. Since the Social Services (NI) Order 1993, the Department of Health and Social Services has the power to devolve responsibility for statutory services to the new community Trusts. Child care services are therefore purchased and delivered through non-elected administrations, thus escaping a great deal of party politics but at the same time preventing direct accountability to their communities. Neither are education services directly accountable to elected members; they are organised with a strong separation between predominantly Protestant and predominantly Catholic schools. (For further description of Northern Ireland's educational system, see McEwen and Salters 1995 and Osborne et al. 1987.)

Because of these differences in structure, direct comparisons between services and the implementation of children's legislation are difficult to make. From another perspective, however, these differences allow for 'case studies' of different ways to organise services. Health and social services in Wales, Scotland and England are frequently criticised for failing to work together. In Northern Ireland they are part of the same structure. Many of England's councils will maintain a two-tier structure: can the larger councils responsible for education and social services deliver more effective services, and provide a wider range, than smaller unitary local authorities manage to do in Wales or Scotland? Can the smaller unitary authorities in Wales and Scotland adopt a 'corporate' approach? Is co-ordination and co-operation enhanced when all local authority services are the responsibility of one body?

The following chapters

To understand the Children (Scotland) Act 1995, the particular context of Scotland's own traditions, laws and approaches is essential. For example, Scottish policy-makers and professionals have (for the most part) stalwartly defended the welfare approach of the children's hearing system against the onslaught from Westminster of more punitive approaches to young people who offend. In education, even with devolved school management, Scottish local authorities retain far more control over state education than their counterparts in England and Wales. Scottish social work services have long had a preventive approach, based on duties laid down in the 1968 legislation that were never replicated elsewhere in the UK. *Chapter Two* will seek to set the Act within its policy context, beginning with the Social Work (Scotland) Act 1968, covering some of the major reports and inquiries in the 1990s and continuing up to the introduction of the Children (Scotland) Bill into Parliament.

Emerging from these past events and trends are certain themes, which encapsulate many of the debates that took place as the Children (Scotland) Bill was formulated, debated in Parliament and enacted: targeting of services; 'working together' and 'partnership'; children's rights; and 'welfare versus justice'. *Chapter Three* will provide an overview of such themes, consider the policy context of Chapter Two in light of them, and provide more discussion of specific recommendations made.

While Chapters Two and Three provide the policy and thematic context for the Bill, there is also a political dimension that is further described in *Chapter Four*. Chapter Four charts the immense political efforts made to have a Bill introduced into Parliament, an aim finally achieved in 1994, and then follows the political events as the Bill made its way through parliamentary procedures. The chapter considers the Bill's parliamentary process by describing three areas of contention: parents' physical punishment of children; a new child protection order to exclude an alleged abuser; and the introduction of a new category for children's services, 'children in need'.

Chapter Five provides a basic analysis of the Act, considering some of the key changes within the Act in relation to the four themes that so influenced it. *Chapter Six* continues with a comparison between the three new pieces of children's legislation in the UK—the Children Act 1989, the Children (NI) Order 1995, and the 1995 Act—with a particular focus on what Scotland can learn from these other pieces of legislation. The concluding chapter (*Chapter Seven*) will consider some issues for the future of the 1995 Act and its implementation.

This book was written at a time when final guidance on the Act had just emerged from The Scottish Office and when full implementation was imminent. The analysis offered and questions raised herein are thus influenced by that particular moment in time, with an in-depth study of local authority policy and procedures not yet possible.

The book is written from a particular, social policy, perspective. It is not written from a child's perspective, nor from that of a parent. An excellent legal analysis of the Act has been written by Norrie (1996) and specifically on the children's hearing aspect (Norrie 1997), and no attempt will be made to duplicate that here. The book will cover many of the areas less written about in Scotland—that is, Chapter 1 of Part II of the Act, which includes provisions for 'children in need' and children's services plans. Less attention will be given to the private law sections of the Act, not because they are not critically important (they are) but because analysis of them has already been undertaken by experts in the field (Norrie 1996). Further, the areas focused on in this book are those particularly concentrated on by the author when working on the Act as it went through Parliament and after. The book's view on the parliamentary process is inevitably partial: given how recent the legislation is, it would be an indiscreet civil servant who revealed all that went on in The Scottish Office in terms of policy debates. Such a political history will have to wait for some time.

No one can yet know what the Act will mean for children, young people and their families. This in itself suggests the need for consistent and regular monitoring. It suggests the need for the issues addressed and questions asked in this book to be re-visited in the future. Importantly, it suggests that the Act should be monitored and examined from the perspective of *children and families* following implementation.

> Perhaps there should be more opportunities for children to voice their opinions. Maybe adults just aren't letting children have a say. Children should not only have an opportunity to say how they feel about political issues that affect them such as education, the juvenile justice system or the NHS, but in the smaller issues that surround their lives such as the way their local park is set out, the newspapers and magazines that they read or what is on the school dinner menu. After all, children are experts on their lifestyle and in issues that affect them, so why shouldn't they have a say.
> (Julia Press, Steering Group member of Article 12, in Hill and Tisdall 1997. ii–iii).

Chapter 2

◆

TWENTY-FIVE YEARS OF CHILD CARE POLICY

UNTIL the 1995 Act, the Social Work (Scotland) Act 1968 was the foundation of child care legislation in Scotland. Largely based on the Kilbrandon Committee's Report and expanded by a 1966 White Paper, the 1968 Act introduced such key foundations of child care services as the general duty to promote welfare ('Section 12') and the children's hearing system, both unique to Scotland. The Act created unified social work departments within local authorities.

The Children Act 1975 made a range of changes and additions to child care law, particularly in relation to adoption, but it was not until 1988 that a comprehensive review of the Scottish child care system was undertaken, leading to the publication in 1991 of the widely-respected *Review of Scottish Child Care Law* (Scottish Office 1991).

Between 1968 and 1991 pressures, needs and demands on children, their families and the child care system had changed—there was greater awareness of child abuse; increased economic pressures on many families; calls for more punitive approaches to young people who offend; ebbs and flows in the degree of state intervention in families; and growing attention paid to children's rights. Fundamentally, however, the system established in 1968 was maintained and developed, seeking to adjust itself to changing circumstances and demands. The smooth path of policy revision, however, was rocked in the early 1990s by numerous scandals, reports and inquiries that generated far more doubt about the Scottish child care system than had been suggested by the Review.

Perhaps the event that focused public and media attention most harshly on the Scottish child care system was the 'dawn raid' to remove children from their homes in Orkney (27 February 1991). The events in Orkney led to a lengthy and expensive inquiry headed by Lord Clyde, and a large volume replete with recommendations laid before Parliament in 1992 ('Clyde Report' 1992). On the same day that Lord Clyde's Report was submitted to Parliament, Sheriff Kearney's extensive report on Fife child care policies ('Kearney Report' 1992) was also submitted. While the Clyde Report received considerably more media attention, both reports made recommendations with potentially profound effects for the Scottish child care system.

In the early 1990s, a flurry of other reports was published. For example, the Finlayson Report suggested improvements in such areas as training and inspection for Children's Reporters. Two reports on residential care, one from the Social Work Services

Inspectorate (SWSI) (the 'Skinner Report' (SWSI 1992)) and from CoSLA and trade unions (1992), focused attention on the 'Cinderella' service and its deficits.

By the time the White Paper, *Scotland's Children: Proposals for Child Care Policy and Law* (Social Work Services Group (SWSG)), was published in 1993, it reflected not only the recommendations of the child care law review, but also the criticisms of the child care system in the intervening years. In its introduction, the White Paper noted two other documents: the Scottish Law Commission (SLC) report on family law (1992) and the final SWSG consultation on adoption law, issued in June 1993.

This chapter will provide a brief overview of these documents, reflecting on their impact on services for children. The history from Kilbrandon to the 1990s will be less thoroughly detailed, as this has been comprehensively documented and discussed in such sources as Martin et al. (1981), Murray and Hill (1992), and Younghusband (1978). Similarly, discussion of issues of family law before the Scottish Law Commission's Report will be minimal; readers are pointed to the seminal work by Wilkinson and Norrie (1993) for further information. The focus will be on the child care system, and the greater emphasis on the various reports and policy documents emerging from the series of reviews, scandals and inquiries in the 1990s. (See Figure A for the progression of policy documents referred to in this chapter.)

Figure A: Policy 'history' to the Children (Scotland) Act—key documents

Kilbrandon Report (1964)
↓
Social Work and the Community (White Paper) (1966)
↓
Social Work (Scotland) Act 1968
↓
Review of Scottish Child Care Law (1991)
↓
A flurry of reports in the 1990s:

The Report of the Inquiry into the Removal of Children from Orkney in February 1991 (The Clyde Report) (1992)

The Report of the Inquiry in Child Care Policies in Fife (The Fife or Kearney Report) (1992)

Reporters to Children's Panels: Their Role, Function and Accountability (The Finlayson Report) (1992)

Caring for the Future (1992) and *Another Kind of Home* (The Skinner Report) (1992)

Report on Family Law (Scottish Law Commission) (1992)

The Future of Adoption Law in Scotland (Consultation Paper) (1993)
↓
Scotland's Children: Proposals for Child Care Policy and Law (White Paper) (1993)

The Kilbrandon Report: setting the scene for the Social Work (Scotland) Act 1968

In 1961, a Committee under the chairmanship of Lord Kilbrandon was appointed by the Secretary of State for Scotland, with the remit:

> to consider the provisions of the law of Scotland relating to the treatment of juvenile delinquents and juveniles in need of care or protection or beyond parental control and, in particular, the constitution, powers and procedures of the courts dealing with such juveniles, and to report. (Scottish Home and Health Department (SHHD) and Scottish Education Department (SED) 1964: 7)

The Committee's conclusions led to a revolution in the juvenile justice system in Scotland.

Lord Kilbrandon and his Committee were examining a fairly conventional system in the late 1960s. The 1908 Children Act had separated juvenile courts from adult courts: juvenile courts could deal with children in need of care and protection as well as young offenders. Specially constituted juvenile courts had been allowed by the Children and Young Persons (Scotland) Act 1932, with suitably experienced justices. The legal system emphasised rehabilitation rather than punishment for children; the welfare of the child was expressly stated as one of the major considerations for juvenile courts.

The Kilbrandon Committee, however, concluded that the system was not working particularly well. Even though juvenile courts had been allowed for in the 1932 Act, only four had been set up in Scotland. Only 16% of young people who offended went to such courts, with 32% going to sheriff courts, 45% in burgh (police) courts, and 7% in other justice of the peace courts (SHHD and SED 1964). These various courts differed extensively in their procedures, in their decisions and in the resources that they could command (Bruce 1982). Care and protection proceedings were held in the courts, but they were relatively rare. The Committee felt a uniform system was needed. Further, the Committee did not feel that the court system suited the realities for young offenders. For example:

- Most young people pleaded guilty to their offences, so there was little need for the courts to make a judgement on the facts.
- With its concentration on the criminal act itself, a court could not consider the complete welfare of the child and act accordingly.
- The court system was usually unable to work well with parents, with its adversarial process and the limited disposals available.
- In the pleas for mitigation, parents and children were more likely to minimise the criminal act and the possible problems behind it than to have an open discussion.
- The courts were unable to follow up their disposals (unless the young person came before the court in a separate situation), to modify, curtail or extend them as needed for the young person.

Thus the court system was unable truly to take into account the best interests of the child.

The Committee recommended a completely new system for young people. It was based on the assumption that all children appearing before juvenile courts—whether for care or protection, or for offending—were all exhibiting symptoms of the same difficulties:

> the true distinguishing factor, common to all children concerned, is their need for special measures of education and training, the normal up-bringing process having, for whatever reason, fallen short. (SHHD and SED 1964: 13)

The new system had to work closely with parents, because 'the most powerful and direct' (*ibid* 99) positive influences on young people came from their homes. Given the need to work with parents and to 'treat' the child, the Kilbrandon Committee proposed a radical separation of decision-making: decisions on guilt and innocence would remain with the courts but a separate system of 'juvenile panels' would make decisions on care. Only an official called the 'reporter' could refer cases to the panel. Local panels would themselves be made up of volunteer lay people. A 'matching field organisation' would provide care and supervision for the children judged to need it by the panel. Since the process was seen as an educational one, these functions were to be performed by a new social education department set up within the education authority. (For a fuller analysis of the Kilbrandon Report, see Martin et al. 1981.)

The publication of the Kilbrandon Committee's report gave rise to a great deal of comment. Opposition was expressed by some, such as the Sheriffs Substitute Association and the Association of Child Care Officers (Bruce and Spencer 1976; Morris 1974). Overall, however, the Kilbrandon recommendations met with considerable support. The combined forces of those sheriffs who praised the recommendations, the respect felt towards members of the Kilbrandon Committee and particularly Lord Kilbrandon, the commendation within the press and The Scottish Office, all helped to propel the proposed new system forward. Indeed, acceptance of the Kilbrandon proposals became 'an issue for national identity', being heralded as bringing Scotland 'into the mainstream of world penal reform' (reported in Morris 1974: 353).

The Social Work (Scotland) Act 1968

The Kilbrandon Report was published during a time of change. The Labour Party's victory in 1964 brought new Ministers into the Scottish Office, and from that point there grew a more revolutionary change in the system than even Kilbrandon had proposed. The changes to juvenile courts became linked to the unification of personal social services.

At that time, social workers and social work services were dispersed across a range of statutory and voluntary agencies. Few had professional social work qualifications.

A consensus had been growing that common methods, theories and objectives could be found across all social work activities, irrespective of the particular client group. What was needed, according to this consensus, was a co-ordinated system of social work training and services.

When the White Paper *Social Work and the Community* (SED and SHHD 1966) emerged from the Scottish Office, it brought forward Kilbrandon's recommendations with a notable difference. Rather than a social education service situated within the education department, a separate and comprehensive social work department would be created in local government. The new department would not only service the new children's hearing system, but bring together social work services for people of all ages. Voluntary organisations would no longer have the same responsibility to provide social work services; local government would take on a statutory responsibility to provide and co-ordinate them.

The resulting Social Work (Scotland) Act 1968 provided the legislative foundation for social work departments, with the requirement for local authorities to have a social work committee and a director of social work. The new departments were made responsible for 'fieldwork' and a range of services: residential, day and domiciliary care. An important feature of the 1968 Act is the duty in Section 12 (1):

> It shall be the duty of every local authority to promote social welfare by making available advice, guidance and assistance on such a scale as may be appropriate for their area, and in that behalf to make arrangements and to provide or secure provision of such facilities (including the provision or arranging for the provision of residential and other establishments) as they may consider suitable and adequate, and such assistance may be given to, or in respect of, the persons specified in the next following subsection in kind or in cash, subject to subsections (3) and (4) of this section.

The duty is further specified for children in Subsection (2) (a):

> a person, being a child under the age of eighteen, requiring assistance in kind, or in exceptional circumstances in cash, where such assistance appears to the local authority likely to diminish the need—
>
> (i)   to receive him into, or keep him in, care under this Part of this Act, or
>
> (ii) of his being referred to a children's hearing under Part III of this Act.

Social work departments thus had a general duty to provide services to promote social welfare, and a specific requirement to help children unequalled in other UK legislation.

The new system of children's hearings was implemented in April 1971, largely as suggested by the Kilbrandon Committee. As set up by the 1968 Act, the children's hearing system had three key actors: the Children's Panel itself; the social work department; and the Reporter to the Children's Panel. Lay people volunteered to become part of the local authority's children's panel and, if selected by the Secretary of State (having been nominated by an independent committee called the CPAC), received training. The White Paper specifically advocated attracting a wide range of community members to panel membership (and wider than had been suggested by the Kilbrandon Report), to include those 'whose occupations or circumstances have hitherto prevented them from taking a formal part in helping and advising young people' (1966: 20). The social work department of the local authority investigated cases on behalf of the Reporter, and implemented any measures of care imposed on a child by the hearing. The Reporter was a senior local authority officer, with experience in both legal and child care issues. The Reporter was responsible for examining cases brought to his/her attention (referrals), and assessing whether a child was in need of compulsory measures of care and should therefore be brought before a children's hearing.

Any individual or agency could refer a child to the area Reporter. After investigating the referral, with the help of social work and potentially education, health and other agencies, the Reporter could decide:

a) to take no further action;

b) to ask the local authority to advise, guide and assist the child and his/her family on a voluntary basis; or

c) bring the child before a children's hearing.

The third option required that a child must appear to be in need of compulsory measures of care, according to the Reporter, and that there was sufficient evidence for at least one ground of referral. Nine official grounds of referral were established by the 1968 Act. These can be encapsulated into four main types: if the child was alleged to have committed an offence; if the child had been truanting from school; if the child needed 'care and protection', for reasons such as parental neglect or falling into 'bad associations', or at risk of harm in a household; or if the child was 'out of control' of the parent. (In legislation after the 1968 Act, other grounds were added to make a total of twelve.)

A children's hearing was an informal tribunal where three panel members (one of whom acted as chairperson) discussed the background and circumstances of the child referred by the Reporter, with the child and his or her family. Then the hearing made a decision on the compulsory measures of care it considered necessary, if any. Appeals against the grounds of referral or the children's hearing decisions were heard by a Sheriff. All supervision requirements were to be reviewed annually. A review could be recommended by a local authority sooner, or requested by a child or parent at any time as long as three months had passed since the requirement was made.

The maximum age for an initial referral to the hearings system was sixteen but a child could remain within the hearings' jurisdiction until the age of eighteen. Depending on the type of court and proceedings, certain young people between the ages of sixteen and eighteen could be sent to the children's hearings for disposal or the children's hearings could be asked for advice. The Lord Advocate *could* direct the prosecution of any child above the age of eight in court, if the case was serious. These cases generally involved offences against the person and were serious ones such as murder or rape. A court hearing could also be required for young people under sixteen, when offences were committed jointly with adults, as being technically necessary for proof.

The Social Work (Scotland) Act 1968 and its children's hearing system revolutionised child care and juvenile justice in Scotland. While arguably Scotland had been trailing behind England and Wales before 1968 (Martin et al. 1981), the new legislation propelled Scotland into the vanguard of change. In fact, parallel English and Welsh proposals never made it to the statute book, and the two systems diverged substantially. The Scottish system had a strong welfare basis, while the English and Welsh system retained a justice approach further strengthened by later legislation.

Nevertheless, Scotland had to pay attention to legislation from England and Wales, with the implementation of the Children Act 1975 which applied across Great Britain. This Act was seen by some as the apex of state intervention in the family (Fox Harding 1991a). Children's welfare became the first consideration in adoption and care cases. Influential research of the time (e.g. Tizard 1977) suggested that 'permanency' in secure substitute homes (adoptive or foster placements) was better for children than leaving them in deprived homes or seeking to return them later to their natural parents. Reasons to dispense with parental consent for adoption were expanded in the 1975 Act. Even if a child was in 'voluntary' care, parents would have to give notice if they wished to remove their child after the child had been in local authority care throughout the preceding months. Foster parents could apply to adopt the child placed with them after five years.

While the Children Act 1975 made certain important changes to adoption in Scotland, other adoption legislation existed. They were brought together, modified and co-ordinated to form the Adoption (Scotland) Act 1978. An adoption order transferred all parental rights in relation to a child to the adopting parents. A freeing order was introduced in 1984, after being legislated for in Section 18 of the 1978 Act. This order dealt with the natural parents' agreement (or not) in advance of an adoption petition. This issue would then not have to be dealt with in the adoption process. Before an adoption order was granted, the natural parent could seek to revoke a freeing order. When implemented, a major problem with freeing orders was the time delays involved in obtaining them (Lambert 1990).

Scottish local government itself faced considerable upheaval in 1975. Mainland social work departments became part of the new nine regional authorities, often requiring amalgamation of smaller departments and readjustment of roles, procedures and management. While on the mainland regional authorities became responsible for services such as education and social work, fifty-three mainland District Councils were responsible for services such as housing, leisure and recreation. In contrast, there were three all-purpose Island authorities. Such structural changes were another significant step in rationalising and structuring public children's services, but also created divisions between different types of services.

Reviewing children's legislation

While Scotland may have blazed the trail legislatively in the 1960s by revolutionising juvenile justice and social services, it trailed behind in the 1980s. It took events in England to create an impetus for a full-scale review of Scottish child care law. In 1984, the 'Short Report' on children in care was produced by the House of Commons Social Services Committee. While not doubting the good intentions of workers and agencies, it was critical of the lack of resources and skills available to promote children's well-being both in their communities and in local authority care. The report stated that English and Welsh child care law was in desperate need of reform and specifically suggested that child care law be rationalised into a simplified and coherent body of law.

The government responded by establishing an inter-departmental working group and an intensive consultation exercise between July 1984 and September 1985. The group reported with 223 recommendations to clarify, consolidate and improve child care, health and welfare legislation affecting children (Department of Health and Social Security (DHSS) 1985a). In turn, the DHSS produced a White Paper in 1987, entitled *The Law on Child Care and Family Services*. The White Paper based its proposals for a new legislative framework largely on the recommendations of the review.

There were other influences on English and Welsh reform. In 1988, the Law Commission produced its final report on the law relating to children involved in custody, guardianship and wardship proceedings. Research had depicted a condemning picture of current practice in child care, and these findings had been brought together and published by the DHSS in 1985. Court decisions had established various rights of children and parents. For example, *Gillick* v *West Norfolk Health Authority* [1986] AC 112 has established 'Gillick' competency for young people: children under the age of sixteen, who are judged to be of sufficient age and understanding, can consent to medical treatment, without their parents' permission. Decisions by the European Court of Human Rights established parents' rights to access to children in care and that parents should be able to participate in planning and decision making for their children (see Ryan 1994).

The spate of high-profile child abuse cases in the 1980s had a profound effect on child care law reform. The criticisms of social work practice raised in the respective inquiries can be summarised into six areas (Hill 1990):

- the child was not considered as the 'client'
- risk factors were not identified
- assessments of the family had been non-existent or superficial
- work with parents had been poor (difficulty in accessing the family home; social workers had been too ready to believe the best of parents, or had over-identified with them; the concern to provide practical help had obscured the need to keep watch over a child's progress)
- there was poor regard to procedures and law, as well as a need to change both

- there was a failure of inter-agency co-operation.

Yet another inquiry was set up in 1987, in Cleveland, but this inquiry differed in several ways from its predecessors. First, the alleged child abuse was of a sexual nature rather than physical. Secondly, for once not only the actions of social workers but also those of other professionals were considered and criticised. Thirdly, the social workers were not accused of failing to intervene, but of having intervened too much and too forcefully (Hill 1990). The events that resulted in the inquiries, and the inquiries themselves, attracted considerable public attention and created a clamour for change.

Given all this attention to child care in England and Wales, the pressure grew in Scotland for law and practice to be examined. In 1988, the Secretary of State for Scotland established a working group to review child care law:

> to identify, in the light of developments since the implementation of the Social Work (Scotland) Act 1968, options for change and improvement in child care law which would simplify and improve arrangements for protecting children at risk and caring for children and families in need ... (Scottish Office 1991: para. 1.1)

The review group would also assess resource implications for any proposed amendments to law, and report. The review group was firmly focused on public child care law in Scotland, and not on family law or adoption law.

The review group itself was chaired by a civil servant in the SWSG and included social work, legal and research officers from the Scottish Office. An observer from the Scottish Law Commission was present. Various representatives of social work, the children's hearing system and the courts were part of the working group, as well as a solicitor and the Scottish Manager of the British Agencies for Adoption and Fostering. A range of other professionals formed sub-groups working on particular areas. In total, there was a strong predominance of social work and children's hearing experts on the group and no representation directly from education, health, nor children and parents involved in the system.

The review group undertook extensive consultation across Scotland on its recommendations, with well over a hundred replies. When the review group reported (in 1990, publishing in 1991) it contained ninety-five recommendations and costed a 15–16% increase per year in spending if they were implemented. A brief overview of the recommendations is contained in Appendix 2, and further discussion provided in the next chapter.

Even though it provided a wealth of suggestions, the review group clearly felt that incremental rather than radical change was needed:

> Our examination of existing law led us to the conclusion that it was fundamentally sound and met the main needs of children and their families. There was no need for wholesale revision or restructuring. ... there was considerable scope for improvement. The interfaces between various support

agencies need to be clarified and defined to ensure the inter-agency co-operation which is necessary to meet the needs of children and their families who require care or support. Changes require to be made in order to meet social needs and pressures which have emerged or become more pronounced since 1968. (Scottish Office 1991: para. 1.15)

The report itself was not met without criticism. The satisfaction expressed about existing law was not echoed by Scott (1989), who felt that far more needed to be done to rationalise and clarify intersecting legislation. Largely, though, the report was welcomed as an important step towards revised legislation, policy and practice. The report's conclusion, that the law was fundamentally sound, was put to the test by events in the 1990s.

Inquiry into the removal of children from Orkney in February 1991

Press attention to the series of events in South Ronaldsay, Orkney, was ferocious and unrelenting, with aggrieved parents and their supporters heavily criticising the agencies involved and particularly targeting the Orkney Social Work Department (SWD) and one particular social work manager. The resulting public outcry was vociferous, as represented by the thousands of supporting letters and presents sent to the children in question. On the one hand, the events in Orkney were unusual: allegations of 'satanic ritual abuse' were thrown around in the media; the local authority was small, with limited resources; and the community itself was minute, remote and isolated. On the other hand, the events in Orkney were symptomatic of the child care system in Scotland. Orkney raised familiar concerns—for example how to deal with suspected child abuse, how agencies should work together, parental rights, and the balance between welfare and judicial decisions. Although it occured in a remote and small local authority, key people in social work were involved throughout Scotland: civil servants in the SWSG of the Scottish Office, and mainland Reporters and SWDs. Indeed, events in South Ayrshire, where eight children were removed from their families due to allegations of child abuse and the children's hearing system was thus activated, were much influenced by events in Orkney—as were the responses to them (Kelly 1996). The impact of Orkney was felt throughout Scotland.

What actually happened in Orkney? Lord Clyde was given the remit on 20 June 1991 to inquire into the actions of the agencies involved, mainly in relation to the removal of nine children from four families, around 7 a.m. on 27 February. An evaluation of the actual allegations of abuse was specifically excluded from his remit. No evidence was ever heard in court concerning the allegations. Thus no one officially knows the nature of the abuse inflicted on the children, nor indeed whether any abuse occured at all.

A great deal, however, is known about the actions of official agencies leading up to, during, and after the removal of the children. To understand the reasons for the nine children's removal, Lord Clyde considered the removal of seven *other* children from their family in November 1990. Known as the 'W' children in the report, these younger siblings were taken to mainland Scotland under Place of Safety Orders (PSOs) after allegations of inter-sibling sexual abuse by one of the children. Their father was at that time imprisoned for sexually abusing certain of his children. The removal of the W children itself was highlighted in the media, and Mrs W received substantial local support.

The Royal Scottish Society for the Prevention of Cruelty for Children (RSSPCC), a long-standing and respected voluntary organisation, was contracted by Orkney SWD to interview the W children. From joint interviews of the children by a RSSPCC worker and police from the Northern Constabulary, the agencies involved came to believe that organised sexual abuse might be occuring in South Ronaldsay involving not only the W children but also children of other families. Assisted by the police and seconded social workers from Strathclyde and Central Regions, the nine children were removed from their families under Place of Safety Orders (PSO) obtained from a Sheriff. All but two of the resident parents were detained by the police for questioning. Taken to the Scottish mainland, the children were medically examined but 'no positive evidence' was found of sexual abuse.

The children were placed, for the most part separately, with foster carers in Highland and Strathclyde Regions. One exception was the eldest boy, who was placed in a residential school. In less than a month, the children were each interviewed between five and ten times, by RSSPCC workers and the police. Co-ordinators were appointed for each Region.

Meanwhile, on Orkney, the children's hearing system was activated by the PSOs. The Acting Reporter organised a 'business' meeting for the children's hearings, on 1 March, which dispensed with the need for the children to attend (although this decision was not binding on the actual hearings, which took place on 5 March). The hearings considered two different situations: the children's detainment in places of safety, and their grounds of referral. The parents all disputed the grounds of referral, and the hearings granted a warrant to continue detaining the children for twenty-one days. The parents appealed against the warrant but were refused. At the appeal, four curators ad litem (representing the child's best interests in litigation) were appointed for the children from the four families. Further children's hearings were held on 25 March, which continued the warrants to detain the children. Again, the warrants were appealed and a Sheriff confirmed the warrants.

The proof of the referral grounds was heard by Sheriff Kelbie on 3 April. The following day, Sheriff Kelbie held that the proceedings were incompetent and the evidence was never heard. The parents had refused to accept the referral grounds, so when the Acting Reporter filled in the necessary forms, he wrote that the children's hearings were satisfied that the children had not been able to understand the grounds. Sheriff Kelbie held that the grounds would have had to be explained to the children by the chairman at the children's panel for the forms to make that statement—thus children had the right to attend the children's hearing and the hearing should not have dispensed with their presence. Sheriff Kelbie went further, expressing his views on the evidence, how the children had been interviewed, the merits of the applications and the detainment of the children. As all the cases were conjoined, the children were returned home the same day.

The Acting Reporter appealed against Sheriff Kelbie's decision to the Court of Session, and won (*Sloan* v *B* [1991] SLT 530). The Sheriff's decision on incompetency was considered unfounded, and he was firmly criticised for expressing his views on the evidence: '… the sheriff had been in clear breach of the elementary rules of natural justice and had disqualified himself from taking any further part in the proceedings …' (531). While the case was remitted back to the sheriff court however, the Acting Reporter decided not to proceed with the case.

Lord Clyde was highly critical of almost all the professionals involved in the events, finding few of the principal actors beyond criticism (14.110). He found flaws ranging from poor management to improper regard for the law and misguided interviewing methodology. He regretted that the evidence had never been heard, that the professionals had closed their minds to possibilities other than organised sexual abuse, and that parental and children's rights had been insufficiently met. All in all, he listed 194 recommendations at the end of his Report. (For summary of recommendations, see Appendix 3; the recommendations are further discussed in the next chapter.)

Inquiry into child care policies in Fife

While the Orkney Inquiry resulted from a particular series of events affecting a handful of families, the Fife Inquiry was instigated due to broader policy and practical tensions between different agencies in the child care system—tensions that had been brewing for some time in the local authority.

In 1985, a revised policy statement entitled 'Services for Children and Families' was issued by Fife Region's social work department. The document emphasised:

- the importance of keeping families together when this could be done without risk to the children
- the need to investigate all alternatives before removing children from their homes and placing them in local authority care
- proper care planning and maintaining links with children's own homes, due to concerns about children 'drifting' in local authority care
- if residential establishments were used, they should ideally be located in the region
- children should not be removed from home for educational failure or offending unless there were additional factors.

In implementing this policy, social workers who recommended a residential care placement needed to have their reports counter-signed. If a child was in residential care for six months, then a review was to be held to try and find a non-residential alternative. Social workers were encouraged to write reports for the Reporter and Children's Panels that contained information only relevant to the grounds of referral, rather than more global comments. Statistics of children in care dropped drastically in Fife with the implementation of this policy, putting it consistently as the lowest user of such measures within Scottish Office statistics.

While the policy document itself was seen as no more than established good practice, it was the implementation of the policy that created the furore:

> the tendency to over-simplify the approach of the social worker to the intricate and difficult discipline of child care and to impose this simplified approach in a rigid and dogmatic manner which, thus imposed, alienated others involved in child care such as, on the one hand the Children's Panel and the Reporter, parts of the Hearings System and on the other hand, other professionals directly involved in child care … It also gravely inhibited the discretion of the professional social worker who worked directly with the child and was in touch with the child's needs. ('Kearney Report' 1992: 616)

The alienation of other agencies was so strong that Fife Children's Panel made representations to the Social Work Services Group (SWSG), and in response the SWSG sent two advisers to conduct an inquiry. Reporting in 1988, the Advisers concluded that the SWD appeared to be fulfilling its statutory duty to implement children's hearing decisions *but* they had certain recommendations for the department, such as:

- it should examine its internal communications because staff did not accurately know the intention of policy and procedures
- it should more explicitly acknowledge the central role of the children's hearing system, and social workers should provide comprehensive information to the Reporter and children's hearings
- it should take steps to encourage positive use of residential care, and should 'try and test' alternatives before transferring resources from conventional residential care.

The SWD refused to accept these recommendations.

The situation worsened, until a further inquiry was announced in the House of Commons, in March 1989. Unlike the Orkney Inquiry, the Fife Inquiry was held in private and oral evidence itself lasted nearly twenty months (a preliminary hearing on 11 April, then hearings from 8 May 1989 to 24 January 1991). The Fife Inquiry was chaired by Sheriff Kearney, a renowned expert on children's hearings and associated law (see Kearney 1987). When the Kearney Report was published, it was an immense tome of 780 pages and contained numerous recommendations.

Fundamentally, Sheriff Kearney laid the blame on the almost 'religious orthodoxy' (613) in implementing the social work department's policy. He also, however, perceived problems in legal and professional roles. As a result, he made specific recommendations in relation to referring cases to the children's hearings, and (lack of) Children's Panel representation on Fife Council's Social Work Committee, and general recommendations to examine the efficacy and functioning of the children's hearing system, social work training and the accountability of Children's Reporters.

Specific issue reports—Children's Reporters, residential care, adoption—and family law

Reporters to Children's Panels: Their Role, Function and Accountability (1992)

Alan Finlayson, a Children's Reporter himself for 20 years, was commissioned by SWSG to study aspects of the Reporter's job and functions. Begun in September 1990, the report was published in 1992—thus carried out and published in the maelstrom of the Orkney and Fife Inquiries. Many of its recommendations fit into the considerations and suggestions made by those inquiries' reports.

The report began, as would be expected, with a strong message supporting the hearing system. At the same time, Finlayson recognised the need to review the Reporter's role and consider change. Between 1980 and 1989, referrals had increased by a third but, most dramatically, non-offence referrals had grown by 113% (8). This workload on child care and protection had not been predicted by the Kilbrandon Committee, and the system needed to consider its practices and policies in light of this substantial increase. Non-offence grounds tended to create considerably more work—from attending case conferences to framing referral grounds (11).

Not unexpectedly, good collaboration between the professionally-independent Reporter, the local authority and the Children's Panel was recommended (viii; Chapter 3). The particular inability of children's hearings to command educational resources was noted (24).

The training of Reporters was declared 'less than adequate' (ix) and 'haphazard' (38) and Finlayson recommended national certification. Qualifications should be prescribed for Reporters. Reporters' particular difficulties in small local authorities were raised: '… the solitary nature of the post, the independent role, a sense of isolation, problems relating to appropriate deputising arrangements in the absence of the Reporter and lack of practical experience of the complex issues which individual cases may raise' (ix). Finlayson reflected on the proposed reorganisation of Scottish local authorities, which would create even more, smaller local authorities and thus potentially widen the number of Reporters facing these problems (49). Finlayson debated the establishment of a National Reporter's system, but decided against it—for it would endanger the system's principle of being locally based, thus weakening the relationships between Reporters and panel membership, and the local Reporter's influence on local government's support and services (x; Chapter 9). Rather, he advocated an Inspectorate of Reporters, operating as an independent unit within the SWSG (x).

The discretion of the Reporter was an essential part of the welfare approach of children's hearings, focusing on the individual child and the individual situation. But as had been suggested by the Fife Inquiry, the degree of variation in Reporters' practice was a matter of concern. Finlayson recommended that practice be 'quantified, analysed and, where appropriate rationalised' (ix). A generally recognised system and code of practice should be generated for Reporters (45).

Residential care: *Caring for the Future* (CoSLA and Unions 1992), and *Another Kind of Home* ('Skinner Report' (SWSI 1992))

Both these reports were published at the end of 1992, depicting a depressing and critical picture of Scottish residential care. The first of these, *Caring for the Future*, considered aspects of staffing and services associated with providing residential care. The report considered all residential care, including that for children, elderly people and adults with learning difficulties. The Skinner Report concentrated on residential care for children, based on a SWSI inquiry into the provision and quality of such care. These reports added to the growing number of reports across the UK demonstrating considerable problems with residential care (e.g. Department of Health 1992; Howe 1992; Hughes 1985; Levy and Kahan 1991; Utting 1991; Wagner 1988).

Caring for the Future made twenty-six recommendations to improve the qualifications, training and support for residential care staff. Salaries and conditions should be improved for residential care staff, and the existing boundaries between different areas of social work services should be reviewed. *Another Kind of Home* made similar recommendations. The Report was also concerned with selection and recruitment of staff.

Another Kind of Home set out eight fundamental principles for residential care:

(1) individuality and development
(2) children's rights and responsibilities
(3) good basic care
(4) education
(5) health
(6) partnership with parents
(7) child-centred collaboration
(8) a feeling of safety. (21)

When discussing the second principle, the Skinner Report recommended that children in care should be given a statement of rights and responsibilities. The statement would cover the eight fundamental principles and be given to the young people before, or at least on, admission to a residential home. Other recommendations covered advocacy support in complaints procedures and funding for Who Cares? Scotland, the organisation of young people and children with experience of local authority care.

Other rights of children were recognised. For example, children's homes should help young people maintain a sense of their own identity. Children should have security for personal possessions and privacy in telephoning. Staff should be trained in racial awareness. Young people and children should have an opportunity to express their views on their preferred type of placement. If the preference was an informed one, and from an older child, it should be followed if possible.

The separation of 'rights and responsibilities' into a separate principle can be misinterpreted, to see children's rights and responsibilities as *distinct from* the other principles. Complaints procedures, statements of rights and responsibilities, involvement in decisions and advocacy are all children's rights, but so are the rights to health, identity and education. While the inclusivity of children's rights was not spelt out in the Skinner Report, the list of 'what young people should be able to expect' (19) can be seen as enunciating just such a broad view of children's rights in residential care.

The call for improved inter-agency collaboration was made in numerous parts of the Skinner Report. Education and social work departments should review their arrangements for overseeing the educational needs of children. The high rate of children in care who were excluded from school was criticised. Local authorities and Health Boards should ensure liaison arrangements are effective in addressing the health needs of this typically mobile group of children. The Skinner Report recommended that local authorities publish plans on social work services for children and their families, based on agreement between education and social work committees and in consultation with Health Boards and relevant voluntary agencies.

The Scottish Office consultation paper: *The Future of Adoption Law in Scotland* (SWSG 1993b)

The consultation paper was the product of numerous preceding consultations and an inter-departmental working group. Fundamentally, it underlined a shift from perceiving adoption as a service for parents to recognising it as a service for children. Numerous proposals were put forward that promoted key rights for children, for example:

- a child aged twelve or over would be entitled to independent legal representation in adoption proceedings (9.12)
- adoption legislation should recognise the right of a child of any age to express views and have these views taken into account (9.14)
- in children's hearings, a safeguarder should be appointed to represent a child's best interests (4.11)
- time-scales should be tightened, particularly in contested cases, so as to avoid unnecessary time delays (9.13-9.29)
- the *paramount* consideration in adoption should be the child's welfare (e.g. when the court is granting an adoption order (1.13); in all aspects of adoption legislation (1.13)). Consultees were asked whether or not there should be a prescriptive welfare test (1.19).

One exception to the paramountcy of a child's welfare was in dispensing with parental agreement (1.16). Suggestions were made to formalise procedures for gaining parents' consent, to ensure that their rights were met (3.12, 9.3). Advice, counselling and information should be available for birth parents (8.18, 8.29). The court and adoption agencies would need to consider alternative orders to that of adoption (1.13, 1.14). If children were adopted, support must also be available for adopting parents (8.7, 8.26).

Report on Family Law (No. 135) (SLC 1992a)

While controversy raged over child protection and the children's hearing system, the Scottish Law Commission (SLC) was embroiled in its own controversy. Its consultation over family law had considered the abolition of parents' right to administer 'reasonable chastisement' to their children—and the public debate was hot and furious.

Its review of family law, however, went far beyond corporal punishment. Its aim was to create a:

> single, comprehensive Act which would be arranged in a logical coherent way. If this measure were combined with a new consolidation of the law on local authorities' powers and duties in relation to child care the result would be a comprehensive Scottish code of child and family law. (1)

The SLC report recognised the connections between private, family law and public law (e.g., referral to children's hearings (56)). It listed other developments, including the *Review of Scottish Child Care Law*, the Fife and Orkney Inquiries, and the Finlayson and Skinner Reports (134).

In relation to children, the SLC summarised its recommendations as such:

> The Commission believes that Scottish family law could do more than it already does to protect children from parental violence, to stress parental responsibilities rather than parental rights, to stress that both parents normally have a parental role to play in their child's life even if they cannot live together, to respect the reasonable views of children in matters affecting their upbringing, and to remove the last remnants of legal discrimination against the children of unmarried parents. (1992b: 1)

The SLC recommended a specific statement on parental responsibilities. Parents would only have rights in order to fulfil their responsibilities, recognising the centrality of the child and a child's status as a person (rather than, as in the past, as parents' property). Weighing both sides of the issue, the SLC recommended that both natural parents of the child should automatically have parental responsibilities and rights, irrespective of their marriage or not, in the absence of any court order regulating this (14). Marriage was not the relevant criterion when considering children's need and right for both parents. This emphasis on joint parenting was further underlined by the recommended change from 'access' and 'custody' orders to 'contact' and 'residence'. This alteration would underline the continuing responsibilities of both parents, unless specifically altered by the court. Indeed, one of the specified parental responsibilities was to 'maintain personal relations and direct contact with the child on a regular basis' (154), if the child was not living with the parent.

The SLC suggested that any person making a 'major decision' in relation to parental responsibilities, should have due regard to the child's views, 'having regard to the child's age and maturity' (19). Third parties, however, were not bound by this requirement for fear of their rights being prejudiced by a failure of a parent or guardian to consult a child (19). The need to take account of children's views was also featured when considering court orders in relation to parental responsibilities. The SLC concluded that children's views should be taken into account by the court (54).

In its recommendations on children's views, the SLC created a presumption that children over twelve would be of sufficient age and maturity. The use of age twelve was justified as preserving a 'valuable feature of Scottish common law' (18) and as following psychological evidence. The SLC added that the legislation would have to be drafted so as to avoid the impression that the views of children under twelve were never important (19). Whether it was actually possible to avoid this impression remained a question to those unpersuaded. Further, unnecessary orders should be avoided and orders should only be granted if it appeared the most effective way of safeguarding and promoting a child's welfare (51). Court rules should be revised to avoid delay in proceedings (58).

Going to the lengths of conducting a national survey, the SLC comprehensively discussed what the law should do in relation to parents' corporal punishment of children. It recommended, in the end, a clarification of law. If criminal or civil proceedings were brought against a parent striking a child, it should not be justified as exercising a parental right if the child was struck: with an object; or in such a way as to cause or risk causing injury; or as to cause or risk causing pain or discomfort that lasted for more than a very short time (33). Although the media reports often seemed to ignore or misunderstand this point, the SLC *did not* recommend that parents would commit a criminal offence if they smacked their child—unless that smack met the criteria listed above. (See Chapter Four for further details.)

While the status of illegitimacy had very few remaining legal repercussions, the SLC recommended abolishing it as an outdated concept (128). Further, the report made other recommendations directly relating to children in relation to the guardianship of children and the administration of children's property.

The White Paper, *Scotland's Children*: *Proposals for Child Care Policy and Law* (SWSG 1993a)

The chorus recommending revised children's legislation had reached a crescendo by 1993. The numerous inquiries and reports had accumulated over 400 recommendations, many of them suggesting an overhaul of children's legislation considerably more drastic than had been advocated by the child care law review.

The White Paper, *Scotland's Children*, was finally issued by the SWSG in August 1993. The timing meant that many interested parties were not available for immediate comment, as it was the time of Scottish school holidays. With its associations with the Orkney Inquiry, however, the document still garnered press attention and organisations developed their responses.

The White Paper covered a number of areas in child care, ranging from a revised 'general welfare duty' from Section 12 of the Social Work (Scotland) Act 1968, to services for children with and affected by disabilities, child protection and children's hearings. It set out eight principles for child care, which were to be applied to those who may need social work support:

1. Every child should be treated as an individual.
2. Children have the right to express their views about any issues or decisions affecting or worrying them.
3. Every effort should be made to preserve the child's family home and contacts.
4. Parents should normally be responsible for the upbringing and care of their children.
5. Children, whoever they are and wherever they live, have the right to be protected from all forms of abuse, neglect and exploitation.
6. Every child has the right to a positive sense of identity.
7. Any intervention in the life of a child or family should be on formally stated grounds, properly justified, in close consultation with all the relevant parties.
8. Any intervention in the life of a child, including the provision of supportive services, should be based on collaboration between all the relevant agencies. (6–7)

Somewhat confusingly, 'key requirements' were laid out on page 19 of the White Paper, which echoed ideas about 'individuality and development', 'rights and responsibilities' and also specified the particular services of education and health.

While the White Paper mentioned the SLC Report and Adoption Review, it did not include proposals in relation to them. This gap concerned many organisations, who were hoping for co-ordinated family, child care and adoption legislation. The Scottish Office, contacted by the press, insisted that the door was not closed on legislation beyond child care—but the White Paper provided few clues on exactly what such co-ordinated legislation would contain. In fact, the White Paper gave few concrete, specific details on what precisely child care legislation *would* contain. As demonstrated by the promises for the 'general welfare duty' described in the next chapter, the words sounded hopeful but without the precision to be judged fully.

A White Paper is usually a step towards new legislation, and this was expected in Scotland. Events will be picked up again in Chapter Four, which will consider the political process leading up to and following the introduction of the Children (Scotland) Bill into Parliament.

Reflections on twenty-five years

The Kilbrandon Report revolutionised Scottish child care, creating new systems and new approaches setting it firmly apart from elsewhere in the UK. This separate system became a matter of pride for many in Scotland, an issue of national identity. This sense of separateness may have helped its more preventive, welfare-based approach to survive against the onslaught of more punitive and restrictive policies developed in England and Wales. At the same time, English influences have altered Scottish child care—for example, the English child abuse inquiries heightened social work's attention to child protection work (as did Scottish child abuse inquiries, which were not made public), parts of the Children Act 1975 also applied to Scotland, and indeed English reports, research and consultations helped create the pressure for Scottish child care law to be reviewed in 1988.

As the *Review of Scottish Child Care Law* recognised, the lives of children and their families had changed since the 1960s. Philosophies for child care also modified during those decades. The Kilbrandon Report suggested a more interventionist role in families, as well as a more preventive one. In its own way, the Children Act 1975 legislated for a considerable role in state intervention. It represented the legislative peak for the movement towards permanency planning, where concern was expressed for children 'drifting' in care. By the time of the review group's report, this had been somewhat modified by the emphasis of 'partnership with parents' whenever possible. Development of family centres (supporting children in their families), family therapy and day-care for younger children grew in the 1980s, with more or less influence on Scottish child care more generally.

By the time of the review group, the role of social work to support families was emphasised and with it the need for social work's resources to be used as positive support—whether it be residential care or home supervision—for children and their families. Meanwhile, the use of residential schools declined. The need to have regard to a child's wishes and feelings, their rights to complain and to challenge decisions on their care, began to emerge and gain strength. Child abuse and reported failures of services to address it became regular media headlines, and crisis child protection work became an ever-increasing workload both on social work departments and on children's hearings. While the children's hearing system may have been set up largely with the needs of young people who offend in mind, by the time of the review group's report, children's hearings were increasingly dealing with children referred on child protection grounds. Thus, while philosophies had modified over the years, so had the work of professionals within the child care system.

Fundamentally, however, the foundations of the Scottish child care system established by the Kilbrandon Report and the Social Work (Scotland) Act 1968 remained and were supported by review group's report published in 1991. The foundations, however, faced a new shock in the 1990s due to the series of scandals, inquiries and reports which challenged the welfare base of the children's hearing system and threw into disarray the gradualist conclusions of the child care law review.

Media attention focused hard on social work services' handling of child protection; it also feasted on the SLC's consideration of parental physical punishment of children.

After the considerable wait for the White Paper, many were grateful for its arrival and appreciative of certain of its provisions. At the same time, the White Paper was criticised for its vagueness, its narrow focus on child care, and its lack of substantial change. Its failure to incorporate adoption and family law was noticed as a particular gap, as creating a truly 'seamless' system required more than revised pathways. It could be seen as a direct product of the various reports in the 1990s, and perhaps their victim too, as the policy makers were weighed down by their 400-plus recommendations. A lot was resting on the first complete overhaul of children's legislation for over twenty-five years.

Chapter 3

◆

THEMES AND ISSUES

THE previous chapter provided a relatively straightforward view of events in Scottish child care; this chapter seeks to bring out the developing trends and questions that so affected the formation of the Children (Scotland) Act 1995. As alluded to in Chapter One, certain themes have dominated Scotland's services for children and their families for decades. Four will be discussed below: the targeting of services; 'working together' between agencies and between professionals and parents; children's rights; and the 'welfare versus justice' debate. The discussion will bring in the different policies and reports, tracing developments and shifts within these themes over the years.

A general or targeted approach?

Section 12 of the 1968 Act was a much admired difference from legislation in England and Wales (Cooper 1983). It created a *positive* welfare duty, allowing room for truly preventive measures. Indeed, the relevant Scottish Office guidance specifically referred to initiatives to strengthen community resources and networks.

The Social Work (Scotland) Act 1968 may have created the possibility of a positive welfare duty, but implementation was more problematic and less revolutionary. Local authorities found themselves working within limited budgets, and social work departments found that the new children's hearing system created a heavy workload. The considerable call on their services and support required them to prioritise their work. As a result, crisis work tended to take priority and preventive measures were curtailed. Child care was now part of a department required to meet all client groups' needs; thus child care services had to compete with others for scarce resources (Murray and Rowe 1973). However, the possibilities of the 'general welfare duty' could be called upon, and certain initiatives were possible under its banner (see Cooper 1983; Martin et al. 1981).

In the 1990s, the interpretation of Section 12 was put to the test by the inquiry into Fife's child care policy. One contemporaneous book described Fife's policy in this way:

> This policy stressed voluntarism and a move from statutory involvement. The aim of the policy was to reduce the need for families to have their children

taken into care and, where families needed advice or guidance, to organise services in a way which reduced the need for statutory involvement (Ross and Bilson 1989: 137)

Indeed, Subsection (2) specifically required Section 12 services to be directed towards diminishing the need for care or referral to the children's hearings (see Chapter Two). Even when a child was referred to the Reporter, the Fife SWD sought to provide appropriate assistance so as to obviate the need for the Reporter to refer the child to a children's hearing. Sheriff Kearney concluded that such an interpretation did fit Section 12; the problem was the *inappropriate* diversion of children from the hearings (579). For example, certain of the managerial 'gate-keeping measures' (such as 'simplistic' statistical monitoring) limited main grade social workers' discretion (e.g., see 614).

Published while the Fife Inquiry was on-going, the *Review of Scottish Child Care Law* (1991) praised the 1968 Act for encouraging preventive work and seeking to maintain children within their families. The review group felt that law should reflect this more positive promotion of welfare in the 'general welfare duty'. It suggested revising Section 12 of the 1968 Act, so that children under 18 years would be offered assistance that 'appears likely to a local authority to promote the child's or young person's welfare' (rec. 1). The specific 'negative' goals in Section 12 of keeping children out of care or from being referred to a children's hearing should be deleted. Indeed, local authority care and children's hearings should not be considered 'the last resort to be avoided at all costs' (para. 2.2), as Section 12 (2) suggested. Rather, both forms of state intervention and support should be seen as 'positive elements of planning for a child's care' (para. 2.2). Specifically, the review group proposed that respite services should be provided under this new general welfare duty, rather than under 'voluntary care'. This move would underline that respite services were more about supporting children in their families than providing accommodation. The review group hoped that the revised duty would help prevent family breakdown (recognising the rising statistics over past decades) and include children with disabilities (hitherto given no specific place in mainstream child care legislation).

When the *Scotland's Children* White Paper was published in 1993, its proposed changes to Section 12 of the Social Work (Scotland) Act 1968 echoed the recommendations of the child care law review, suggesting a more positive formulation:

> The Government therefore proposes to change this duty towards children, to enable local authorities to assist any child during his childhood or any young person under 18 where this is necessary for his or her welfare. This assistance will be directed to:
> - supporting the care of the child in the community
> - helping to keep families together by providing assistance to the parents or others responsible for looking after the child; and
> - providing advice, services and assistance for rehabilitation after a period in care. (9)

No further details, however, were given. The paragraph concluded by simply stating that the revised duty would be complemented by existing powers to provide services, and that guidance would set out the full range of services. The government's promise merely echoed the child care law review; it added very little that was new, and had few specifics.

The 'scope of services' outlined on page 11 of the White Paper gave another clue as to the government's intentions for targeting. Eight areas were specifically mentioned, ranging from day care for young children to provision for children with disabilities. But, given the mention of universal services such as health and education in the 'key requirements' (19), whether this 'scope' would be inclusive of all children or targeted towards some was unclear.

Some targeting was evident for particular children. For example, the White Paper did not accept the full extent of the child care law review's recommendation on after-care. It suggested a smaller population, promising to extend the local authority duty to children under the age of nineteen who had been in care immediately before school leaving age (and not age twelve, as suggested by the child care law review). Local authorities would have the discretionary power to provide help for those over the age of nineteen, up to the age of twenty-one. The targeting rationale was clearly stated: 'This will have the effect of concentrating services on those who have recently left care, whose problems are greatest (the 16–18 year olds)' (18).

Over twenty-five years, then, the 'general welfare duty' of Section 12 maintained considerable support in principle, but arguably had not fulfilled its preventive potential. By 1993, the rhetoric of prevention was strong in policy circles, but so were the pressures of limited resources and the efficiency discourse of targeting resources on those 'most in need'.

Working together—inter-agency collaboration

Although 'local authorities' was the terminology used in the Social Work (Scotland) Act 1968, this was interpreted to mean the new social work departments. This provided clarity as to which administrative unit would have specific responsibilities, particularly in relation to the considerable powers for child protection. On the other hand, this created an administrative distinction between the different departments in the local authority. The 'matching field organisation' of the children's hearings was *not* part of a local authority's education department, as the Kilbrandon Committee had proposed, but in its own separate department, with its own management, financing, professional ethos and priorities. Co-ordination with, and call on, education resources soon became an issue (Bruce and Spencer 1976; Scott 1975). Co-ordination was also problematic with health, which did not have the same administrative boundaries as local authorities and their social work departments.

By the time of the child care law review, the call for improved inter-agency collaboration had grown loud. The need for it was stated in the review report's introduction, and threaded through numerous sections in its following chapters. Health, education and social work should be required to work together, for children in care or who were subject to compulsory measures of care (para. 10.2). The connections between courts and children's hearings should be strengthened, so that courts should seek advice of children's hearings when an application for parental rights, freeing or adoption is being considered and the child is subject to a supervision requirement (para. 11.11 and Chapter 17). Children's hearings should have access to education resources, and social work and education departments should work more closely to tackle the problem of children who fail to attend school (para. 13.12). Children's needs were not being met when agencies did not work together to make resources available.

Yet the review group felt that its remit rendered it unable to recommend specific duties to bind service agencies outwith children's hearings or social work departments to co-operate or provide services. It did recommend amendment to health and education law (rec. 36). But once again, the boundaries of responsibilities prevented a clear vision of a comprehensive service focused on what children need, rather than one based on the structures of the services themselves.

Inter-agency collaboration was considered so important in the White Paper (1993) that it was required by its eighth principle, and the key requirement for 'child-centred collaboration' on page 19. Specifics were outlined in numerous places about such collaboration. For example:

- education and health to be considered in care reviews (13)
- health or education establishments accommodating children would be required to notify the local social work department about any child who had not had, or was unlikely to have, contact with a parent or guardian for three months (15)
- a code of practice to promote and monitor the welfare of children living away from home, particularly to encourage close liaison between social work, health and education (15)
- government-funded demonstration projects to reduce the risk and incidence of youth homelessness, bringing together social work, housing, employment and social security (18)
- co-operation between social, education, housing, health and financial support for children with disabilities (21)
- co-operation between agencies over child abuse, with specific mention of Child Protection Committees and guidance (23)
- co-operation for children's hearings, e.g. with education services for young people who truant (36), for young people who present 'especial problems' in developing personal self-control (40) and for young people who offend (42).

Education and health dominated the references to inter-agency collaboration within the White Paper, with housing only referred to in relation to young people who were homeless and children with disabilities. Voluntary organisations were mentioned particularly with reference to services for children who offend, children with disabilities and day care, and more generally with reference to financial support from the Scottish Office (40) and children's services plans (46). No comment was made in relation to leisure and recreation, and the police service was mentioned very rarely.

A specific means to facilitate inter-agency co-ordination, at least among the major players, was outlined: children's services plans. Nestled in the White Paper's final chapter, the government would introduce a new duty on local authorities to publish such plans. They would contain:

- a clear appraisal of the strengths and weakness of current services
- an assessment of further needs
- an estimate of likely available resources
- a statement of strategic objectives for service development
- a review of innovative developments. (46)

Consultation would be required with education, housing, health, police, the children's panel and the voluntary sector (46). Given the list of consultees, the responsibility for the plans, and presumably thus their coverage, lay with social work and not the broader 'local authority' initially indicated—for why else would 'social work' be left out of the list to be consulted? Unlike the Skinner Report (SWSI 1992), no specific mention was made that the plans should be jointly agreed by local authorities' Education and Social Work Committees. Consultation would be specifically required with local and national organisations representing children and their families, and information should be provided to children and their families on available services (46).

Over twenty-five years, then, the development of children's services encouraged both specialisation and growth. As a corollary, though, this progress has created problems of collaboration and co-operation. By the 1993 White Paper, the calls for improved inter-agency work had led to both rhetorical exhortations and certain practical recommendations, like children's services plans.

Working together—partnership with parents

Working with parents is a principle established as far back in Scottish child care services as the Kilbrandon Report. The Kilbrandon Committee argued that the new system must work with parents, because they had such influence on children. Further, the Committee clearly set out that the reasons for children's problems were rooted in some lack or failure in a child's upbringing:

> … the true distinguishing factor, common to all the children concerned, is their need for special measures of education and training, the normal up-bringing processes having, for whatever reason, fallen short. (Scottish Home and Health Department (SHHD) and Scottish Education Department (SED) 1964: 13)

Thus, the children's hearings required not only children but parents to be present at a Children's Panel. A strong emphasis was placed on creating an informal atmosphere within the hearings, to facilitate open discussion and consensual decision-making. In early research, parents' reactions to the process and decisions of the hearings seemed positive (e.g. Bruce 1975). Later research (Petch 1988) pointed out that the hearings tended to assume that families, and particularly parents, were a unit; they did not adequately explore the possibility of differences, disagreements and dissension between parents.

Martin *et al* (1981) found a mixture of styles and approaches at children's hearings. At one extreme, they found panel members using sarcasm and sermonising, with family involvement minimal. At the other end, they found children's hearings functioning with empathy, understanding and genuine dialogue. While Martin *et al* were concerned about the negative style of some hearings, they found children and parents much less condemning. Although the children's and parents' comments were not free from criticism, they tended to be positive about their participation:

> There is a sense of having been listened to, a sense of having been allowed to express themselves, a belief that panel members were genuinely interested in the views expressed and were helpful in their intentions. (1981: 270)

Similarly, Erickson's (1982) research with 105 children, referred on offence grounds, found that most children expressed satisfaction with their participation levels.

The powers of local authorities to intervene in families, through their social work departments, expanded vastly under the Social Work (Scotland) Act 1968. Social work staff could ask for Place of Safety Orders (which allowed for children to be removed from their homes) from Sheriffs or Justices of the Peace if children were deemed in urgent need of protection. The children would then have to be referred to the Reporter. Local authorities could assume parental responsibilities through an administrative procedure, with parents offered little opportunity to state their opposition.

In certain situations, there were ambiguities between those who had responsibility for the child. For example:

- Who held parental responsibilities when a children's hearing decided a child should be on 'home supervision'—a compulsory measure of care which the social work department must implement, but where the child remains at home?
- Who had parental responsibility when a child was in 'voluntary care'? Section 15 of the 1968 Act required local authorities to provide accommodation for children, under various criteria, usually with the agreement of children's parents or guardians. The child might be looked after by the local authority, but who had the power to make decisions: local authority staff or the parents?

The child care law review (1991) addressed these issues in considerable detail. For example:

- Parents should be more fully involved in 'voluntary care' (para. 4.7).

- Parents should be kept aware of decisions when a child is under emergency protection (para. 14.17).
- Children's Panels should emphasise more strongly the positive role expected of parents, particularly if the child is on a home supervision requirement (para. 16.2).
- In 'voluntary care', place of safety warrants or supervision requirements, the presumption should be that parents have access to their child unless specified otherwise (rec. 10–12).
- Parents should have the right to attend care reviews, unless local authorities specifically and justifiably excluded them (rec. 20).
- Parents should have the right to see children's hearing reports (rec. 86), an omission which had long been criticised in the children's hearing system.
- Parental rights should only be taken away through a court procedure (rec. 40) (see discussion below).

With some dissension, the review group recommended that parents be recognised as having full parental responsibilities and that a child would not be 'in care' when the child was at home, even if on a supervision requirement (rec. 70); children detained in a place of safety should be in the care of a local authority (rec. 62).

While the Children Act 1975 can be seen as the apex of state intervention, the child care law review had clear messages about working with parents. In the first instance, children should be supported within their families. If children were to be accommodated outwith their families, partnership with parents should be extended as far as in the child's best interests. The responsibilities of parents and local authorities should be clarified, and procedures tightened so as to be clear when parental rights are being taken away. Should parents be dissatisfied, they should have access either to judicial decisions (i.e. to appeal a children's hearing extension of a place of safety warrant) or complaints procedures (rec. 28–30). The review did not address the thorny question of who 'qualified' as a parent. Given increased co-habitation, rather than marriage, the report did not consider the position of unmarried fathers who at that time had no legal right to attend their children's hearings (unless they fell within the definition of 'guardian' under the 1968 Act). Some account was taken of a child's relationships beyond their parents, with concern that relatives would also have contact with children in voluntary care. But the review appeared to reflect little on how the system might need to change to reflect the changing realities of marital patterns and a child's own network of relationships. It was the Scottish Law Commission's report (1992a) that concluded unmarried fathers should *automatically* have full parental responsibilities and therefore rights.

The 1993 White Paper produced 'partnership with parents' as a 'key requirement' on page 19, and backed it up in numerous places within the document. Particular attention was paid to partnership with parents, when the child was in local authority care. Taking on the child care law review's recommendations, contact between parents and child should be encouraged and parents should always have reasonable access (6 and 10). As suggested by both the review and Lord Clyde's Report (17.2), children who are the subject of an emergency child protection order should be in the 'care' of a local authority, but on-going parental responsibilities (unless taken away by the court) should be recognised (26). Again, partnership with parents was raised for children with disabilities (20), stating that 'some children need extra-ordinary care to live ordinary lives with their families' (20). Fundamentally, working with parents was seen as the best way to promote the child's welfare (7). Following the SLC, the White Paper accepted that both parents should normally have a role in their child's life, even if the parents were not living together (3). The concept of 'parental responsibilities' was accepted, specifically recognising the rights of children:

> There is a marked shift away from children being viewed as the property of their parents: parents do not 'own' children. They should be valued as individuals in their own right whose wants and needs must be taken seriously. (5)

The need to work with parents, in order to work effectively with their child, has thus long been accepted in Scottish services. Over the years, the extent to which the state intervened, and how it viewed parents' rights in relation to their children, shifted back and forth. By the 1990s, children were seen as separate individuals from their parents, but also as generally benefiting from having both parents in their lives. Service providers and courts needed to recognise and support parent–child relationships better, it was concluded—as long as this was in the best interests of the child in question.

Children's rights

Even though it was an English case, the Maria Colwell case (Secretary of State for Social Services 1974) had a considerable impact on child protection in Scotland. Maria Colwell had died, at the age of eight, after prolonged ill-treatment by her mother and stepfather. Maria had previously been in care, and then returned by social services and the courts to her mother's home—against Maria's obvious wishes. The reaction was to give the protection of children a higher priority above the maintenance of parents' bonds with their children. Someone was needed, it was decided, to be solely concerned with a child's welfare. In England and Wales, the guardian ad litem system was established by the Children Act 1975: a professional who would represent and report a child's best interests in care proceedings. An equivalent was contained within the Act for Scotland (amending the Social Work (Scotland) Act 1968): a 'safeguarder' (the term later established in rules) could be appointed in cases where a conflict was conceived between a child's and parents' interests. The provision was not implemented in Scotland until 1985.

The creation of a 'safeguarder' was a recognition that, particularly in child protection cases, a family could not necessarily be treated as a unit. Other examples showed a similar recognition. The Children Act 1975 placed regard to children's views on a more official footing for children in local authority care and adoption: due regard had to be given to a child's wishes and feelings. The Adoption (Scotland) Act 1978 established that a 'minor' child (aged twelve for girls and fourteen for boys—changed by the Age of Legal Capacity (Scotland) Act 1991 to twelve for both girls and boys) could consent—or not—to being adopted. The gaps in relation to children's participation, however, were considerable. While parents could ask to place children in 'voluntary care', children had no say in the matter. When local authorities took on parental responsibilities for a child, children had no official right to state their views. Children had no right to state their views if their parents applied for an access order, once the local authority had taken over parental responsibilities. The right of a child to welfare was recognised far more than a child's right to participate.

The United Nations Convention on the Rights of the Child helped to change that imbalance and raise the profile of children's rights more generally. The UN Convention itself identifies three key principles (1):

- all rights guaranteed by the Convention must be available to all children without discrimination of any kind (Article 2)
- the best interests of the child must be a primary consideration in all actions concerning children (Article 3)
- children's views must be considered and taken into account in all matters affecting them subject to their age and maturity (Article 12).

Other articles can be divided into three areas: participation, protection and provision. In total, the Convention brings together fifty-four articles concerning civil, economic, social and cultural rights (see Appendix 1 for the English text of the Convention). Article 1 establishes that a 'child' under the Convention is defined by age: 'every human being below the age of eighteen years', unless a child is considered an adult legally at an earlier age (age of majority). The Convention states in its preamble that children have equal value to adults. At the same time, children also need special safeguards and care. For the sake of their development, children should grow up in a 'family environment' and due account should be given to traditional and cultural values. (For a detailed analysis of the Convention, see Hill and Tisdall 1997 and Veerman 1992.)

Unlike some other countries (such as Belgium), UK ratification of international conventions does not automatically incorporate those conventions into the domestic legal system. The UN Convention thus has no legal force in the UK (the European Convention on Human Rights does apply in the UK, but only if a ruling on a case is obtained from the European Court on Human Rights in Strasbourg; the Labour Party is committed to incorporating the ECHR into domestic law, but not, so far, the UN Convention). The sole 'enforcement' is through the requirement of states to submit regular reports to the UN Committee on the Rights of the Child. The UN Convention has only rhetorical, and not legal, power in the UK. The rhetorical power, though, has been used to galvanise and facilitate new institutions, approaches and practices towards children in the UK.

The child care law review group wrote that it was making a strong commitment to both the European Convention on Human Rights and the UN Convention on the Rights of the Child. Children's welfare was the first principle laid down in the report: a child's best interests should be the primary consideration in child care law (para. 1.13). One of its foundation principles included 'the rights of children to participate in and if necessary challenge decisions related to their care' (para. 1.13). Children aged twelve and over should have the statutory right to attend their care reviews, with requests from younger children considered. Not only should children be given these rights, but they should be prepared for their reviews—thus providing support to the right to attend (rec. 19). The setting of the age of twelve has no justification in the report, and indeed Scott (1989) argued that setting such an age boundary is arbitrary—a matter discussed in the previous chapter.

Following the strong tradition in Scottish law and services, the report made numerous recommendations to meet children's welfare. But it also sought to approach a child's welfare from the child's perspective. So that a child could feel comfortable and able to speak, children's hearings should be able to exclude parents from parts of the hearing (rec. 82). Official attention to children's welfare should be expanded into different locations: if a child had not had parental contact for over three months in health or educational establishments (rec. 6); if a child was accommodated for schooling (rec. 7); increased inspections of independent residential schools on welfare grounds (rec. 8). The role of the safeguarder should be more tightly constructed (rec. 85) and safeguarders should have 'proper training and preparation for their tasks' (para. 20.12). Particular regard was given to avoiding time delays in children's hearings proceedings because: 'A child's perception of time differs significantly from that of an adult …' (para. 15.1). Thus specific time limits were suggested for referrals to children's hearings (rec. 65–66) and adoption/ freeing (rec. 95). Warrants should be rationalised, in part to ensure that they were not misused to detain children for twenty-four weeks (rec. 58). The rights of children from ethnic minorities were specifically mentioned, although due regard to their racial and cultural background should be *supplemental* rather than overriding local authorities' overall welfare duty (rec. 27). The report strongly recommended that a Child Welfare Commission be established, in order to monitor, advise and recommend on children's welfare and rights (rec. 88).

The increased awareness of child abuse and the ever-growing workload as a result of child protection cases led to recommendations acknowledging that families could not necessarily be considered as single units. For example, the report discussed excluding an alleged abuser from the home, rather than necessarily taking away the child (although recognising that the alleged abuser was not always a parent). However, the report concluded that no new legal order to exclude an alleged abuser should be made available, as the alleged abuser had not been found guilty; the only options were to improve private law (where spouses etc. can apply for an exclusion order) and an alleged abuser voluntarily excluding himself/ herself (para. 21.11). The report appeared to hold adults' rights to tenancy and their civil liberties higher than children's welfare and their own rights to their homes.

While the child care law review may have mentioned the United Nations Convention on the Rights of the Child within its introduction, the Clyde Report goes into considerably more detail on its potential impact on child care procedures. For example, revised guidelines on child protection should begin with a clear statement of basic principles. These principles should address not only the rights and duties of parents, but also children's rights (15.60).

Just as the Clyde Report identified numerous gaps in working with parents and considering their rights, it repeatedly criticised failures to meet children's rights. For example, the nine children at the centre of the events in Orkney had not been treated individually. With minds already fixed from the W children's allegations, PSOs were obtained with no explanation of how the criteria might apply to each individual child (5.22). In Fife, Sheriff Kearney found that the individual needs of children were ignored in the requirement on social workers to reduce use of residential care (612). The Fife SWD ignored the value of residential care for some children, at particular ages or stages in their lives.

Lord Clyde felt that further consideration should be given to appointing safeguarders in child protection cases, with a wide-ranging role:

> … including the making of investigations, following the child through the implementation and review of decisions, following up the case to ensure that the child's needs are attended to and reviewed when necessary, securing that the child is informed of the grounds for referral, representing the child at hearings before the Sheriff and later before the Children's Hearing, and advising the child on the child's rights and interests. (17.13)

Such tasks would require further training and particular expertise of safeguarders, and they need not be appointed in every case. The suggestion of a 'Child Advocate', with an even wider and longer-term role, was not accepted by Lord Clyde, at least until the enhanced safeguarders were tried out. Oddly, no clear justification was given in the report for this decision beyond that the safeguarder would mostly fulfil the role of a Child Advocate (17.17).

Lord Clyde saw no tension between the safeguarders' primary mandate to represent the child's best interests, and representing the child's views. Throughout the process, children's views should be considered: 'An express obligation to consult the child where appropriate would assist in securing that the child himself is not overlooked in the process and procedure of the various agencies professing to secure his welfare' (17.7), a comment reminiscent of the Cleveland Report: 'The child is a person and not an object of concern' (Butler-Sloss 1988: 245). The interviewers were generally accused of following their own agendas, thus failing to pursue matters that the children raised (14.87). Lord Clyde also commented on the delicate balance between listening to children's allegations but not accepting them blindly:

> The allegation is not to be put lightly aside. That the person making the allegation is a child is not to be taken to detract from the attention to be paid to it. It is to be taken as seriously as an allegation made by an adult. But it still requires to be scrutinised, assessed and evaluated. (13.20)

While parents and children should ideally both consent to interviews, 'at the least an informed consent' should be obtained where possible from the child (17.51). Such attention to children's views requires considerable respect for children and their wishes.

The Clyde Report recommended specific changes in the system, to protect the children's welfare. Certain recommendation were similar to those of the child care law review: for example, the parents' right to be present throughout children's hearings should be qualified when the child's interests require their exclusion (18.32). In other ways, Lord Clyde went further than the review, such as his recommendation that serious consideration should be given to a new power of the Sheriff to exclude a suspected abuser from contact with the child (15.51). The child's own ability to act should be further advertised both to professionals and children themselves: a child could self-refer to the Reporter or take refuge in a place of safety (16.8). The press should be further restrained in attending and reporting on children's hearings (18.35–18.38). While outwith the remit of the inquiry, the legalisation of 'safe refuges' for children should be considered (17.33).

Sheriff Kearney's report outlined a potential conflict between rights completely unacknowledged in the UN Convention itself: what if one child's rights appear to conflict with other children's rights? He wrote of the potential tension between social work and education, where social work works with individual children—and usually those that are 'problems' for education—while educationalists have responsibilities both for individual children and children as a group (600). No suggestions, however, were made as to the resolution of such conflicts.

Just like previous policy documents, the White Paper in 1993 relied heavily on the UN Convention in its introduction. The White Paper attributed its eight principles largely to the Convention, and indeed the Convention's influence can be seen within them. Children's views were highlighted in numerous places, from the Secretary of State's foreword, 'I am keenly aware of the need to listen to children', to The Scottish Office's own attention to children's views in formulating the White Paper (4), and the handling of residential care complaints (43). In fact, the last words of the final chapter are 'the right of the child to be heard' (47).

Attention to the child was strengthened by promises about children's hearings—although most were provisional or vague. For example, the power to appoint safeguarders would be 'emphasised' (33) and the child care law review's suggestions followed in relation to safeguarders' reports. In making an emergency Child Protection Order (CPO), a Sheriff could appoint a safeguarder for the child (25). The Scottish Office would further consider whether parents could be excluded from children's hearings in order for the child to speak his or her views, whether children (and parents) could receive reports, and whether hearings could prevent distraction and interruptions by third parties (33).

Two requests from children were accepted: a new order to exclude an alleged abuser, and 'safe refuges'. As discussed above, the child care law review had decided *not* to recommend a court order to exclude an alleged abuser. Lord Clyde had drawn attention to such a new order but had not gone as far as firmly recommending it. The White Paper did. The new order would be one option among child protection measures, and would be available on application to a Sheriff. (27) The allowance for 'safe refuges' was a reaction to evidence gathered by ChildLine Scotland, Scottish research (SCAFA 1990) and young people themselves. Legislation would be amended so that people and places who took in a child who had run away, for example, would not be guilty of 'harbouring' (28).

Welfare versus justice

One of the government's reservations about the UN Convention related to children's rights to legal representation. Article 39 (d) of the Convention states that:

> Every child who is deprived of his or her liberty shall have the right to prompt access to legal and other appropriate assistance, as well as the right to challenge the legality of the deprivation of his or her liberty before a court or other competent, independent and impartial authority.

The government reserved its right to continue the practice of the Scottish children's hearing system, where a child could not be legally represented within an actual children's hearing (although they could have legal advice prior to a hearing and appeal against a hearing's decision to the court).

The government justified its reservation thus: 'Children's hearings have proved over the years to be a very effective way of dealing with the problems of children in a less formal, non–adversarial manner'. With the aim of encouraging the children and parents to speak for themselves, it was feared legal representation would lead to the lawyers speaking (rather than the family members), a greater formality in the proceedings (making family members hesitant to speak), and a more adversarial process (e.g. see Bruce and Spencer 1976). A child and/or parent could bring along a 'supporter' who could be a lawyer, but the person would not function as a legal representative and the legal representative would have no right to attend the hearing. No legal aid would be available for the lawyer to attend the hearing.

Concerns had been raised early on in the life of the children's hearings about whether children's and parents' procedural rights were being met. Even though strongly supporting the hearing system, Martin *et al* (1981) themselves expressed concern that not all hearings were following the established procedures, and thus failed to uphold children's and parents' rights. Panel members were often hesitant to discuss sensitive issues with families, such as child abuse. Children and parents needed to be told clearly their rights to dispute the grounds of referral, their rights to appeal, and the reasons for their hearing's decision.

The debates go beyond questions for children who offend. Children's hearings also deal with children in need of care and protection, and the balances between welfare and 'due process' have been central to the intense scrutiny of child protection procedures in the 1990s. In Scotland, courts have long been able to grant emergency orders to local authorities to remove children from their parents, and these have been a focus for lively debates about 'due process' and controls on the welfare discretion of social workers. The administrative procedure by which local authorities gained parental responsibilities did not follow legal standards that would be required by court procedures: that is, the right of 'defendants' to put their case, to have legal representation, or to receive legal aid if needed. Parents could object by sending a 'counter-notice' to local authorities, and the case could eventually be brought to court. But the system could be difficult for the parents to negotiate. The child care law review recommended strongly that parental rights orders be removed from local authority discretion:

> The court is a more appropriate forum for decision-making on parental rights, exposing the local authority's grounds to rigorous and impartial legal assessment and giving parents the right to object at the time should they wish to exercise it. (para. 11.4)

Parental rights—for example, to access their child in care—were to be stated explicitly in law. Regulations should be made by the Secretary of State on care reviews (rec. 22). Full grounds of referral should be made at a children's hearing, following a place of safety warrant (rec. 56). Parents needed to have these in order to make an appeal to the Sheriff. With this tightening of procedures, the discretionary element around decisions based on a child's welfare was circumscribed. The child's welfare would still remain primary, but intervention would have to be justified more carefully and certain processes followed.

The welfare basis of Scottish child care, however, was to be kept. For example, the review group left no room for doubt of its support for the children's hearings system:

> One of our guiding principles in undertaking this review has been that the operation of the children's hearing system on the whole is successful and that any proposals for reform should build upon that success. (page 27)

The review group considered the procedures for emergency protection, and felt that the balance between orders, warrants, the children's hearings and recourse to the courts did meet justice requirements (para. 14.2). The review group noted the rights of appeal against the decision of a children's hearings as satisfactory safeguards to the parents' and child's rights to a judicial hearing (para. 20.7). The balance between welfare and justice might need some slight readjustment, with time-limits set on place of safety orders (rec. 55), and timing of Children's Panels (rec. 57), but the balance was seen as essentially fair.

Lord Clyde did not agree with the conclusions of the review group. The discretionary scope of PSOs was too wide (16.2). PSOs should only be given if children face a 'real, urgent and immediate risk' of suffering 'significant harm' (16.5). The Orders should only be enforceable for three days (16.33), and should be obtained from a Sheriff or Justice of the Peace (JP). The Sheriff should take on more of the discretionary decisions on children's welfare, with the power to attach specific orders in relation to medical examinations and access or contact. The whole processing of the revised emergency orders (Child Protection Orders) should be removed from the children's hearings to the judicial setting (18.21). At every decision point, parents/guardians, children and safeguarders should be able to apply for recall or variance of the order (16.28 and 18.20).

Lord Clyde was quick to affirm the continuing support for the children's hearing system, making a distinction between emergency CPO procedures and the longer-term decisions on welfare in relation to compulsory measures of care (18.45). Given the sensitivity of those involved in the children's hearing system, however, and the considerable changes recommended in remit and procedure, unsurprisingly Lord Clyde's recommendations on these points gave rise to considerable debate. Lord Clyde appeared to be dissolving the traditional separation between decisions on welfare (hearings) and decisions on fact (courts), to make another distinction between short-term and long-term decisions on welfare. Short-term welfare decisions on emergency child protection would also largely be in the courts' jurisdiction. The children's hearings would retain their power over longer-term decisions.

The recommendations appeared to counter the firm support of the system voiced by Lord Hope in the Court of Session appeal:

> The genius of this reform [the establishment of the system], which has earned it so much praise which the misfortunes of this case should not be allowed in any way to diminish, was that the responsibility for the consideration of the measures to be applied was to lie with what was essentially a lay body while disputed questions of fact as to the allegations made were to be resolved by the sheriff sitting in chambers as a court of law. (*Sloan* v *B* [1991] SLT 530 at 548)

Sheriff Kearney repeated this quotation of Lord Hope's in the Fife Report, and indeed wrote of the legal system's perception of the children's hearing system: 'More generally we believe that the Children's Panel on the one hand and the Reporter on the other hand because their concerns are principally with children may sometimes be regarded as less significant in our legal system than they might be' (625). At points such as these, it would have been useful for Lord Clyde and Sheriff Kearney to have commented on each other's reports.

Lord Clyde dwelt on the tension between the public interest in criminal prosecution and children's welfare. The separation of the children, their frequent interviewing and their isolation, were largely justified by the need to gather evidence (14.18). Lord Clyde had no question that the child's interests must come first:

> In some cases a prosecution may be in the best interests of the child. In others the continuation of a criminal investigation, let alone the insistence on a prosecution, may be damaging, to the child and in those cases the public interest in securing a conviction must give way to the paramount interest of the child. (15.52)

Given the children's traumatic experience of being removed from home, agencies should have considered other alternatives and had a sounder basis for their decision. Not only children's welfare had been risked, but also the rights of families and parents as outlined in the European Convention on Human Rights (16.1–3).

The shifts between welfare and justice can be seen from three directions within Lord Clyde's report. One, the familiar tension between courts and children's hearings was played out, with the final recommendation that emergency child protection be removed from the children's hearings' remit. Two, the welfare discretion of professionals was re-balanced, towards more judicial discretion over welfare decisions (e.g. access, medical examinations, appeals) and a considerable tightening of legal and policy requirements (e.g. removal of children only in emergencies). Parents' and children's rights needed to be given more regard, and the judiciary was one way to ensure this. Children's welfare still had to be protected—the judiciary would simply have increased concern with it. Three, *less* judicial involvement, on the other hand, might be required with reference to criminal prosecution. Children's welfare was the paramount consideration, above the need to gather evidence.

Sheriff Kearney's report addresses the first two of these directions, but from different viewpoints, and thus he arrived at different conclusions. One, that children's hearings should take on more responsibilities, as suggested by the child care law review. Children's hearings should be able to consider the long-term care of children, and not just SWDs and courts (598). Even though the Kearney Report considered child protection referrals to the hearings, no suggestion was made that the hearings were unable to deal with them. Two, welfare discretion of main grade social workers was to be *encouraged*, not diminished:

> Of course the social worker's discretion is not absolute. Social workers must work within various limitations including those of general and particular policies and they are affected by the available resources. But the consideration that such limitations exist must not take away from the essential duty of the social worker to remain alert to the needs and wishes of the individual child in the individual situation and to the most appropriate means of being able effectively to address these needs. (613)

The Kearney Report was criticising not legal constraints, but internal bureaucratic and management ones. Still, its avowal of social work *welfare* discretion can be seen as substantially different to the Clyde Report's recommendations for greater policy and judicial control. To what extent was this difference caused by the nature of the inquiries: Sheriff Kearney's remit to consider policy, which he did through examples of cases, versus Lord Clyde's remit to consider individual cases to evaluate policy?

The legacy of Lord Clyde's report can be clearly seen in the 1993 White Paper. At the beginning, the Secretary of State wrote: 'The White Paper sets out proposals for improving legal procedures to safeguard the rights of children and families, particularly in situations where emergency action is being considered'. The seventh principle clearly defined the 'default option' as children living with their families, only to be interrupted on 'formally stated grounds' (7). Child protection orders would be taken on the basis of 'significant harm', and not a child's welfare (25)—considerable grounds had to be established before a local authority could so intervene.

An elaborate procedure was set out in the White Paper addressing the relationship between emergency child protection and the children's hearings (29). While the constant provision for appeal, recall or variation by parents and children clearly reflected the Clyde Report, the White Paper did not go so far as to remove emergency child protection completely from the children's hearings. The new CPOs would replace PSOs, still to be applied for to a Sheriff, but to last only for three days if unimplemented. If a CPO was obtained from a JP, it would have to be confirmed by a Sheriff within twenty-four hours. Children's hearings would have to consider the CPO within at least two 'working days', with a full consideration of grounds of referral within eight 'working days'. Further time limits were laid down in relation to subsequent hearings and appeals (26–27). The process was complex indeed, and the initial reaction of those involved in the system was critical of children potentially being caught up in complicated parallel processes of appeals and children's hearings.

The court would be given the discretionary powers to grant ancillary orders, specifying and regulating examinations, interviews, access, communication and disclosure of a child's whereabouts, as had been suggested by Lord Clyde. The White Paper specifically recognised that this would take on matters 'presently largely governed by local authority practices' (26). Areas of welfare discretion would thus be removed from social work and taken on by the courts.

The discretion of a local authority to take on parental responsibilities was also removed, and placed with the courts (4), a move advocated for in the child care law review and widely accepted amongst professionals. The response was less sure about the proposal for short-term Child Assessment Orders. Only local authorities could apply for these orders to a sheriff, which would only be granted for up to seven days (28). The response was emphatically critical to the White Paper's approach to the children's hearings. The White Paper clearly set out to reassure, with more than a page praising the system. For example:

> The children's hearing system has a vital and continuing part to play at the centre of child care in Scotland. It has shown itself to be soundly based and at

the same time capable of adapting to major changes. It has won the confidence and support of judges, lawyers, social workers and other services as a sensitive and practical way of dealing with children's problems with the law. (30–31)

What particularly alarmed advocates of the children's hearing system was the structure of the White Paper. Recommendations were spread across Chapters Five to Seven: The Protection of Children; Children's Hearings and the Reporter; and Children and Young People in Trouble. Was child protection being hived off from the children's hearings, as suggested by Lord Clyde? Was the punitive approach to children who offend spreading to Scotland from England, so that a basic principle of children's hearings ('needs and not deeds') would be threatened?

Beyond the changes in child protection, little was new. By the time the White Paper was published, the government's intention to centralise the Reporter system was known (33)—with mixed reception by professionals and against the Finlayson Report's recommendation (1992). The tightening of Reporters' qualifications, training and policy/procedures had already been much advocated. The Kearney Report's recommendations for greater panel involvement in local authority decision-making and knowledge of local resources was a familiar suggestion (31). The children's hearings would continue to deal with young people over sixteen, under particular circumstances, but with the promise of additional resources and training to help meet these older children's needs. Where did the White Paper lie between the Clyde and Kearney Reports? Somewhere in between, with evidence of greater judicial scrutiny and decision-making but less than had been recommended by the Clyde Report.

Reflections on twenty-five years

While particular issues generated considerable attention at specific times, the tensions between protecting rights and promoting welfare has a long history in Scottish law and services. The distinction set up between the 'welfare' children's hearings and the 'justice' courts provides a structural focus for these debates (see Allen 1996; Campbell 1977; Martin et al. 1981; Morris and Giller 1987). In practice, pragmatic compromises are made between the 'welfare' and 'justice' approaches. The children's hearing system includes numerous aspects of 'due process'; court proceedings for children who offend still tend to have some regard to children's welfare. For the practitioner, the 'best' solution can be to try and bring the two sides closer together (King and Piper 1990). The Scottish system can be seen as making various balances and re-balances between 'welfare' and 'justice' considerations.

As children's hearings took on more and more responsibility for child protection decisions, these tensions took on a new focus in policy documents, inquiries and media attention. The European Court of Human Rights and the UN Convention on the Rights of the Child provided outside impetus to reconsider these issues. In the end, the White Paper advocated keeping the fundamentals of the welfare–justice divide in the children's hearing system, but recommended the addition of numerous checks and balances in structures and specified rights.

The rights of children had become part of the legislative and practice discourse by the 1990s. While Scotland had long worked with the concept of children's welfare in family, child care and adoption legislation, children's right to participate was increasingly recognised formally in law and in policy.

Another addition to the discourse around children's services was the need to be 'child-centred'. As children's services grew and developed, so did the number of professionals and agencies that could be involved in the lives of children and their families. Children could either find themselves overwhelmed by professionals and confused by the plethora of service criteria and provision, or lost 'through the cracks' of the often fragmented array. By the 1990s, virtually every policy document on children's services contained more than one recommendation to improve inter-agency collaboration. Better collaboration could ensure services actually met the needs of children and their families.

Scottish child care services have a strong history and adherence to the 'general welfare duty' which had always promised the possibility of preventive rather than crisis-driven services. While the promise of Section 12 has perhaps never been fully realised, in the 1980s and 1990s Scottish child care services were becoming overwhelmed by the pressures of emergency child protection. The need to shift towards prevention was constantly advocated in the child care literature, but social work services found themselves constrained by funds, by encouragement to 'target' services on those most in need, and harsh media attacks on their handling of individual child abuse cases. The transition to a more 'preventive' approach was hampered by the very real needs of children in desperate situations and the developed structures and practices of child care services.

Chapter 4

◆

THE CHILDREN (SCOTLAND) BILL IN PARLIAMENT

THE policy history to the Children (Scotland) Bill can be looked at from two perspectives: first, what can be euphemistically called the 'paper trail' and second, the 'political trail'. The last two chapters addressed the paper trail: the long path of documents beginning with the 1968 legislation and culminating in the publication of the Bill on 24 November 1994. This chapter will explore the political trail, examining some of the political events that led to the final introduction of the Bill into Parliament. The examination will go further, following the Children (Scotland) Bill's progress through Parliament.

'The political trail' to the Children (Scotland) Bill

Several starting points can be identified in the political history of the Bill. In one sense, it could begin as far back as the immense political will and organisation of Scottish politicians, peers and influential policy makers, which pushed the Social Work (Scotland) Act 1968 through Westminster while proposals for the English and Welsh equivalent floundered and died. It could also begin with the concern of influential local authority staff and representatives, opinion-makers and politicians about the scandals and inquiries in the 1980s and 1990s affecting child care services. But for this description, the trail will start at the Children Act 1989 for England and Wales.

New children's legislation for England and Wales was introduced into Parliament in 1988, and made law in 1989. It brought together aspects of family and child care law that affected children, with certain amendments to adoption legislation. The Children Act 1989 contained some sections that applied to Scotland: namely, those relating to day care (registration and inspection of childminders, and day care reviews). The Children Act 1989 was implemented in 1991, with twelve volumes (including two introductory ones) of detailed Department of Health guidance, a clear monitoring strategy with an intensive and extensive research programme, monitoring committees and annual reports to Parliament.

While the government had not yet ratified the UN Convention on the Rights of the Child while the Children Bill was going through Parliament, the Convention was used extensively in Parliamentary arguments and key children's rights were established in the Bill. When the government came to write its first report to the UN Committee on implementation of the Convention, it claimed that the Children Act 1989 was the key legislation that put children's rights into policy (UK Government 1994). When the Lord Chancellor introduced the Children Bill into the House of Lords in 1988, he described it grandly as: 'the most comprehensive and far reaching reform in child care law which has come before Parliament in living memory' (Hansard 6.12.88, Co. 488). Service providers and others involved in Scottish and Northern Irish children's services began to ask: where was *their* new and improved children's legislation?

When the Children Act 1989 was going through Parliament, a cross-party group of MPs and Peers worked together to improve the Bill—the UK All Party Parliamentary Group (APPG) for Children. Encouraged by the International Year of the Child (1979), Baroness Faithfull had established the UK APPG to draw attention to children's issues in Parliament. Baroness Faithfull herself had been a Director of Social Services before accepting her peerage.

APPGs are relatively informal groupings, which can obtain official standing through registering in Westminster. APPGs differ widely in their composition, their funding, their activities, and their effectiveness. The foundational concept of these groups is the collaboration of backbench parliamentarians of different parties, on a particular issue.

While APPGs are officially composed of parliamentarians, they are often originally conceived by, lobbied for and serviced by outside organisations. So, for example, the APPG on Parenting Matters was established in 1994, instigated by a voluntary agency. Part of the considerable influence and activity of the APPG on Penal Affairs is attributed to the diligent servicing of the group by NACRO (National Association for the Care and Resettlement of Offenders). Certain APPGs are well-funded by industry or charitable sources; others function on small budgets gathered from parliamentarians' donations.

Funding, commitment and servicing of the group have considerable impact on the extent of an APPG's activities. Most APPGs flourish when key legislation is contemplated or going through Parliament. The legislation provides a focus for the group's work, and a means to co-ordinate an all-party response on amendments. Certain APPGs have regular meetings, and themselves produce various reports and briefings. Others are moribund.

The effectiveness of APPGs can depend on several factors. As they are relatively loose coalitions, the leadership of the APPGs is critical. For example, Baroness Faithfull was held in considerable esteem in the House of Lords as someone who knew about children's social services. She put considerable effort into the UK APPG, encouraging key Peers to join and become regular members, and to organise the activities of the APPG. The reality of APPGs is that, while the official membership can be quite large, their effectiveness is usually reliant on a core group of motivated, active parliamentarians.

The impact of an APPG on issues is greatly influenced by its composition. The UK APPG for Children benefited from Baroness Faithfull sitting on the government's benches in the House of Lords. APPGs that are predominantly made up of opposition members lack the same impact on government thinking and policy. APPGs have greater influence if they are perceived as all-party groupings, rather than of one party alone (particularly if the party is the main opposition). Certain APPGs are seen as predominantly filled with Peers, while others are more closely aligned with the House of Commons. When parliamentarians overcome some of the traditional rivalries between the Houses, an APPG is likely to be more effective.

For an outside body, APPGs provide a means to communicate with politicians with particular interests, and to develop a concerted approach to policy issues. Parliament can be an opaque bureaucracy to those who are not part of it, and APPGs can provide vital information and contacts. Politicians have access to the media, to official and unofficial government channels, to which many outside agencies may not.

As the wait for Scottish children's legislation lengthened, the idea was generated to create a Scottish APPG for Children. While the UK APPG for Children contained Scottish members and had shown interest in Scottish children's services, a solely Scottish group could concentrate on the large range of issues for children and families in Scotland. Children in Scotland, the national agency for organisations and individuals working with children and their families, took on the role of recruiting politicians to establish such a group, prompted by the unique nature of Scottish legislation and services for children, and the imminent need for revision. The Scottish APPG was formed, with the dual leadership of Dr Norman Godman, MP (Labour) and Lady Saltoun (Cross-Bench). This was a deliberate move to encourage members of both Houses to join the group. The all-party nature of the group was further encouraged by the election of Vice-Convenor MPs, Margaret Ewing (Scottish Nationalist Party (SNP)), George Kynoch (Conservative), and Jim Wallace (Liberal Democrat). Initial funding of the group was provided by certain members of Children in Scotland providing some seed money and offering other supporting services. The Scottish APPG was officially established in July 1993 and embarked upon a series of meetings, beginning with consideration of *The Future of Adoption Law in Scotland* (June 1993), responding to the White Paper *Scotland's Children*, and meeting with young people from Who Cares? Scotland. The Scottish APPG was preparing for a Scottish children's bill.

Local government reorganisation, however, was given priority over a children's bill in the 1993-94 Parliamentary year. At the time, the government was faced with the difficulty of having only eight Scottish Conservative backbenchers available to sit on the committees that give detailed consideration of Bills. While the government could substitute non-Scottish MPs to sit on such committees, a public outcry would result if they were too numerous. This small number of backbenchers thus created something of a bottle-neck, and this was a strong reason why the government limited the introduction of Scottish Bills during a Parliamentary session.

The Scottish APPG used the Local Government (Scotland) Bill to raise the profile of Scottish children's legislation. Amendments were put forward in both Houses, which sought to elicit commitments from the government to introduce legislation in the next parliamentary session. Amendments were also put down that dealt with substantive concerns for children's services in the Bill (e.g. for specialised services) but, as expected in such a highly politicised area as local government reorganisation, these were not incorporated into legislation. But in some ways, the Local Government (Scotland) Bill enabled children's agencies in Scotland to become familiar with the parliamentary process, and provided time for the Scottish APPG to consolidate.

The large upheaval that would be caused by Scottish local government reorganisation provided a dilemma for those calling for Scottish children's legislation. On the one hand, early legislation would find local authorities still struggling to adapt to their new structures and boundaries. On the other hand, child care legislation had not been substantially updated since 1968. The numerous inquiries, reports and papers had generated over 400 recommendations. If these were not acted upon, they would quickly become out-dated. If the opportunity was not taken to introduce children's legislation in 1994–95 there was no guarantee that another opening would be available in following years. On balance, the membership of Children in Scotland and the Scottish APPG decided, children's legislation needed to be introduced.

Even though a year had passed since the *Scotland's Children* White Paper, a place in the 1994–95 parliamentary calendar was still at risk. The Scottish APPG identified the need to lobby the government, and set up a meeting with Lord Fraser of Carmyllie (then Minister for the Scottish Home and Health Department) in May 1994. Attended by the APPG convenors and other key members, the group put forward its case for the introduction and comprehensive content of the legislation.

The groundwork had already been established for this meeting, as Scottish Office civil servants had been openly kept abreast of the APPG's briefings and in fact had sent representatives regularly to its meetings. Lord Fraser clearly himself wanted children's legislation to be put forward in the next parliamentary year: the Scottish APPG was strengthening his hand. The meeting added some important pieces to the political jigsaw. First, Lord Fraser was debating the potential range of the Bill, indicating the possibility of more limited legislation than had been covered in the Children Act 1989 for England and Wales. Secondly, he was also angling for a strong statement of all-party support for such legislation, so as to use the new Scottish procedures.

Through the 'Taking Stock' procedures outlined in 1993 (Scottish Office 1993), the government had sought to deflect the forces for Scottish devolution and independence by offering new mechanisms within existing parliamentary procedures. The Scottish Grand Committee had been dusted off, and would be composed of all Scottish MPs, have the power to meet in places other than Westminster, and to call in Ministers who were not Scottish MPs. The Scottish Grand Committee would have regular debates and could hold the first real discussions on new Bills (called the 'second reading'). The 'Taking Stock' procedures also allowed for the formation of a 'Special

Standing Committee', which could take written and oral evidence on a Bill. Further, when a Scottish Bill reached the House of Lords, the detailed look at the Bill could be held 'off the floor of the House', in a committee located elsewhere in the House of Lords.

Lord Fraser's questions to the Scottish APPG suggested that the government was looking for a popular piece of legislation to be the 'guinea pig' for the new procedures. This would require all-party consensus, particularly as the Labour Party had an immense majority in the Scottish Grand Committee and could possibly disrupt the whole procedure if they sought to vote against the Government in a debate. A Children (Scotland) Bill, backed by an all-party consensus for such legislation, could provide a successful means to inaugurate the new procedures.

The prospects of a Bill were looking more favourable, but Lord Fraser could make no commitment to saving a place in the new parliamentary year. Other Scottish Bills were jockeying for position, and a *Scotsman* story on 1 July 1994 suggested that a Criminal Justice Bill would be introduced in 1994–95—with no mention of Scottish children's legislation.

The reaction of children's agencies in Scotland was firm and swift. A letter to the press was co-ordinated between fourteen children's organisations in Scotland, declaring: 'It is, in our view, unthinkable that space should not be made within the coming parliamentary session'. *The Scotsman* decided to run with this reaction as its lead story (MacAskill, 7.7.94). The ensuing public response was substantial. In the next few weeks, more letters were written to the newspapers and further articles published. Public attention had been drawn to the risk that children's legislation might once more be ignored by the parliamentary agenda.

As the announcement of the new legislative schedule neared, the fate of the legislation still was unknown. No guarantee had been given that legislation would be introduced. Rumours abounded. What is generally thought to have tipped the balance was the failure of the government to gain support for Post Office privatisation. As such, a gap appeared on the parliamentary schedule, just before the Queen's Speech. Time could be found for a Scottish children's bill.

When the Queen spoke on 16 November, no mention was made of Scottish children's legislation. Not until the (then) Prime Minister, John Major, made his speech to Parliament later that afternoon, was Scottish children's legislation officially announced. Finally, the promise had been made that Scotland would have its new, revised children's legislation.

The parliamentary process

The late inclusion of the Children (Scotland) Bill in the parliamentary schedule had a considerable disadvantage. Until the Bill had a definite place, it was not drafted. The Children (Scotland) Bill that was first laid before the House on 24 November 1994 was thus a quickly drafted document and, although a commendable effort in a short time, was filled with technical inaccuracies and conceptual difficulties. While undoubtedly welcome by almost all throughout Scotland, clearly many of the provisions within the Bill were problematic and incomplete.

A deal had been struck between the Scottish parliamentary parties (largely made possible by members of the Scottish APPG) to use the new Scottish procedures for the Children (Scotland) Bill (see Figure B for stages and dates of the process). Thus, the 'second reading' debate on the Bill took place in the Scottish Grand Committee on 5 December. Lobbied for by the Scottish APPG and others, a Special Standing Committee was organised. Anyone had the opportunity to write in their views to the Committee, and the Committee itself asked certain individuals and groups to give oral evidence and answer questions over three days. The Committee was headed by William McKelvey, MP, and mostly contained MPs who later served on the Committee that gave line-by-line consideration to the Bill. When the Bill was debated in the House of Lords, the Committee Stage was taken off 'the floor of the House', and detailed consideration given in the nearby Moses Room.

For those uninitiated to the Westminster parliamentary process, it can be both confusing and inaccessible. The jargon of different parliamentary procedures abounds, key opportunities to influence and inform debates are hard to identify, and the timetable is subject to change and vagueness. In fact, dates are often not set until the last moment, and people are often reliant on word of mouth for arrangements (even MPs and civil servants). Information, such as new amendments, is vital but yet often very expensive and hard to access unless parliamentarians or civil servants provide it. Despite the important of this stage in policy making, the voices of those perhaps most affected by the legislation—children, their families and service providers—can be the least heard in the parliamentary process.

Recognising this difficulty, a Consortium for the Children (Scotland) Bill was formed on 18 November 1994. Jointly facilitated by Children in Scotland and the Scottish Child Law Centre, the Consortium set its remit on its first meeting: to seek the most effective legislation for Scotland's children and their families. The Consortium grew to over fifty organisations, including statutory, professional and voluntary organisations. The Consortium sought to bring the views of children and families to the notice of the policy makers through (a) its members that worked directly with children and families; (b) its members who represented children and/ or families; (c) young people and parents attending Consortium meetings; and (d) seeking to facilitate communication between children and their families, and the press and parliamentarians. The Consortium worked closely with the Scottish APPG, whose core members were active in all stages of the parliamentary process. By the end of the Parliamentary stages, the Consortium had developed over a hundred amendments put forward by Parliamentarians, had innumerable meetings with MPs, Peers, and civil servants, and provided detailed commentary on the Bill's provisions.

What happened to the Bill as it went through Parliament? The interactions between process and outcome are perhaps best illuminated by looking at examples of particular

Figure B: The Parliamentary process for the Children (Scotland) Bill

House of Commons

First Reading	Bill became available	24th November 1994
Second Reading	First Parliamentary debate on the Bill, which could discuss both what the Bill did and did not contain Occurred in Scottish Grand Committee	5th December 1994 (Edinburgh)
Special Standing Committee	Small number of MPs considered written and oral evidence	Oral evidence taken on: 6th February 1995 (Glasgow) and 13th February 1995 (Edinburgh)
Still called the Special Standing Committee, the Committee Stage of the Bill	Small number of MPs considered the Bill line by line These MPs could put forward amendments for the first time, and vote on them	8 Sittings, usually on Tuesdays and Thursdays: 21st February 1995-13th March 1995
Report Stage/ Third Reading	Revised Bill available Although technically separate stages, these were taken on the same day Taken 'on the floor' of the House of Commons, so all MPs could have contributed to debates and voted	1st May 1995

House of Lords

First Reading	Revised Bill was available	3rd May 1995
Second Reading	First House of Lords debate on the Bill Taken 'on the floor' of the House of Lords	9th May 1995
Committee of the Whole House off the Floor of the House	All Lords could attend the Committee, for line by line consideration of the Act First opportunity for Lords to put forward amendments and vote on them Held in Moses Room, 'off the floor' of the House of Lords	3 Sessions: 6th June 1995-13th June 1995
Report Stage	Another opportunity for Lords to put forward amendments and vote on them Taken 'on the floor' of the House of Lords	5th July 1995
Third Reading	Another opportunity for Lords to put forward amendments and vote on them Taken 'on the floor' of the House	12th July 1995

House of Commons

	Consideration of Lords' amendments	19th July 1995

Royal Assent

	HM the Queen signs Bill (required for Bill to become law)	19th July 1995

provisions. Three are considered below which, from the Consortium's viewpoint, can be seen as examples of 'successes', 'failures' or 'promises'.

A 'success': the exclusion of alleged abusers order

One of the more dramatic 'successes' in the parliamentary process was the inclusion and modification of a new type of child protection order: the exclusion of an alleged abuser order.

As mentioned in Chapter Three, Lord Clyde suggested the further consideration of such an order in his report on the Orkney Inquiry. The White Paper, *Scotland's Children*, had taken up this recommendation, proposing an exclusion order as one option amongst child protection procedures. In a consultation on the White Paper, young people had expressed their anguish at being taken out of their homes for emergency protection:

> Just when you need your Mum most you get taken away.
>
> Why bother if this is what happens?
>
> The rest of your life stops too—my school trip was cancelled. (SWSG 1994: 11)

While support was growing in Scotland, previous meetings with the Scottish APPG had already indicated the controversial nature of this provision. Certain key MPs and Peers were very concerned about the civil liberties of the alleged abuser, who at the stage of exclusion would have not been found guilty of a crime.

Realising that this issue was likely to be difficult in Parliament, the British Association of Social Workers in Scotland had agreed to service a working group on this issue. The membership of the group included a range of agencies, including ChildLine Scotland and Who Cares? Scotland to ensure that the views of young people were considered. The group produced a booklet outlining the principles supporting the exclusion order and key elements that should be included in any proposal. The booklet was widely distributed to Scottish MPs and Peers. Fortunately, the Scottish Labour Party officially decided to support the provision in principle.

When the Bill was introduced into Parliament, it contained provision for an exclusion of an alleged abusers order, largely based on matrimonial home provisions (domestic violence orders). However, Consortium members realised that an emergency order would not be possible under the provisions. A minimum of forty-eight hours would be required between an application and the granting of such an order, due to provisions for the alleged abuser to be heard or represented before the Sheriff. While clearly protecting the civil liberties of the alleged abuser, this time gap was directly contrary to one of the main purposes of the exclusion order—to prevent children from being removed from their homes, whenever possible, so as to prevent the trauma of being taken away from support and familiar surroundings. If a child was judged to be at risk of imminent 'significant harm', concern for the child's safety would necessitate removing the child for at least those forty-eight hours.

This need for an emergency exclusion order was raised by several MPs at the first major debate on the Children (Scotland) Bill, in its Second Reading Debate. The next stage, however, was arguably the most critical for the order's development—written and oral evidence. The Consortium here was able to help build a consensus around the need for an emergency order. The Consortium submitted its own evidence and gave oral evidence, based on the collective views of its members. Numerous Consortium members also chose to submit their own evidence. Thus MPs received a chorus of support for an emergency order. Even more influential was the oral evidence given by young people, which had considerable impact on the MPs. Young people from Who Cares? Scotland firmly supported the need for an emergency order, as one option amongst child protection procedures. As one young man said: 'It doesn't matter if it's 2 days or 2 weeks. If young people are the victims of abuse, we are the victims to start off with and it feels as if we are getting the blame for being abused' (Hansard 6.2.95, Col. 49).

Several MPs thus took on the emergency exclusion order as an important issue, which resulted in considerable support in the next stage of the Bill—the detailed consideration in the Committee Stage of the House of Commons. Here, Jim Wallace (Liberal Democrat) and Maria Fyfe (Labour) both put their names to a range of amendments drafted by the Consortium.

The Consortium had gathered that a major barrier to the emergency order was the government's concern that it would contravene the European Convention on Human Rights—particularly Article 6 (1) requiring a 'fair and public hearing'. Thus the Consortium decided to obtain a Counsel's Opinion on whether provision for an emergency order would be against Article 6. The Opinion was submitted just in time for the debate on the emergency order in Committee, and was given to all participating MPs and the civil servants. The Opinion was not a clarion call for change, but still sided on the legality of an emergency interim order:

> I am of the view that such a provision may not fall foul of the terms of the [European] Convention. I have come to this view with some hesitation, particularly because of the draconian nature of the proposal for the person excluded and because of the extreme importance of an individual being given the opportunity to be heard or make representations. (Moir 1995)

It also appeared that certain influential civil servants were themselves seeking to work out a functional emergency order. At the Committee Stage, Lord James Douglas-Hamilton (leading for the Bill in the Commons) said the Government would consider the provision.

At Report Stage, Jim Wallace put down a shortened amendment for an exclusion order. His speech was well-informed and persuasive, bringing out all the salient points. Other MPs spoke in support. Finally, Lord James Douglas-Hamilton stood up and announced that the government had accepted the need for an emergency order in principle, but had not had time to work out the details of such a provision. Amendments would be introduced at a further stage.

While the result in the House of Commons was positive, the House of Lords' stages remained. Several Peers were still antagonistic to the exclusion order in principle, let alone the addition of an emergency order. The Consortium worked to try and change their minds, but was not surprised to hear some Peers criticising such provisions in the House of Lords' Second Reading Debate. At Committee Stage, the government introduced amendments for an emergency provision as promised. The debate on the exclusion order, however, hardly attacked the need for such a provision (certain major opponents being silenced due to other events)—instead only advocating more positive change to make the orders more effective. The battle for an emergency order was thus won, and the Bill proceeded to become law with these provisions included.

In certain senses, the 'success' was a minor one. The exclusion order, even if used to its best advantage, is unlikely to be used often as there will be salient concerns for a child's safety if he or she remains at home. Problems remain in the legislative phrasing and criteria (see Chapter Five). On the other hand, the number of matrimonial homes orders have increased in recent years, as the judiciary becomes more comfortable with them and they have often proved workable and useful.

Importantly, the exclusion order represents a vital recognition of children's rights in two ways. First, the order provides some re-balancing between the rights of children and those of adults. A child's right to the familiarity, comfort and advantages of their own home, networks and environment is supported, which will not always be supplanted by adults' rights in relation to civil liberties. When a conflict occurs between the rights of an adult and the rights of a child, the child's rights may sometimes prevail. Second, young people's right to have their views given 'due regard in all matters affecting them' (Article 12 of the UN Convention) was operationalised over this particular provision. The views of the Who Cares? young people, when meeting and giving evidence to MPs, was possibly the most influential in persuading several MPs to fight for an emergency exclusion order. Children's views made a difference.

A 'failure': restriction of parents' corporal punishment of children

When the Scottish Law Commission (SLC) published its Family Law Report in 1992, it recommended changes in the law concerning parents' corporal punishment of children (see Chapter Two). While Section 12 of the Children and Young Persons (Scotland) Act 1937 prohibits physical punishment by adults of children, it provides the following exception in subsection (7):

> Nothing in this section shall be construed as affecting the right of the parent, teacher, or other person having the lawful control or charge of a child or young person to administer punishment to him.

This exception has been substantially curtailed for teachers in state schools by amendment of education law in 1986 (in a large part due to an adverse ruling from the European Court on Human Rights), and for those who have the 'lawful control or charge of a child' (e.g. residential care workers) by local authority policies. Parents retain their right to punish their children, unless the punishment is considered 'unreasonable' by the court.

The SLC's suggested changes would not have banned corporal punishment—despite the media's (incorrect) revival of the 'smacking debate' (i.e. whether parents should be allowed to 'smack' children). The SLC recommended a further restriction of a parent's defence, if accused of assaulting a child (1992a: 156):

> In any proceedings (whether criminal or civil) against a person for striking a child, it should not be a defense for the person to establish that he or she struck the child in the purported exercise of any parental right if he or she struck the child—
> (a) with a stick, belt or other object of whatever description; or
> (b) in such a way as to cause, or to risk causing—
>   (i) injury; or
>   (ii) pain or discomfort lasting more than a very short time.

To test the distinctions between different types of physical punishment, the SLC had commissioned a public opinion survey in 1991. Interviewees were asked to consider the differences between smacking with an open hand and hitting with a belt, stick or other object, for children of different ages. The survey found support for smacking a child, but not for hitting children with an object (e.g. only 3% thought it should be lawful for a parent to hit a three-year-old with an object). The SLC felt this was quite conclusive support for the above restriction.

In the White Paper, *Scotland's Children*, the government had remained silent on the issue of parents' corporal punishment. When the Children (Scotland) Bill was introduced into Parliament, it too lacked any provision paralleling the SLC's recommendation.

Consortium members decided early on to prioritise this issue. After considerable debate, the Consortium as a group decided to lobby for the SLC proposal to be included in the Bill. Several members would have preferred an outright ban of corporal punishment, but the SLC proposal was thought to have a better chance of success—due to the high status of the SLC, its careful analysis of and consultation on the issue, and the relatively conservative objective of the proposal. Furthermore, an attempt had been made when the Children Act 1989 was going through Parliament to ban corporal punishment, and it had been unsuccessful. Children 1st (formerly the Royal Scottish Society for the Prevention of Cruelty to Children) offered to take the lead for the Consortium on this matter.

From the first debate in the Scottish Grand Committee, the Scottish Labour Party decried the absence of the SLC proposal. In her closing speech for Labour, Maria Fyfe MP criticised:

The Government should not dodge the issue of lawful and unlawful methods of corporal punishment. The law should be worded clearly. That may be difficult to achieve, but we should not avoid our responsibility: we have the Bill before us at long last and we should attempt to address that problem. (Hansard 5.12.94, Col. 45)

During evidence-taking, several organisations underlined the need for the SLC proposal, including the Association of Directors of Social Work, the Consortium and the SLC itself. While Norman Godman, MP (Labour), expressed his concern for the limited change of the SLC proposal, two Conservative backbenchers thought the SLC proposal would go too far. For example, Bill Walker, MP, provided this scenario at the Special Standing Committee:

On Friday in London, I saw a mother with a child, a pram, a toddler and an umbrella. She tried to stop the toddler from going off the pavement and on to the road by using the umbrella. I fear that that could result in a prosecution if a nasty person... (Hansard 6.2.95, Col. 23)

Kathleen Marshall, one of those giving evidence for the Consortium, did not accept Bill Walker's scenario: 'I do not see how that example could conceivably be seen as physical punishment. That mother was simply restraining the child from running on to the road—she was not punishing the child' (Hansard 6.2.95, Col. 24). Even at this early stage of the Parliamentary process, common arguments for and against the SLC proposal were outlined (see SLC 1992a for summary of arguments).

The Association of Directors of Social Work (ADSW) constructed a new clause to ban physical punishment of children 'looked after' or provided with day care, which was put forward by Maria Fyfe at the House of Commons' Committee Stage. Five other MPs on the Committee has also put their name to the new clause: a large number, but they were all Labour MPs. Given the atmosphere of the Committee, this display of Labour opposition made it unlikely that the new clause would succeed. Lord James Douglas-Hamilton, leading for the government in the House of Commons on the Bill, saw little need for the new clause in relation to residential care: the prohibition was already contained in residential care regulations. For day care, Lord James saw no reason to take away a parent's right to authorise day care providers to use physical punishment (as had been allowed for by a court case in England).

The calm progress of the debate soon broke down. Phil Gallie, MP (Conservative), interjected with an expression of his disregard for Labour MPs' support for the amendment: 'I ask my Hon. Friend the Minister to close his ear to the claptrap we have just heard ...' (Hansard 14.3.95, Col. 624). When Maria Fyfe moved to withdraw the amendment, MPs such as Phil Gallie refused: an unusual move, but one which prevented the amendment being resubmitted at a later (and hopefully more favourable) stage in the Bill's progress. The amendment was voted down by the Committee.

With this taste of the fight to come, Children 1st, on behalf of the Consortium, sought to mobilise the maximum amount of support for the SLC proposal in the next stage of the Bill: the Report Stage. Unlike Committee Stage, new clauses are argued *first* at Report Stage, which gives greater likelihood of a full, well-attended debate. While the new clause still only listed Labour supporters, other opposition parties were purposefully enlisted in support. George Robertson MP (Labour, then Shadow Secretary of State), introduced the new clause to the House, enumerating the numerous arguments for the SLC proposal: e.g. that 'much child abuse was corporal punishment gone wrong', the Government's obligations under the UN Convention and the European Convention on Human Rights, and the respected SLC Report itself.

Phil Gallie was not impressed by such arguments. He saw the amendment as a conspiracy against parental rights, and looked favourably on Singapore, 'where the use of corporal punishment has wiped out crime' (Hansard 1.5.96, Col. 57). Margaret Ewing, MP (SNP) was disdainful of these views, saying:

> Needless to say, I do not want to pursue many of the points that he [P. Gallie] raised, as the arguments that he deployed were similar to those advanced on issues such as the abolition of slavery, about slavery being good for slaves, who would not be able to cope with freedom; or how it was good to keep pushing young boys up chimneys because it gave them employment. (Hansard 1.5.96, Col. 58)

Beyond the drama of the debate, the details of the SLC proposal were also questioned. Would hitting a child with a pencil be a criminal act? Was the proposal still likely to be confusing to parents? What would constitute a 'very short time' in the suggested new clause?

In the Government's reply, Lord James Douglas-Hamilton stated four central reasons against the clause: it was unenforceable; it missed the legal point (saying that the law required 'evil intent' for a crime to have been committed); it lacked objectivity; and it limited the court's power to take into account all the facts. Before a Consortium representative could find an MP to contest this last point by Lord James, the new clause had gone to the vote. MPs who had heard nothing of the debates rushed through the corridors to vote. The results were a foregone conclusion: 193 supporting the new clause, and 260 against. The votes were neatly divided amongst party lines— opposition parties voting for the new clause, and Conservatives against.

Unlike the exclusion order, the House of Lords had always looked more hopeful to the Consortium than the House of Commons, for the SLC provision. An active group of Peers had been working to ban corporal punishment for years, and Children 1st was able to tap into this well-briefed and dedicated coalition. Further, this group included Peers from outside Scotland. This provided the slight possibility of mobilising more attention and even the remote possibility of a vote against the government. Attention to the Children (Scotland) Bill had been difficult to gain generally from non-Scottish Peers (with the notable exception of Baroness Faithfull). Even when those like Baroness Faithfull were active, they would be politely hesitant as non-

Scots. But the SLC proposal might just be the issue that could provide some fireworks in the House of Lords.

Unfortunately, at the time the Peers had been warned not to risk the Bill. Rumours abounded that the Conservative majority might fall in the House of Commons. If the House of Lords sent the Bill back to the House of Commons, which the Commons would not accept, a to-and-fro between the Houses could result. If the government fell, and an election was called, the Bill could be caught un-enacted. Several Peers warned the Consortium not to push too hard. Certainly, such tactical concerns made it less likely that Peers would vote against the government.

As always, the greatest hope for an amendment was to persuade the government to accept it rather than to rely on a vote. While previous debates had considerably dimmed this hope, Lord Fraser would be leading on the Bill in the House of Lords. The Bill was the responsibility of Lord Fraser, and further he was a lawyer, likely to be influenced by the legal arguments of the SLC. Perhaps the Government would rethink its position?

When the SLC proposal was put forward at Committee Stage in the House of Lords, full all-party representation was behind it. Lord Henderson of Brompton led strongly on the amendment, with Baroness Faithfull rising to support it. At that point, however, the concerted approach was breached. Lord Macaulay of Bragar, who was leading on the Bill for the Labour Party, spoke out against the vagueness of the proposal. Lord Fraser agreed with Lord Macaulay, and Lord Henderson withdrew the amendment.

Lord Macaulay's attack on the proposal was a surprise to many, as George Robertson himself had led on the amendment in the House of Commons. By the time a revised amendment was put forward in the Report Stage in the House of Commons, Lord Macaulay felt able to support it.

The fate of the SLC proposal was finally sealed by Lord Hope's disapproval. Lord Hope was held in high regard for his legal knowledge, as the then Lord President and Lord Justice General. He had made his maiden speech in the House of Lords at the Second Reading of the Bill, and clearly chose his interventions carefully to concentrate on legal issues. So when Lord Hope said that the courts did not find it difficult to detect cases where 'abusive forms of severe punishment were used' (Hansard 5.7.95, Col. 10), the proposal had little chance. Indeed, when the vote was taken, it was 128 against and 87 for the amendment. The battle had been lost.

The corporal punishment issue demonstrates the tactical decisions involved in parliamentary work, which in this case were ultimately unsuccessful. The biggest chances of success were already lost when the government failed to replicate the SLC proposal in the White Paper and then the Bill's first draft. The Consortium decided that the SLC proposal was the most likely to be successful, even though most of its members would probably have supported a clear ban on corporal punishment. As such, though, the Consortium's arguments had to cover the complexities of the SLC proposal, and deal with its lack of clarity. The official support of the opposition parties for the SLC proposal was in itself a small success (as this could be referred to again should there be a change of government), but when the amendments were put forward only with Labour supporters in the House of Commons, the Party lines were firmly drawn. When the Conservative MPs most likely to be sympathetic to the SLC provision spoke out against it, the chance of swaying the government seemed even smaller. The all-party support in the House of Lords provided a boost for the proposal, but Lord Hope's rebuttal firmly closed the possibility of its success. The progress of the amendments through Parliament exemplifies the intricacies of balancing party politics, the influence of key people and Government backbenchers, and the difficulties of causing any real change in 'uncontroversial' Scottish legislation without government support.

The arguments that the SLC proposal lacked clarity do seem to have some merit. Critical terms in the proposal would have required court interpretation. Perhaps it was misleading to describe the proposal as greatly 'clarifying' the law on physical punishment. Perhaps a truer explanation of the proposal was the moving of the line on what was acceptable: the defense against assault would be more circumscribed. Whether the case being taken to the European Court on Human Rights (Jackson and Meade, 10.9.96) will require introduction of the SLC proposal in time is unknown. The case involves a then nine-year-old boy, caned by his step-father, to the extent that he was reportedly treated for his injuries. Perhaps it will take another European Court decision for Scottish law to constrain further the right of adults to punish children physically.

A 'promise': children in need

The new duty towards 'children in need' lacks the drama of the physical punishment debate. While the Bill was going through Parliament, it was difficult to interest the media in 'children in need', while they were only too eager to report on whether smacking would be banned. Yet the new duty creates a potentially far more radical change for Scotland's children and their families.

As described in Chapter Three, the White Paper had indicated that a new 'positive' general welfare duty would be constructed in order to update Section 12 of the Social Work (Scotland) Act 1968. In response to the White Paper, children's organisations had requested greater clarification. Not until the Children (Scotland) Bill was introduced into Parliament was this clarification given, and children's organisations were dismayed by it. The Scottish Office had decided to import the category of 'children in need' from the Children Act 1989. All specific references to children were deleted from Section 12 of the 1968 Act, and Section 12 amended so that assistance would only be provided for those over eighteen years. Under the draft Bill, local authorities would have to 'safeguard and promote the welfare of children in their area who are in need' and seek to do this by supporting children in their families.

The proposed new duty pivoted on the definition of 'in need'. After considerable searching, the definition could be found in the 'interpretation of Part II', way back at the end of the draft Bill:

> ... being in need of care and attention because—
>   (i)   no-one has parental responsibility for him;
>   (ii) he is lost or abandoned;
>   (iii) for whatever reason, the person who is or has been caring for him is not safeguarding or promoting, or is not adequately safeguarding or promoting his welfare; or
>   (iv) he is disabled.

For 'children in need', a child was defined as under eighteen.

This definition was *not* the same as that found in the Children Act 1989:

> ... a child shall be taken to be in need if—
>   (a) he is unlikely to achieve or maintain, or to have the opportunity of achieving or maintaining, a reasonable standard or health or development without the provision for him of services by a local authority under this Part;
>   (b) his health or development is likely to be significantly impaired, or further impaired, without the provision for him of such services; or
>   (c) he is disabled. (Section 17 (10))

This last definition was at least less stigmatising than the proposed Scottish one. While still phrased in terms of 'impairment' and negative development, this definition did not presume that 'children in need' were largely in need because of parental failings. What parent would want to access say, respite services, under the Scottish definition?

From the beginning, civil servants in The Scottish Office indicated that the Government would probably be willing to modify the particular definition of 'children in need'. This flexibility was welcomed, but it did not address the more fundamental issue of having such a targeted category in the first place.

While 'children in need' may have been heralded in England and Wales as a considerable improvement in promoting preventive services, it received no such response in Scotland from most organisations working with children. England and Wales had never had the equivalent of Section 12, and the Consortium certainly felt the new category was a retrograde step. Furthermore, the experience in England and Wales of this duty had been less than positive—in part due to lack of resources but also due to problems inherent in the category itself. These conceptual difficulties could be groups into three areas:

(1) vague definition of 'children in need'
(2) potential stigmatisation of the category
(3) failure to facilitate preventive services.

(For further discussion of these in a Scottish context see Chapter Five and for English and Welsh research findings, see Chapter Six.)

The Consortium tried hard to persuade The Scottish Office to reconsider. When little hope seemed evident there, the Consortium sought to do what it could through the parliamentary process. Its written evidence suggested deleting the new category and retaining a more general local authority duty to safeguard and promote the welfare of children in a local authority area. This could be supplemented by a statutory code of practice, outlining a minimum range of services that should be provided, that could be made part of the new statutory duty for local authorities to make children's services plans.

The government's concerns were evident from the beginning. In the House of Commons Committee, Lord James was quick to underline the government's commitment to providing 'support services for children and their families' (Hansard 28.2.95, Col. 375). But the government saw the need to target attention on priorities, in the face of increasing demand. Lord James offered to give attention to further amendments in this section. 'Children in need' had already become caught in the parliamentary timetable. By the time 'children in need' was being debated, considerable pressure had mounted for the proceedings to advance more quickly: other Scottish legislation was piling up, unable to go through until Scottish Conservative backbenchers were freed to sit on other committees. So by the time this new amendment was being discussed in the Committee Stage, the pressure was on for speed.

Anticipating the government's further amendments, the Consortium readied its arguments, but not a suggested rephrasing, for the Report Stage of the House of Commons. This was an unwise move. In part due to its genuine attempts to address all the issues raised in Committee, government amendments were delayed. The government put down over forty pages of new amendments and clauses at the end of Thursday evening—leaving only the weekend for interested parties to consider them (and many MPs are not in the House on Friday or Monday mornings). Opposition MPs were irate at the opening of the debate on Monday evening, and the government apologised. But when it was discovered that no amendments had been put down by the Government on 'children in need'—not even one on which a discussion could be justified, where opposition MPs could bring up their arguments—the opportunity had been lost. Those concerned were left with a promise that 'children in need' amendments would be put forward in the House of Lords.

By the House of Lords, the Consortium felt it was time to act tactically. In Committee, the Consortium took one more chance at having the 'children in need' category deleted, drafting an amendment that was put forward by the Earl of Mar and Kellie. Lord Fraser refused to accept the amendment with a clear message about non-intervention and targeting:

> … we need a suitable trigger. We do not want a local authority to have *carte blanche* to intervene when it is not necessary. Some assessment of need is surely

appropriate and we cannot expect local authorities to promote the welfare of children where such action is not required, and, perhaps more importantly, where it is not desired by the child's family. (Hansard 6.6.95, Col. 51)

Lord Fraser pointed to the government's own amendment to the definition of 'children in need', which replaced the initial, highly stigmatising definition with that of the Children Act 1989 (see above)—with one exception. 'Children in need' would not only include children with a disability, but also children adversely affected by a disability (thus including siblings, and young carers, for example).

The government made a range of changes along the way. In one of the more dramatic 'successes', Lord James took his own initiative (after a lengthy conference with the civil servants during the Committee) and accepted an opposition/Consortium amendment on principle. 'Children in need' services would have to have 'due regard to a child's religious persuasion, racial origin and cultural and linguistic background'. The Consortium suggested amendments to specify particular services that 'children in need' must have, paralleling the specifications of the Children Act 1989. Only one specific service was accepted: what became Section 27, where local authorities must provide day care, after-school care and holiday care for 'children in need'.

Further promises were made in relation to the new provision, which would be contained within guidance:

- preventive services will be included within the range of services for children 'in need'
- respite services will be included in children's service plans
- 'one-stop' assessments will be put forward in guidance, to prevent unnecessary duplication of assessments, e.g. with the range of assessments required for those with special educational needs.

Implementation of 'children in need' will be a topic further discussed in the next chapter. But certainly, its importation into Scottish children's services seemed both unjustified and unexpected. Despite some attempts by children's organisations and support by Parliamentarians, it simply did not garner the attention of other more 'media-worthy' and emotive provisions. The particular workings of Parliament precluded an intensive debate on its implications, and the Consortium was left trying to elicit promises and additions to something with which it fundamentally disagreed.

However, the government's promises do hold weight. Hansard can be referred to in court, to help guide interpretation. The government can be held publicly to its statements in Parliament, and such a promise can often be the best outcome realistically hoped for in parliamentary lobbying. 'Children in need' may suffer from its vagueness, but this very vagueness at the very least provides the possibility that Scottish local authorities could do things differently.

The thorny problem of resources, however, remained. The government put forward £4 million, in its financial memorandum to the draft Bill, for all the new welfare provisions. Given the debt many local authorities were already facing, such financing would hardly permit them to cover the costs of change, let alone new duties. Yet somehow local authorities must continue to meet the needs of children and their families.

Concluding thoughts on the parliamentary process

The Children (Scotland) Bill was introduced into Parliament because of the propelling force of all-party support. The Scottish APPG for Children was formed in order to create pressure for the legislation, and lobbied ministers, sent out press releases and held meetings to forward this aim. Key parliamentarians worked to persuade their party leaders to prioritise the legislation, and opposition parties agreed to use new procedures (which most only reluctantly accepted) positively to allow the legislation parliamentary time. The Bill was introduced in a fanfare of consensus and hopeful speeches. For example, the (then) Conservative backbencher Raymond Robertson, MP, told the Scottish Grand Committee: 'I am ready to listen and I do not approach the Bill in a dogmatic and doctrinaire way' (Hansard 5.12.94, Col. 26). Maria Fyfe, MP agreed with Raymond Robertson in her closing speech for Labour. But this hoped-for avoidance of party politics was scarcely evident as the Bill proceeded through Parliament.

In order to maintain its majority on the House of Commons Committee, the Conservative side was stacked with Scottish Office ministers. Beyond voting with the government, none contributed to the debates in the Committee and indeed most of them steadily worked through their portfolios throughout the meetings. Another noisily opened his mail throughout one morning, leaving piles of envelopes on the floor. There were strong indications that Conservative backbenchers on the Committee were told most firmly not to put forward amendments, not to lengthen debates, and to do nothing to slow down the Committee's timetable. At times, these MPs did not abide by the Whip's wishes (and at one occasion Phil Gallie supported extended after-care provisions), but they were seriously limited from the promised 'adequate discussion of such an important Bill' (Lord James Douglas-Hamilton, Hansard 21.2.95, Col. 215). The scrutiny of the Bill soon clearly and firmly divided on party lines, not only in voting but also in putting forward amendments.

The parliamentary process arguably did not suit the detailed scrutiny required of the Bill. So many technical gaps were found in the Bill, that eventually the Consortium/opposition were supporting amendments just to help cover the worst of these gaps. Certain Parliamentarians were talented and dedicated, seeking to ensure the government respondent was actually answering the questions and addressing the issues behind amendments; yet so many issues were greeted with the same arguments from the government time and time again, without account being taken of the reasons for the amendment. Important points were thus never really wrestled with during the process. The timetable of the parliamentary procedures, confusing to the uninitiated and apparently unpredictable even to those in Parliament, precluded in-depth consultation and consideration of new amendments and clauses. For example, when the Bill was taken in Committee in the House of Lords, not all the Peers were aware of its first meeting and the turn out was very low (although arguably those who attended were the most committed).

Perhaps of most concern was the place of children's and families' views in the parliamentary process. At this stage of formal policy making, the Consortium found it difficult to ensure that such views could be heard, let alone be influential. Because the draft Bill was unavailable for consultation before the parliamentary process began, young people and their families could not be consulted on the detail of the legislation. The parliamentary timetable made it difficult to arrange meaningful consultations with young people and families as the legislation progressed. When meetings and debates were held in Parliament, funds were not available for young people to lobby there directly—the money for travel, overnight and subsistence.

More positively, though, other means were used. Press conferences were arranged with young people and families. Some young people and parents participated in the Consortium. The media helpfully provided some information about the public being able to send views into the evidence-taking Committee. The evidence-taking itself was a vital innovation in recognising children's and parents' rights: as already mentioned, the young people's organisation Who Cares? Scotland were asked to give oral evidence, as were (anonymously) parents and a young person involved in the Orkney Inquiry. Holding the Scottish Grand Committee and evidence meetings in Scotland greatly facilitated young people's attendance. Attempts were made by the Consortium to include young peoples' and families' views in amendment briefings, and to prioritise their concerns. Still, the parliamentary process was scarcely child-friendly, and arguably worked against the realisation of Article 12 of the UN Convention—the right of children to have their views to be given due regard in all matters that affect them.

The Children (Scotland) Bill was heralded as putting the UN Convention into Scottish law. The rights of children were referred to throughout the Parliamentary process, and certain key changes made to facilitate them: e.g. the recognition of cultural, religious, and linguistic rights for children in receipt of 'children in need' services. But while the UN Convention held rhetorical power, the European Convention on Human Rights seemed much more persuasive to the Government. As was indicated by the exclusion order debates, the Scottish Office was determined to avoid another lost European court case and paid careful attention that the legislation would not do so. Without such an enforcement mechanism as the European Convention has with the European Court, the UN Convention is a much weaker standard in the UK.

Chapter 5

◆

AN ANALYSIS OF THE ACT

THE final result of the Parliamentary process was a lengthy Act—105 Sections and 5 Schedules—with many cross-references and containing numerous changes from the original Bill. The Act takes forward several familiar themes and incorporates much of what was already considered good practice. It contains many changes that have long been advocated, and others that have been resisted.

What it will actually mean in practice, and most particularly to children and their families, will depend on the Act's implementation. An initial analysis of the Act, as it stands after its passage through Parliament and as rules, regulation and guidance are finalised, provides some indication of its opportunities, disadvantages to guard against, and key areas for interpretation and decision-making.

In this chapter, the Act will be considered in light of the issues raised in Chapter Three. Certain provisions will be highlighted: for example, children in need, children's services plans, the rights of children to be heard and the new thresholds for child protection orders. The chapter will not attempt an exhaustive analysis of all provisions, for that task is one for far more than a chapter and probably more than a book. Readers are encouraged to consider other interpretations of the Act, as provided in exquisite legal detail by Norrie (1996) or other legal interpretations (Cleland and Sutherland 1996), or in simplified form by the Scottish Child Law Centre (1995), Children in Scotland (1995, 1996c) or British Agencies for Adoption and Fostering (1996). The analysis below differs significantly from these, for it focuses on areas given little attention in other interpretations and is constructed primarily from a social policy perspective. A summary of the Act's provisions can be found in Appendix 4.

Three general points about legislation and associated guidance may be useful. First, a fundamental distinction exists between 'duties' and 'powers' in law. A *duty* to provide a certain service, or to take a certain action, is binding on a local authority. Flexibility can exist around the interpretation of certain aspects of the duty (e.g. how to define a 'child in need'), but the duty itself must be fulfilled or the local authority risks an adverse court ruling. A *power*, on the other hand, means that a local authority *can but does not have to* provide the service, or take a certain action. In times of resource constraints, there are fears that powers may not be acted upon. Second, terminology can have specific legal meaning and is not necessarily consistent across sections of the legislation. So, for example, 'parent' has a particular meaning under the 1995 Act, attached to someone legally having parental responsibilities and rights, which may not match common usage of the term. 'A relevant person' includes particular people who have rights in relation to children's hearings, but the same people are not necessarily 'a relevant person' in relation to parental responsibilities orders. Third, rules, regulations and directions associated with the Act are *prescriptive*: i.e. courts, children's hearings, local authorities etc. *must* abide by them. While local authorities must perform their functions under the Act's guidance, they have discretion as to whether they follow it in a particular case. They may have to justify any deviation from guidance, if challenged. Guidance does not have the power of law, however, and the power to interpret the law lies with the courts.

Those most 'in need'?

In its sections on child care law, the 1995 Act can be seen as encouraging the targeting of children's services. Help from, or intervention by, the local authority has been circumscribed, with the justification of ensuring a more effective service for those who will receive it. For example:

- Children can only stay in 'safe refuges' for a maximum of seven days, or in exceptional prescribed situations, up to fourteen days (Section 38). These time-limits were specifically justified by the government as encouraging focused work and to clear the refuge places for other children (Hansard 12.7.95, Col. 1806–7).
- Local authorities' duty to provide after-care support was only extended by one year up to the age of nineteen for young people who were 'looked after' (Section 29): '… we want to see services improved for those who most need them and not simply spread resources more widely … We do not want to dilute this focus' (Hansard 6.6.95, Col. 55).
- The new criterion of 'significant harm', in order to obtain court orders for child protection, can be seen as tightening the criteria for service intervention (see discussion in Chapter Six).
- In contrast to the former Place of Safety Orders (PSOs), the new Child Protection Orders (CPOs) will only be granted in a perceived emergency and will only be available for a short time.
- The new Child Assessment Orders (CAOs), described further below, have a lower threshold of harm than CPOs, but they too have a tight time-frame of no more than seven days.

A trend can be seen in these provisions to limit the duration of both intervention and support in the lives of children, young people and their families.

The most obvious targeting lies with the new duty to safeguard and promote the welfare of 'children in need' (Section 22). Its implementation and interpretation will potentially have the most widespread effect on children and their families.

Children in need

Section 22 requires local authorities to:

(a) safeguard and promote the welfare of children in their area who are in need; and

(b) so far as is consistent with that duty, promote the upbringing of such children by their families, by providing a range and level of services appropriate to the children's needs.

Such services can be provided to the child, to the child's family or a member of the family. Assistance can be 'in kind' or, in exceptional circumstances, in cash. The assistance can be free or families can be asked to repay it, depending on their financial means.

As discussed in Chapter Four, this Section was originally seen as largely replacing Section 12 of the Social Work (Scotland) Act 1968 in relation to children. The 1995 Act had in fact repealed the specific mention of children within Section 12, leaving Section 12 as:

(1) It shall be the duty of every local authority to promote social welfare by making available advice, guidance and assistance on such a scale as may be appropriate for their area, and in that behalf to make arrangements and to provide or secure the provision of such facilities ... as they may consider suitable and adequate, and such assistance may ... *be given in kind or in cash to, or in respect of, any relevant person,*

(2) *A person is a relevant person for the purposes of this section if, not being less than eighteen years of age, he is a person in need requiring assistance* ... [italicised sections being the changes added by Schedule 4, para. 15 (11) of the 1995 Act]

The government seems to have heeded some of the concerns expressed (see Chapter Four), and the guidance on 'children in need' somewhat unexpectedly states that Section 12 of the 1968 Act can still be applied to children (Social Work Services Group (SWSG) 1997a: 1). The official message from the SWSG appears to be that the general duty is further specified by the 1995 Act's 'children in need'.

A specific definition is given for 'children in need', although it must be gathered from various sections of the Act. A 'child' is defined as under the age of eighteen, and a child is 'in need' because:

(i) the child is unlikely to achieve or maintain, or to have the opportunity of achieving or maintaining, a reasonable standard of health or development unless there are provided for him, under or by virtue of this Part, services by a local authority;

(ii) his health or development is likely significantly to be impaired, or further impaired, unless such services are so provided;

(iii) he is disabled; or

(iv) he is affected adversely by the disability of any other person in his family. (Section 93 (4)a)

The definition of 'children in need' was nearly a straight copy from the Children Act 1989: the difference being the Scottish addition of children 'adversely' affected by disability. The definition seems to have been lifted without due consideration of the difficulties it has caused in England and Wales, a subject that will be explored in further detail in the next chapter.

The definition can be seen as a legislative rationing device, rather than an administrative one (Tunstill 1995: 658). No local authority in the past provided all social work services to all children universally, but functioned with some administrative thresholds and criteria by which to distribute scarce resources. The 'children in need' definition, however, is not clear enough to rest solely in primary legislation—nor is it intended to. Local authorities will have to decide further exactly what type of characteristics or situations are likely to 'impair significantly' or 'further impair' children, and what are reasonable standards of 'health or development'. The definition in itself appears somewhat circular in (i) and (ii), as these subsections depend on services being provided by a local authority: i.e. you are not a 'child in need' unless there is a service that would address your need. Some services are specified in the Act—safe refuges, day care, child protection when a child is at 'risk of significant harm', children's hearings with their grounds of referral—but the 'range and level of services' indicated in Section 22 are not defined in the Act.

The guidance provides little help in further defining 'children in need', and the guidance for children's services plans takes the approach of identifying groups of children and suggesting types of services. Even 'health' and 'development' are not minimally defined in legislation or guidance, although they are in the 1989 Act. The new duty towards 'children in need' provides little protection for children's services, at a time of huge cuts in local authority spending, smaller local authorities with correspondingly smaller budgets and fewer economies of scale. 'Children in need' could easily be defined as a very narrow, very targeted and thus highly stigmatising category of children.

The vagueness of the definition does however provide local authorities with the possibility of providing flexible and effective services that best met the needs of children in their communities—the positive side of 'decentralisation'. It also means that, with thirty-two local authorities across Scotland, children in one area could be offered vastly different services to children in another area. The flexibility could bring with it considerable inequity, to the considerable disadvantage of some children. The possible migration of families, children and young people to councils with better services might well increase far beyond the levels that existed before local government reorganisation. Again, small local authorities with small budgets could easily become overwhelmed and have to cut back on their original intentions.

No consideration seems to have been given to alternatives other than identifying children by groups (Annex A of the guidance on children's services plans (SWSG 1997a) suggests groups such as 'children/young people who misuse substances/alcohol' and 'children who live in violent environments'). As the SWSG guidance recognises (1997a), the planning process and the resulting delivery of services might run into difficulties dealing with children who have multiple characteristics of 'need'. Prior to the implementation of the 1995 Act, the difficulties for children who have multiple needs have been demonstrated anecdotally as well as by research. For example, social services have experienced problems in meeting the needs of disabled children who are in residential care, while services for disabled children can find it difficult to deal with children who need protection or who face discrimination because of their ethnic minority background (Hill and Tisdall 1997).

A person is disabled if that person is 'chronically sick or disabled or suffers from mental disorder (within the meaning of the Mental Health (Scotland) Act 1984)' (Section 23 (2)). Specific provisions for children with and affected by disabilities are contained within Section 23, which will be described shortly. This definition of disability has the advantage of being familiar to local authorities, and thus will help ease the implementation of the relevant section. It could conceivably be quite wide, with non-life threatening chronic diseases included. Its appropriateness to children, however, is questionable. Few children are classed as mentally ill, although they may have emotional or behavioural problems: thus the use of the Mental Health Act is unhelpful for most. The use of the term 'chronically' creates a static definition, and thus fails to capture the reality of disability for some children. When children are born with an impairment, there will have been no past history to establish its chronicity, and how it will impact on the children may not be predictable. A clear diagnosis of a child's problems is often not made for several years. Children may experience disability or be affected by disability for short periods. Perhaps most problematically, the definition of disability rests on the individual child, and thus remains firmly within the 'medical model' of disability (see Oliver 1990). Even though the Children (Scotland) Act 1995 went through Parliament at the same time as the Disability Discrimination Act 1995, it fails to incorporate the more up-to-date definition of disability as provided for in that Act[1]. While the disability legislation itself could be accused of not adequately considering its applicability to children, it does recognise the social contribution to an individual's disability.

In providing services for a child 'in need', a local authority must have 'due regard to a child's religious persuasion, racial origin and cultural and linguistic background'. The duty has the familiar qualifications of 'as far as practicable' and 'due regard' and is itself vague, but still will be an important challenge to many Scottish children's services. Candappa (1994) provided thoughtful advice:

---

1 'Subject to the provisions of Schedule 1, a person has a disability ... if he has a physical or mental impairment which has a substantial and long-term adverse effect on his ability to carry out normal day-to-day activities.' (Section 1 (1))

For children from 'black' and other minority ethnic communities there is the question of whether services are ethnically sensitive and accessible to them. For children living in largely 'white' areas and those in pre-school settings where nearly all the children and the carers are 'white', there is a particular need for counteracting the learning of racist attitudes and for providing meaningful experiences of cultural diversity. (229)

Good practice has been built up in many Scottish service areas, such as adoption and fostering, and in certain localities, in addressing such issues. A particular challenge may be posed by the small size of most local authorities. They have smaller budgets than the previous regional councils, are likely to offer fewer services and thus probably operate with constrained options. Local authorities may in fact find it harder to meet their duties if they have only one child or one family from a particular background, than if the community is larger and there are opportuities for economies of scale and community resources. Care also must be taken to avoid eurocentric assumptions (see Thanki 1994) in evaluating 'significant harm' or what services should be provided. Guidance from the SWSG has identified key considerations in such areas as foster and residential care (1997b), and commissioned a consortium to produce written advice. Children's services across Scotland have had a chequered past in meeting the needs of children and families with diverse backgrounds, and much needs to be learned in order to meet these new duties.

Under Section 27, each local authority must provide day care for children as is appropriate 'in need' aged five or less, and after-school and holiday care for children 'in need'. Local authorities have a power, but not a duty, to provide such care for other children. Local authorities will also have the power to provide 'facilities' (including training, advice, guidance and counselling) for those caring for children in day care or who at any time accompany children while they are in day care. These are the only services specified for 'children in need', and will need to be co-ordinated with the duty to inspect, to register and to review child care services under the 1989 Act (provisions that also apply to Scotland).

The provision of after-care and holiday care for children 'in need' will be much welcomed by many parents of children with disabilities, who have often found it difficult to find and afford good quality care. The duty on local authorities will have to be placed alongside their duties in Section 23 specifically towards children with disabilities. 'Children in need' services will have to be designed so as:

- to minimise the effect of his/her disability on a disabled child
- to minimise the effect of the disability of another family member, on any child adversely affected
- to give those children 'the opportunity to lead lives which are as normal as possible'. (Section 23 (1))

These requirements promote an 'integrative' or 'inclusive' approach to services, and would seem to mitigate against the provision of segregated or stigmatising services for children with or affected by disabilities. This provision could be seen to ease the fear that 'children in need' services will become residual and highly unpopular—for how then could duties under Section 23 (1) be met?

Interactions with other legislation may provide further support to these measures. The Disability Discrimination Act 1995 requires public services (excluding education, and with numerous other exceptions) to be accessible to all disabled people. Taken together with Section 23 (1), would this mean that all local authority services should be accessible for disabled children, from swimming pools to day care? Local authorities are defined corporately, and thus include services such as housing, education and leisure and recreation. The relationship between the Education (Scotland) Act 1980 as amended, which does not contain any promotion of inclusive schooling, and the requirements of the 1995 Act, is not clear but perhaps can be used positively. The words 'to minimise' and 'as normal as possible' in themselves are qualified and imprecise in the 1995 Act—but the potential is worth exploring.

Duties towards children with and affected by disabilities are further specified in Section 23. A local authority must assess the needs of such children (Section 23 (3)), when requested to do so by a child's parent or guardian, so as to provide services under Section 22. Other family members can also be assessed. Further, under Section 24, a local authority must assess a carer's ability to care when requested to do by a carer. The carer may make such a request:

- when a disabled child is being assessed under Section 23
- the person intends to provide a 'substantial amount' of care on a regular basis
- the person is not caring under a contract or as a volunteer, and is a 'natural' person (e.g. not a visitor to the UK).

A local authority must undertake such an assessment before decisions are made, either for a child with and adversely affected by a disability (i.e. under Section 23), or under the Chronically Sick and Disabled Persons Act 1970 (Section 2(1)). The requirement, however, under Section 8 of the Disabled Persons (Services, Consultation and Representation) Act 1986—which is another requirement for the local authority to have regard to the ability of a carer to care—will not apply.

Broadly, including services for children with and affected by disabilities within mainstream legislation was welcomed. The need for assessments was not disputed. However, the particular formulation does have some inherent problems. For example:

- The parent or guardian, and not the child, is the only one who can demand a Section 23 (3) assessment. What if a child wishes to have an assessment, but his or her parent or guardian refuses? (Some options do exist: for example, a child could ask the court for a 'Specific Issues Order', under the private law Section 11 of the Act.)
- No specific reference is made in this section about taking into account children's views, despite this basic principle outlined in the White Paper (SWSG 1993a).

- No specific reference is made in the legislation about informing a carer of his or her right to an assessment.
- Despite the government's good intentions, the assurances given in Parliament that carer assessments for young carers were covered by the Carers (Recognition and Services) Act 1995 have now been questioned. For children under sixteen in Scotland, their right to such a carer's assessment is insecure at the time of writing.
- The legislation contains no obligation to provide a copy of the assessment to the child or parent/guardian, nor to match the 'determination of needs' with the provision of services, nor to construct a time-table for promised services and action.
- The carer's assessment is dubiously worded in the context of children. The assessment is to consider the 'carer's ability to continue to provide ... or care for that child'. This may be appropriate for adults, but if a carer is *not* able to care, a local authority may be required to instigate child protection proceedings or refer a child to a children's hearing. A more appropriate wording would have been to assess carers for their need of services, in order to support their caring.
- The legislation contains no requirement to review, at regular or established intervals, the assessment nor the right of a child, parent or guardian to ask for a review.

Other legislation (e.g. the Education (Scotland) Act 1980 as amended) is more prescriptive in terms of assessment requirements—so precedents did exist for greater definition within the 1995 Act. Given the difficulties found in both community care and education in relation to these issues, firm requirements would have been better expressed in the legislation. Fortunately, certain of these matters (e.g. information to carers about their right to assessment) are set out in the SWSG guidance.

The whole issue of assessment is a problematic one for 'children in need'. A promise was made in Parliament to promote a 'one-stop assessment' (Hansard 6.6.95, Col. 61), and SWSG guidance on 'children with need' and children affected by disabilities does mention the need to avoid unnecessary duplication of assessments by different services, and to consider 'joint assessment' (SWSG 1997a). Indeed, the newly revised educational circular on the assessment and recording of children with special educational needs (Scottish Office Education and Industry Department 1996) also makes mention of the need to consider joint assessment. These steps are welcome, but they provide few details and a divided approach. No *joint* guidance from the Scottish Office departments seemed to be planned, to include at least the major players of health, social services and education. While the assessment duty on local authorities may be corporate (and thus include education as well as social work), this does not include health services. No resolution has been suggested for the various overlapping assessments for children with disabilities by social work, as the child reaches the age of sixteen. Whether a 'one-stop' approach will actually be implemented, across

Scotland, is left to the initiatives of local providers or the local children's services plans.

A significant issue to sort out between 'special educational needs' assessments and Section 23 (3) assessments for children affected by disabilities, will be the difference in categories. A child with 'special educational needs' is not necessarily a child with disabilities, nor is a disabled child necessarily a child with 'special educational needs'. Further, not all children with 'special educational needs' are assessed for a Record of Special Educational Needs: for example, 32.7% of children in special schools were not recorded in 1993 (Scottish Office 1995c). This is a not a new problem for social work and education services. The 'Section 13' assessment required by the Disabled Persons (Services, Consultation and Representation) Act 1986 is based on the term 'disability', and must be considered when a Future Needs Assessment takes place for those with Records of Special Educational Needs.

A child has 'special educational needs' if: 'they have a learning difficulty which calls for provision for special educational needs to be made for them' (Section 1(5)(d) of the Education (Scotland) Act 1980 as amended). A learning difficulty is said to be present if children:

- have significantly greater difficulty in learning than the majority of those of their age; or
- suffer from a disability which either prevents or hinders them from making use of educational facilities of a kind generally provided for those of their age in schools managed by their education authority; or
- who are under the age of five years and, if provision for special educational needs were not made for them, are or would be likely, when over that age, to have a learning difficulty as defined above.

There would seem to be considerable overlap between 'children in need' and 'special educational needs', given that education could be part of a child's 'development'. However, if 'special educational needs' provision is being provided for a child, there may not be other services that the child requires under 'children in need'. While different professionals may be talking about 'need', 'need' can have different meanings to them.

The influence of community care can be traced within the new requirements for assessment. Ideas about 'packages of services' and about 'managing individual cases' have been transplanted into the guidance on children in need (SWSG 1997a). The assessment should be 'needs-led' and not 'service-led'. The focus on assessment within the guidance itself is an indication of community care's influence. Whether some of the lessons from community care's experiences have been taken on board appears less certain.

A clear problem lies with the identification of unmet need. Both the guidance on community care and on children in need suggests that unmet need be recorded, and fed into the service planning process. Such guidance is laudable, in providing important information for planning. Community care services, however, have been understandably loathe to implement this (Browne 1996: 56). If unmet need is recorded in an individual assessment, and the person assessed has access to this assessment, the person could seek a judicial review (Browne 1996: 59). Legal cases, at least in England and Wales, have established the right for users to challenge the failure to provide services for an identified need, and to have the services provided (Browne 1996: 62; Community Care 1997a). This has been questioned by the recent House of Lords decision, where a local authority was allowed not to meet assessed needs because the local authority lacked the resources (*R*. v *Gloucestershire CC Ex p. Barry* [1997] 2 All ER 1; Valios 1997a). If assessors are themselves part of the service administration, they may well be pressurised into not recording unmet need. The SWSG guidance on 'children in need' gives no indication that assessors must be separate from provider management.

Further pitfalls of assessment can be found in the literature on special educational needs. For example, just as with community care, research found that professionals can feel pressured into *not* recording the full extent of a child's needs, if they know the resources are not available (Armstrong et al. 1993; Education Committee 1996). Children's behaviour during assessments can be greatly influenced by their understanding of the assessment's purpose and the professionals' roles. Even when information is provided to children, some see the assessment as punishment for their failures or behaviour. Professionals can be seen by children as finding out what 'is wrong' with the child, and children can be correspondingly anxious: 'I was dreading going. I don't know why. I was nervous and dreading going' (Susan, quoted in Armstrong et al. 1993: 124). While the term 'special educational needs' was specifically chosen to underline the part played by the school in generating a child's special needs, assessments still tend to be located firmly in the individual child and not her/his school or family environment (Hill and Tisdall 1997). The SWSG guidance on 'children in need' and children affected by disability (1997a) however outlines the need to support children and their families, and to provide information. The research on special educational needs indicates both the difficulties and the necessity of this for many children and their families.

The focus on assessment for 'children in need' is familiar from special educational needs services and community care. On one hand, assessments can ensure that suitable services are provided, that provision is regularly reviewed, that everyone is clear about 'who, what and when'. On the other hand, assessments can be used as a rationing device, to delay and diminish demands for services. The SWSG guidance on 'children in need' (1997a) says that not all 'children in need' will require further assessment after an initial 'screening'. This recognition seems welcome when one considers the success of open-door family or youth centres, particularly in areas of deprivation. The SWSG guidance, however, seems then to link services predominantly with assessment, leaving a strong sense that assessment will be the main way to access services for 'children in need', just as it is becoming increasingly so for children to access services for 'special educational needs' (Hill and Tisdall 1997).

The new requirements for assessment must be used to their advantage, and pitfalls avoided. Most importantly, they must not be used as an excuse or a diversion to 'manage the problem' for children in need, so as to miss tackling the community's or society's contribution to the child's situation or needs. There is little point in intense inter-agency collaboration, and numerous meetings between professionals, when there are few services or opportunities to offer children and their families (Tisdall 1997).

Children's services plans

If individual assessments of need and unmet need are co-ordinated with the new duty on local authorities to create children's services plans, than assessments may be purposeful, and numerous opportunities could be opened up for children and their families. Section 19 of the 1995 Act requires local authorities to prepare, consult upon, publish and review plans for all 'relevant' children's services. Local authorities will have to provide their first plans by 1 April 1998. SWSG guidance (1997a) states that the plans should be for three years, with an annual review. Local authorities could choose to review parts of their plans more frequently.

Again, the government clearly wishes to target the plans. A list of 'relevant' services was provided in the legislation, and the government refused to widen it further. Still, the list of services is long. It includes all services provided under Part II of the 1995 Act, which include:

- services for 'looked after' children and 'children in need'
- 'after care'
- safe refuges
- services in relation to children's hearings
- preparation and publication of information
- ensuring welfare of children in residential homes/schools, hospitals and nursing homes
- assessments of children affected by disabilities and of carers' ability to care
- early years services
- child protection.

Further, all services contained within Section 5 (1B) (a) to (o) of the Social Work (Scotland) Act 1968 are to be included. When these are followed up within the various pieces of legislation, they include local authorities' responsibilities for:

- adoption and fostering services
- services for homeless people and in relation to housing
- charging and recovery of costs for services
- children affected by matrimonial proceedings such as divorce, as decided by court
- services for disabled people and people with mental health disorders
- young people on remand or committal for trial/sentencing

- access to 'personal information' in files
- review of early years services, registration and inspection of childminding and day care.

Unfortunately, SWSG guidance does not follow through the various pieces of legislation to define fully for local authorities and other readers exactly what these services under Section 5 (1B) (a) to (o) are—which will thus require considerable work in the local authorities to identify them. For local authorities, the references to and fro between different pieces of legislation are confusing and, without definitive requirements, local authorities could easily produce plans in breach of their legal duties.

The legislation does not *prevent* local authorities from including more services in their plans. Indeed, the SWSG guidance (1997a) lists seventy-two services for possible inclusion. But the Conservative Government had made clear statements about limiting plans: 'Children's services plans are a far cry from a "wish list" and equally from concentration on high volume/low cost services which are designed "simply to stretch the money further"' (Lord James Douglas-Hamilton, reported in Children in Scotland 1996a: 6). Clearly, relevant services only include those provided or contracted out by local authorities—so the plans have no legal requirement to consider the overlap or gaps with non-local authority services such as Reporters for children's hearings, or Health Boards (although guidance suggests it). Local authorities will have duties to *consult* such providers on their plans.

Definitions of 'children in need' and 'need' more generally will be central to the content of any children's services plan. While 'need' is a traditional criterion for the welfare state, it is well-known as a slippery concept. Regard can be given to the extensive literature deconstructing the criterion, such as the much quoted works by Bradshaw (1972) and Doyal and Gough (1991). Bradshaw's work is particularly useful in describing the various ways 'need' can be identified, and in questioning professional ascendancy. He presented a 'taxonomy of need':

- Felt needs: needs identified by individuals themselves. Individuals may not express these needs.
- Expressed needs: needs that are expressed by individuals or groups.
- Normative needs: experts or professionals define an agreed standard. Those individuals or groups who fall below this standard are identified as being 'in need'.
- Comparative need: the needs of a group of individuals relative to those of another group with similar characteristics.

This framework mainly relates to how individuals or groups are identified as being 'in need', rather than specification of what their needs might be. This focus on method may be useful for those responsible for creating children's services plans, in concentrating their minds on their various options for identifying need. Will they canvas individuals or groups in their area? Will they create some benchmark, either seeing themselves or other sources as 'experts', and compare people to it? Will they draw together various indicators of need, and see which groups are worse or better off in comparison to these? The SWSG guidance (1997a) seems to suggest assessing need on the basis of predetermined groups (11), with a concern for geographical equality: local authorities are asked to demonstrate how services are distributed to meet needs in their areas (10).

Who will ascertain needs? In the 'needs' literature, solely relying on experts has been criticised (Smith 1980). The instruments used to identify need have been accused of often being limited and biased (Lishman 1983; Taylor and Ford 1989). Perceptions of need may be unduly restricted as professionals may define need only in terms of the services that are already provided. For example, many health professionals are inclined to see child safety as a matter largely for parental education, rather than addressable by housing or environmental improvements (Roberts et al. 1995). Professionals and officials are not necessarily disinterested parties. They have power, jobs and position to protect, and may use their system of knowledge to impose their ideas on people and to perpetuate their professional status (Hewitt 1992).

Doyal and Gough (1991) are considerably more positive about professionals or experts contribution to identifying need. They argue that individuals alone may not be the best judges of what they need, for they may lack knowledge or information about what is possible. Physical health and autonomy should be considered universal, objective basic needs with a further eleven 'intermediate needs' that contribute to health and autonomy in all cultures. These are:

- safe birth control and child bearing;
- appropriate education;
- economic security;
- physical security;
- significant primary relationships;
- appropriate health care;
- security in childhood;
- a non-hazardous physical environment;
- a non-hazardous work environment;
- adequate protective housing; and
- adequate nutritional food and clean water.

A list such as Doyal and Gough's would require further specification in a local area, but could be manipulated into certain indicators. For example, the Children in Need Working Group in Wales (1995) suggests that local authorities could draw on existing databases held by agencies such as community health and education, use census data or an IT-based geographical information system to help them identify areas where children with priority needs cluster. Such surveys of local needs have been much used in other areas of planning, such as health and housing (Porteus 1996).

Most advice on planning suggests the usefulness of such information. Using pre-existing data can be both cost-effective and relatively quick. Because of the amount of information that is available, analyses can provide a wider range of indicators than assessments requiring the collection of new data. Often this data is collected over time, so that temporal comparisons can be made (Porteus 1996). The disadvantages, however, must also be considered:

- As the data is usually collected for other purposes, the information may not necessarily reflect actual need.
- Such data can inform about the existence of need, but little more about it.
- Data is not always current (e.g. census data is only collected every ten years).
- Different information systems can collect data on the basis of different geographical boundaries (e.g. postcode areas versus electoral wards).
- Analyses can require statistical expertise and technical knowledge that not all local authorities may have.
- Commonly-used indicators tend to emphasise certain types of needs, and not others. For example, indicators of deprivation such as overcrowding, proportion of single parents and high levels of unemployment do not often reflect the needs of rural communities. (Percy-Smith 1996a; Porteus 1996; Statham and Cameron 1994)

Qualitative and community-based needs assessments are often advocated. For example, the SWSG guidance on children's services plans suggests: 'It is also necessary to take into account views of users—and potential users—on existing services, their adequacy and quality and perceived gaps in provision' (1997a: 11). Such consultation is the most likely way to gather in new concepts of need, and to ascertain 'unmet need'. Decisions still need to be made about how such consultation would take place. Is the focus on the collective needs of the community or the aggregate needs of individuals? What community is being considered? The SWSG guidance identifies two groups—present users and past users of services (11). These groups are likely to cross geographical boundaries even within a local authority, being a 'community of interest' rather than a 'spatial community'. Other considerations can be 'communities within communities' (e.g. children with disabilities, or from an ethnic minority, within the general community of service users). Community consultation can be both enabling and empowering, particularly if community members acquire new skills, fresh insights and new knowledge about their community. However, such consultation is not without cost. Certain people participate more easily in such consultations than others: different methods may be required to include the views of those often 'excluded' (e.g. children). Further, fears are often expressed of 'raising expectations' which are then not met. Such problems are not insurmountable but, for successful planning, they need to be addressed (Foreman 1996; Percy-Smith 1996b).

Identifying and assessing need does not answer the question of service provision and distribution. At its worst, assessment and planning can hide the lack of resources and the political manoeuvring. Criticising the process for housing, the Chair of the Association of District Councils said:

> The more we investigate housing need, produce strategies for dealing with it and draw up ever more sophisticated ways of measuring performance the fewer resources we are given to dealing with needs... The most urgent need might be for new rented housing, but it would be a foolish council that made that the centre of its strategy, let alone propose to build such housing itself. (quoted in Hawtin 1996: 101)

The reality for many local authorities is very scarce resources. Planning may be frustrating when much-needed services seem impossible to provide. Perhaps the best possibilities lie in seeking to think creatively—whether that means involving the community in decision-making, pooling resources across departments, or collaborating with other local authorities or the voluntary sector.

Working together—inter-agency collaboration

How will agencies work together, under the provisions of the new Act? As mentioned above, Section 19 (5) lists specific agencies with whom a local authority must consult in preparing its plan:

- every health board and trust in the local authority's area
- voluntary organisations which the authority sees as (a) representing the interests of people who use or are likely to use the 'relevant services' and (b) providing services in the area that could be 'relevant services'
- the Principal Reporter
- the chairman of the area's children's panel
- local housing associations, voluntary housing agencies and other bodies providing housing
- and those the 'Secretary of State may direct'.

Given the rhetoric of children's rights in the presentation of the Act, the failure to include children (and their families) on this list is notable. Consultation with voluntary organisations that represent children and their families is very welcome, but not all groups have representative organisations (e.g. while there are several representative groups of parents whose children are disabled, there are few representative groups for the children themselves). Assurances were given, and are reflected in SWSG guidance (1997a), that local authorities would be expected to consult directly with children and their families.

Co-ordination between health and local authorities may be particularly difficult for some, as health and local authority boundaries are not necessarily coterminous. Some health boards will cover parts of several local authorities. Such local authorities may have a very different range of priorities, different definitions of 'need' and different ideas about co-operation and collaboration. Voluntary organisations may appreciate being consulted, but for some the costs of consultation may be difficult to sustain in a time of scarce resources. Further, voluntary organisations that either already are commissioned by a local authority to provide 'relevant services' or who may wish to in the future should be consulted. It may be difficult for voluntary organisations to disassociate their need for such contracts and commissioning from their view on what children's and families' needs are and what services should be provided.

The legislation is notable in that it contains the verb 'consult' and not 'collaborate' or 'co-operate'. The Social Services Inspectorate (SSI) (1995: 24–25) developed a hierarchy of co-operation, going from weaker to stronger relationships, which provides a useful perspective on the term 'consultation':

- communication: one agency tells another what it intends to do
- consultation: an agency asks another for opinion, information or advice before finalising a plan
- collaboration: a degree of joint working on plans, involving mutual adjustment and agreement on the extent and limits of each others' activities, but agencies provide services independently
- bilateral planning: although each agency retains its own plan, agencies will operate interactively based on common planning
- joint planning: agencies work operationally to the same plan.

This hierarchy provides clarity on what relationships are being considered (although it refers to agencies who provide/plan services rather than other interested groups or individuals). Consultation is a relatively weak relationship, which may indeed be appropriate between certain agencies or groups. Even within this category, consultation can have many degrees. For example, at what point does consultation take place (setting the agenda, setting priorities or on the final draft)? What support will be given for people to be informed of the issues, in order to provide well-thought out replies? How much influence do the different consultees' views have? How are different views resolved? Who has the power to resolve them?

Section 21 of the 1995 Act may provide some impetus for agencies to strengthen their planning and working relationships. When a local authority makes a specific request to another agency, the agency *must* help when the request is compatible with the agency's own obligations and does not 'unduly prejudice' any of the agency's functions. The local authority must specify what help it requires, in carrying out any of its functions under Part II of the Act (which include the preparation of children's services plans, preparing and publishing information and services in relation to children's hearings—see Appendix 4). Certain agencies are specified: any other local authority, a NHS trust, or a Health Board. The Secretary of State could identify others. Further, Section 19 of the Children Act 1989 still applies to Scotland. This requires a local authority to review its early years provision, taking account of representations made by health and any other relevant bodies.

Section 21 may be another example of rhetorical, rather than practical, strength. The qualification provided by the phrase 'unduly prejudice' could be an easy get-out clause for agencies faced with scarce resources, waiting lists and other pressures. The parallel provision in the 1989 Act has not proved strong when tested legally in England (see Chapter Six). Nonetheless, the 1995 Act had not been introduced into Parliament with a remit to legislate for other services, and at least this additional section underlines the importance of co-operation. Indeed, inter-agency co-operation is a principle contained in the White Paper (SWSG 1993a) and emphasised constantly throughout SWSG guidance (1997a–c).

The government has potentially encouraged collaboration and co-operation *within* local authority services. A local authority is defined corporately within the Act, and the government has promised to underline this. So, for example, the SWSG guidance on children's services plans asks chief executives to assume corporate responsibility for the preparation of plans (1997a: 10). The potential of such a corporate definition is impressive, particularly when housing, education, recreation and social services are all within the same unitary authorities. Will children's hearings be able to call on educational services, and actually have them provided, for children on supervision requirements? Will housing services be required to meet the housing needs of 'children in need' and their families? The SWSG guidance (1997a–c) would suggest the answer is 'yes' to such questions. The corporate definition may encourage the sorting out of different pieces of legislation, to provide a 'seamless service' as advocated for disabled children in *Scotland's Children* (SWSG 1993a: para. 4.9). Local authority departments could come to working agreements and coherent plans in such areas as:

- day care inspection under the Children Act 1989 and inspection in relation to educational vouchers under the Education (Scotland) Act 1996
- homelessness and housing (Housing (Scotland) Act 1987)
- children with disabilities, special educational needs and community care: (Education (Scotland) Act 1980 as amended, Chronically Sick and Disabled Persons Act 1970, Disabled Persons (Services, Consultation and Representation) Act 1986 and National Health Services and Community Care Act 1990).

While improved from its draft form, the final SWSG guidance (1997a–c) does not consistently adhere to this corporate definition. It slips into referring to the 'social work department' rather than 'local authority', despite the reality that some local authorities no longer have social work departments. The guidance thus provides little help on potential tensions caused by the shift to corporatism, nor does it provide insight into its advantages. There appears to be no intention to issue the guidance jointly from the relevant Scottish Office departments for education and/or housing. The potential for a corporate approach to children's services could be better exploited.

Consultation and collaboration are also worth considering *within* agencies. Planning can be done solely at managerial or executive level, with little commitment from actual service providers. The potential control of 'street level bureaucrats', in children's and families' actual access and experience of services, should be remembered (Weatherley and Lipsky 1977). More benignly, ground-level service providers may know the intricacies of actual service provision best, and be the ones who need to liaise in particular situations with other agencies. The level of planning, consultation and dissemination needs to be considered, although SWSG guidance makes no mention of this. With smaller authorities, consultation with staff can place extra resource burdens on local authorities; on the other hand, being smaller can provide more potential for people coming together and fewer people to disseminate to.

Working together—partnership with parents

Just as co-operation between services providers is a foundational principle set out in the White Paper (SWSG 1993a) and SWSG guidance (1997 a and b), so is partnership between parents and local authorities. Such partnership can have different meanings and dimensions. It can be understood as promoting voluntary measures rather than compulsory ones, which is reflected in numerous sections of the Act. For example, courts and children's hearings should not make an order or a supervision requirement unless it is better than making none. This 'non-intervention' (or 'minimum intervention') principle would presumably support children and families voluntarily agreeing to work with social work services, rather than making them do so compulsorily. 'Children in need' services are to support children within their families, and parents can receive services in order to best safeguard and promote the welfare of their children. Carers, who may well be parents, can receive their own assessments. 'Accommodation' under Section 25 will not be provided for children if those with parental responsibility are unwilling (or if the child over sixteen years disagrees), and the parent of a child under sixteen can remove the child either without notice, if the child has been accommodated for less than six months, or with fourteen days' notice if the child has been accommodated for longer. Adoptive parents can receive post-adoption support or adoption allowances.

Partnership can also be understood in terms of participation. SWSG guidance (1997a) states that parents should be consulted over children's services plans, their children's assessments and decisions. They should participate in care reviews (SWSG 1997b). For children who are or will be 'looked after', parents' views must be considered (as far as is practicable) when decisions are being made (Section 17 (4)(b)). Local authorities will also have a duty to promote '… on a regular basis, personal relations and direct contact between the child and any person with parental responsibilities …' (Section 17 (1)(c)) for 'looked after' children.

Partnership can also be seen in relation to a sharing, or clear distribution of, responsibilities and rights. Thus, the change of terminology to 'looked after' was deliberately intended to stress parents' continuing role with their children:

> The words 'in care' have also been perceived as giving a particular package of powers to the local authority. This runs counter to our aim of providing a more flexible provision, determined by the individual child's needs and the

responsibilities and rights of their parents. ... local authorities' responsibilities are to be determined by the ability and willingness of each child's parents to meet their own responsibilities. (Lord Fraser of Carmyllie, House of Lords, Hansard 6.6.95, Cols. 30–31)

Local authorities are only to take on full parental responsibilities through the court, and will no longer be able to do so through administrative procedures. Parental responsibilities are to be curtailed primarily by the court or children's hearings, and not through other administrative or professional decisions. If parents are dissatisfied, they have rights to complain or appeal.

Partnership is also encouraged *between* parents. The 'non-intervention' principle applies to private law orders under Section 11. If parents come to a joint decision on residence or contact with their children, the case will not come to court. Unmarried fathers will have a new way to gain parental responsibilities (Section 4), which is supposed to be understood easily and available, and entail minimal cost. They will be able to gain full parental responsibilities (and rights) if they and the children's mothers sign these 'parental responsibilities agreements'. Unmarried fathers would still have recourse to the court if mothers refused to sign. Services may need to consider how to respect and promote such joint parenting, even though parents may not necessarily present themselves as an unit and may indeed live considerable distances apart. Local authority housing, for example, may need to provide multiple housing units for children, if a residence order (Section 11) is made between parents—for example if children will live alternate months with their mother and then their father.

Confusion is possible between parents who do not agree, as Section 2 allows for a person with parental responsibilities to exercise his/her rights without the consent of another person with such responsibilities *unless* an order or some other specification has been given that the parent cannot. The confusion is somewhat alleviated by Section 6, which says that such a person should 'have regard so far as practicable to the views' of another person with parental responsibilities/rights, when reaching 'any major decision' in relation to parental responsibilities/rights. The Section is qualified, however, and 'any major decision' left undefined. Further, this provision seems difficult to enforce and no obvious sanction available if this duty is not carried out (Norrie 1996). These Sections could impact on those services that are trying to respect joint parenting, such as education or social work services. To whom does a school send its reports, receive signatures for permission or call for parents' meetings? How does a foster carer deal with conflicting demands of parents for children being fostered? Piper (1995) pointed out that the emphasis on joint parenting can ignore the gender divides between parenting, and sometimes services like mediation ignore the inexperience or even incompetence of one parent. Just as the 1995 Act encourages services to recognise the individuality of children within a family unit, services may find it necessary to consider, at times, parents as individuals in their partnerships. Legally, they may have to tread this path carefully.

In its promotion of 'non-intervention', the Act risks placing parents' decisions above children's rights and particularly their welfare. For example, if parents come to an agreement in relation to divorce, there is no legal requirement that the child's welfare be the paramount consideration in such issues as where they live or who has responsibility for them. Similarly, the Parental Responsibilities Agreement of Section 4 can be signed between unmarried parents, without any test of the child's welfare. Presumably, such an agreement would count as a 'major decision' in relation to parental responsibilities, so that young people should be consulted by their parents. Still, the protection of children's rights seems far stronger in contested cases (i.e. those under Section 11), than it does in consensual agreements that do not come to court.

Children's rights

As suggested in previous chapters, the government described the Children (Scotland) Act 1995 as fulfilling its obligations to implement the UN Convention on the Rights of the Child: 'The Bill is founded on principles derived from the United Nations Convention on the Rights of the Child...' (The Rt. Hon. Ian Lang, Scottish Grand Committee Hansard, 5.12.94, Col. 4). (For description of the UN Convention, see Chapter Three; for its text, see Appendix 1.) Such principles can be found in numerous locations in the Act:

- The welfare of the child should be the paramount consideration in making decisions affecting the child. Section 11(7), 16(1), 17(1), 95, Sch. 2 para. 16
- Due regard should be given to children's views, subject to their age and maturity. While any child has this right, children aged twelve or older are presumed to have sufficient age and maturity. Sections 6(1), 11(7), 16(2), 17(3), and 95
- No order should be made unless it is better than making no order. Sections 11(7), 16(3), 96, Sch. 2 para. 16
- Due regard should be given to a child's religious persuasion, racial origin and cultural and linguistic background. Sections 17 (4), 22(2) and 95

The avoidance of unhelpful time-delays is not as commonly found in the Act, although this is raised in relation to adoption and is addressed in rules and regulations. In a retrograde step, the requirement for a children's hearing to have regard to a child's religious persuasion has not been maintained from the 1968 Act. If such a consideration, however, were considered part of a child's welfare, the children's hearing must have regard to it.

The welfare test is a familiar one to courts in family law cases, as that developed from Section 3(2) of the 1986 Act (Norrie 1996). Notably, the Act goes beyond Article 3 of the UN Convention, which only requires that a child's best interests be a 'primary consideration' rather than paramount. It also goes beyond that recommended by the child care law review (1991: para. 1.13). On the other hand, the welfare test is specified in the 1995 Act to apply to certain kinds of decisions: for example, when deciding about family law or adoption orders, or decisions for 'looked after' children. Thus, while the welfare criterion may be stronger in the 1995 Act than required by the UN Convention, it only exists in specific situations.

A distinction is made in the Act between adoption and other proceedings. When deciding on adoption orders, the welfare of the child *into* adulthood must be considered. This reflects today's reality that fewer babies are available for adoption and more older children: so that to consider only a young person's welfare in childhood might be a very short perspective indeed. It does raise potential difficulties, however, of establishing what exactly *is* in a child's best interests and predicting outcomes into the future. Even though courts may have developed case law and social workers gained knowledge from research findings and experience, such evaluations are by no means established and concrete. 'Welfare' and 'best interests' are vague terms, with many imponderables (see Eekelaar 1994; Marshall 1997; Reppucci and Crosby 1993). Whoever decides what are children's best interests has considerable power, but there is no clear answer about who it should be (Marshall 1997). While numerous professions may have important contributions to make, including psychologists, health visitors, social workers or teachers, none are inevitably the single source. The discussion of needs earlier in this chapter is also informative, because it highlights the potential clash between the opinion of the expert and the individual. Where do the child's felt or expressed needs fit into the determination of the child's best interests?

Consideration of a child's views in making decisions is another principle consistently paired with the welfare test—thus the Act requires children's views to be part of the determination of their best interests. While the Children Act 1975 included the right of children to be consulted when they were in care or when they were involved in adoption, the extension of this right to numerous other proceedings and services is considered a revolutionary aspect of the 1995 legislation. It brings into Scottish legislation another key article of the UN Convention, Article 12.

But, as in the UN Convention, the impact of a child's views is qualified. The Scottish variation does so by such phrases as 'taking account of the age and maturity of the child'. Such qualification of children's rights recognises children's gradual development in experience and thinking. Younger children's views may be seen as short-sighted or too dependent on others' opinions, for them to be weighed as heavily as adults. (Why both age and maturity are included in the qualification is less understandable, as age seems somewhat redundant once maturity is included. However, this does follow the wording of Article 12.) This qualification weakens the power of a younger child's view. This is further weakened by the frequent provision that children over twelve should be presumed to be of sufficient age and understanding. Children over twelve may have their rights better protected by this presumption, which is positive. Children under twelve may be more at risk. While Norrie (1996) cited cases where the views of very young children were considered, to those with non-legal backgrounds the Section could be read to suggest children under twelve are not presumed to have sufficient age or maturity. It does not consider the advantages of looking at children's views in context: for example, a young child might have a very well-informed and 'mature' view of what type of home they wish to live in but have difficulty working out a nutritious weekly meal plan. The wording for children's views, however, had been consulted upon and agreed in the Scottish Law Commission's Report No. 135 (1992a) and applied in the Act.

The impact of a child's views is also qualified because it is subordinate to the welfare principle. A parent, court, children's hearing or local authority must have 'due regard' and 'as far as is practicable', but they do not have to abide by it. Campbell (1992) worried that adult values tended to constitute what was considered in the child's best interests, and this led to ignoring the child's life and experiences in the present. (For further discussion, see the next chapter.)

Again, this protective stance may beneficially take into account children's development, the responsibility of adults to make decisions and not pass them on to children, and children's rights to be protected. It can mean, however, that children's rights to be heard are engulfed by paternalistic views of their best interests. To take Article 12 seriously in practice, it is submitted, children should be presumed to have a view under the Act's provisions and to have the right to express it. Qualifications of this right should require specific justifications.

Scottish legislation extends children's right to have their views considered into their relationships with parents. Just as parents must consider another parent's view when making a 'major decision' (Section 6), so must parents give due regard to their children's views. The same qualifications also apply, however, as outlined above. Nonetheless, this extension of Article 12 into the private life of families is a new and ideologically powerful step.

The Act goes beyond principles to establish a range of procedures and means to operationalise such rights. For example, children now not only have a duty to attend their own children's hearing, but a right to attend (Section 45). As Gordon (1996) pointed out, however, this may clash with a business meeting's ability to excuse a child from attending his or her own hearing—such a decision cannot be appealed. Parents (technically, a 'relevant person' under the Act), the press and other specified people can be excluded from parts of children's hearings, if in the interests of the child and so the child's views can be heard or to avoid 'significant distress' to the child (Sections 46 and 43). However, again this procedure is weakened because the hearing's chairperson must then explain to the excluded parent the substance of what has taken place in that person's absence (Section 46(2)). If children are worried about possible repercussions of stating their views, they may not feel protected by this requirement.

For both courts and children's hearings, the legislation outlines a process to help operationalise a child's right to be heard, which is further developed in rules of court and children's hearing regulations. For example, when applications for Section 11 orders are contested, a 'Child Welfare Hearing' will be held at an early stage in the procedures where a child's views can be put forward (Rule 33.22A of the Ordinary

Cause Rules 1993 as amended). Anecdotal reports of the Child Welfare Hearing, since its implementation in November 1996, indicate that this provision may be an important practical step in encouraging courts to recognise children's right to have their views considered.

Other provisions can be identified that operationalise children's agency and participation rights. A child who is desperate enough to run away may be able to go to established 'safe refuges'. These could allow children at least some respite, initiated by their own action. Local authorities do not have a duty to establish or fund such refuges, so the possibility of this provision will be at their discretion or others' initiative (Section 38). Children will have the right to sue their parents for failing to meet their parental responsibilities (Section 1(3)). Children themselves can apply to court in relation to child protection measures or Section 11 orders (e.g. to re-establish contact with a birth parent, after adoption). Legal aid is generally available for children (and others), for court proceedings around child protection and/or children's hearings (Section 92). A new subsection is added to the Age of Legal Capacity (Scotland) Act 1991, so as to remove any doubt about the ability of children under the age of sixteen with 'general understanding of what it means to do so' to instruct a solicitor in civil proceedings (Sch. 4, para. 53(3)). The right of a child to consent to, or refuse, medical examination or treatment contained within the 1991 Act is re-asserted (Section 90). This right is subject to a child being of 'sufficient understanding'. Children's rights to a familiar environment and people is supported by the possibility of an exclusion order for an alleged abuser (discussed below and in Chapter Four). The rights of children to be treated as individuals, separate from their parents, and to take their own actions and decisions have increased considerably.

A critical question will be what information children will be given in relation to their rights. Local authorities are required to publish information on their (and voluntary agencies) services by 1 April 1998 (Section 20), but this does not apply to private law provisions. The Scottish Office commissioned the Scottish Child Law Centre to produce information for children on the private law provisions (*You Matter* (1996)), but considerable dissemination would be required across all services providers who come in contact with children. Further, it cannot be assumed that information for children of a certain literacy and comprehension level will meet the needs of all children or all carers. Truly ensuring that people are informed about services and about their rights is a task that requires considerable effort, consultation and monitoring.

Safeguarders could provide information to children involved in certain procedures, although this is not the legal role set out for safeguarders in legislation. As heralded by the White Paper (SWSG 1993a), a safeguarder can now be appointed in a wider range of situations, by courts or children's hearings, when it is considered necessary to 'safeguard the interests of the child in the proceedings' (Section 41). Despite Lord Clyde's recommendation (see Chapter Three), a safeguarder is still not appointable when an application is made for an emergency order. The possibility exists in the legislation for different safeguarders to be appointed at different proceedings, which is unlikely to be in a child's best interests. The continuation of the same safeguarder between courts and children's hearings, if need be, is not guaranteed (although it is encouraged) by the rules. The debate about whether a safeguarder can adequately put forward a child's views, when a safeguarder's role is to report on the child's best interests, is left undecided. Children do not have the right to legal aid to fund representation in children's hearings, although a lawyer can attend and participate. Legal aid is available for children in any associated court proceedings and for advice. The Act allows for further regulations to be made for safeguarders (as well as curators ad litem and reporting officers), concerning appointment, qualifications and training as well as management and organisation. A panel could be established by the Secretary of State. These provisions put off crucial decisions about the safeguarders' role, expertise and management for a future date, and fail to provide any answers to the debates around safeguarders (see Chapter Three).

The Act has much to commend it. The principles, however, are not extended across all of its provisions. In an analysis of these basic principles across the (then) Bill, over one hundred gaps were found and many of these remained unfilled. The Government argued against having an overarching set of principles, saying their mention at specific points would strengthen their application (Hansard, 1.5.95 Col. 93).

Certainly, when the government created an overarching set of principles over more limited areas of the Act (in Section 16 for children's hearings and courts, and Section 17 for local authorities 'looking after' children), they created exceptions that are potentially draconian. For example, Section 17 (5) qualifies the duties of local authorities:

> If, for the purpose of protecting members of the public from serious harm (whether or not physical harm) a local authority consider it necessary to exercise, in a manner which (but for this paragraph) would not be consistent with their duties under this section, their powers with respect to a child whom they are looking after, they may do so.

The rights of 'looked after' children to be heard, to have their welfare or their backgrounds considered (as well as parents' rights for contact and to have their views considered) are removed with no legislative statements about time limits, no recourse to appeal, and with no requirement for a continuing process. What 'serious harm' exactly means is not defined by the Act. Norrie (1996) wrote that the harm can be to property or to a person, or emotional or psychological. The determination of 'serious' is said to be 'harm that is not trivial' (46). Evidently, the phrase will require legal interpretation to judge its parameters.

The government's justification at the time lay with the paramountcy of children's welfare within these sections. Because the paramountcy test was so high, said government ministers, exceptions were needed. The government sought to reassure those concerned. The sub-sections were:

not a separate power to send a child to secure accommodation or to place the child under a supervision requirement. It opens the way to their [courts or children's hearings] exercising their functions for which succeeding provisions of the Bill provide specific authority ... they would continue to have regard to the welfare of the child as an important consideration but not the paramount one. (Earl of Lindsay, Hansard, 12.7.95 Col. 1799)

Such exceptions to children's best interests were not new to Scotland. Secure accommodation had long been a possibility on the grounds of children injuring themselves or others. Kearney (1996) pointed out that a court decision in 1986 (*Humphries* v *S* [1986] SLT 683) said that it could be in a 'child's own interest to be detained in order to prevent him from worsening his position by committing further offences' (7). Such reasoning did seem a roundabout way to bring in protection of the public, arguably in the guise of a child's welfare. What was new about Sections 16 (5) and 17 (5) for Scottish child welfare legislation was the *explicit acknowledgement* of others' interests when making decisions about a child in these situations.

While hopefully these provisions will be little used, theoretically, their inclusion is informative. They bring in concerns about youth crime and violence, traditionally rejected by the Scottish welfare approach in the children's hearings. They suggest difficulties within rights theory itself, in relation to balancing the rights of one child against the rights of other children and whether there can be exceptions to children's rights. They raise questions about the welfare approach, in the extent of discretionary powers and restrictive policies in the name of 'welfare'. The provisions encapsulate many of the difficult theoretical—and practical—questions of how to deal with young people who threaten (or appear to threaten) others.

Re-balancing justice and welfare: children's hearings and emergency child protection

The influence of previous reviews and inquiries can be found strongly in the new arrangements for child protection. While not extricating child protection from the children's hearing system, Lord Clyde's suggestion for increased judicial oversight and decision-making over child protection was heeded. The White Paper's (SWSG 1993a) recommendations were largely followed (with some alterations in times and details). At virtually every stage, parents or children will be able to ask a court to set aside or vary emergency orders (although it should be noted that, in the past, such requests were possible at numerous stages as well). The time-frames are detailed and short for both appeals and procedures. Sheriffs can make decisions not to grant a particular order, but at applications for both Child Assessment Orders (CAO) and Exclusion Orders (EO), they can choose to grant a Child Protection Order (CPO) instead. A diagram of the CPO process provides an idea of its complexity (see p. 93).

If a child or parent applies to a court to have the order set aside or varied, they can become caught up in parallel processes between children's hearings and courts that

Diagram A: Legal steps once application made to Sheriff for Child Protection Order (CPO)

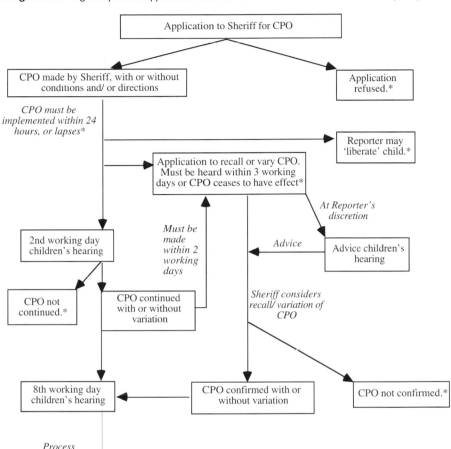

* Points where this Child Protection Order process can end. This would not necessarily preclude applicants or authorities taking other measures, such as referring a child to the Reporter.

could be confusing. The time-table is tight and leaves little room for manoeuvre. It recognises the necessity of avoiding time delays, but fails to acknowledge problems parents and their children may have in operationalising their rights—such practical problems as limited access to telephones, making arrangements with a lawyer on short notice, or literacy difficulties. Simply explaining the various options and procedures to children and their families will be a complex task.

Courts will be able to specify particular directions of the order, in relation to medical examination and treatment, for example, and contact. If there is new evidence and several other conditions met, a Sheriff can review the establishment of grounds of referral (a government response to events in South Ayrshire in the 1990s, see Kelly 1996). Thus, certain procedures have been tightened, increasing recourse is made to judicial decisions, and the rights to procedural justice for children and parents (supposedly) enhanced.

A controversial provision in the Act has re-balanced the traditional (although never in practice absolute) division between justice (court) and welfare (children's hearings) decisions. On appeal, a Sheriff will be able to substitute his or her own disposal for that of a children's hearing (Section 51(5)(c)(iii)). Norrie (1996) provided this explanation:

> One cannot question the Government's good intention, which was to protect the hearing system from challenge on the basis that it is not judicial enough to satisfy the due process requirements in the European Convention on Human Rights, nor can one doubt that the provision may in time destroy what Lord President Hope described in *Sloan v B* 1991 S.L.T. 530 at p.548E as the 'genius' of the system under the 1968 Act, that is to say the complete separation of roles between the children's hearing and the court (though it must be admitted that Lord Hope himself supported the inclusion of this provision …). (90)

The legislation leaves unaddressed the reasons why Kilbrandon initially suggested that courts remain out of welfare decisions: their difficulties in following up on their disposals, their lack of expertise in welfare areas, and their adversarial nature (see Chapter Two). Sheriff Kearney, a respected expert in children's hearings and related laws and author of the Fife Report (1992), suggested the need to introduce welfare decisions back into the courts:

> there is no requirement in the [1995] Act for the sheriffs to conduct a sort of judicial children's hearing although nothing is said to prohibit this and some of us feel such a process to be desirable or even necessary if we are to have any chance of addressing the needs of the child in the light of the overarching principles. (1996: 28)

The survival of the children's hearing system may be threatened, due to this particular re-balancing between welfare and justice. Sheriffs do not have to use their power to set their own disposals, and reports across Scotland suggest that at least presently most Sheriffs have no intention of doing so. But now, under the Act, the possibility is there.

There are those who do not think the 1995 Act has gone far enough in ensuring justice. For example, Sheriff Mitchell (1997) remained very concerned that children's hearings can make decisions based on allegations not proved in court. Reporters can present minimalist grounds, if grounds of referral are taken to 'proof'. Children's hearings do not learn directly from the Sheriff exactly which facts were established at proof and which were not. Sheriff Mitchell was not reassured by Norrie's arguments that the Reporter should ensure that hearings are given new grounds, when relevant. Sheriff Mitchell believed there should be more judicial oversight in hearings: 'It is a fundamental flaw in our system that lay members of the children's hearings are expected to reach correct decisions in law without being assisted or guided by a suitably qualified lawyer' (16). He did not think that Reporters always provided such assistance and guidance.

Further, Sheriff Mitchell was highly critical of the complexity of the system, referring particularly to the new appeal to the Sheriff Principal (Section 51). An appellant can now go to the Sheriff Principal or to the Court of Session. From the Sheriff Principal, there could be a further appeal to the Court of Session if the Sheriff Principal grants permission. Sheriff Mitchell was concerned about the potential for time delay and the potential inconsistency of Sheriff Principals' decisions across the six areas of Scotland. He concluded: '… the sheriff principal can be required to deal with appeals from the decisions of different sheriffs in different processes at different times in respect of the same child' (9). Too much complexity may have been introduced into the system.

New orders and new thresholds

The Act introduces a new term into Scottish law, which requires considerable debate and judicial interpretation to define it: significant harm (for discussion, see Chapter Six). The provisions for orders about child protection are further complicated by slightly different thresholds for different types:

(1) The lowest can be found for *Child Assessment Orders*. (CAOs allow for a child to be taken away for assessment or to require a person to comply with an assessment. The order can last up to seven days, and contact—as well as other conditions—can be specified by the Sheriff. Only a local authority can apply for such an order.)

A sheriff will grant such an order if satisfied that a local authority has *reasonable cause to suspect* that the child is suffering or likely to suffer significant harm. The Sheriff will also have to be satisfied that an assessment is required in order to establish *reasonable cause to believe* a child is so suffering or likely to suffer and that, without the order, an assessment could not be carried out or would be unsatisfactory. (Section 55)

(2) A higher threshold can be found for *Child Protection Orders*. (CPOs allow for a child to be removed or kept in a place, require a person to produce a child, and other specifics. The order will cease to have effect if it is not implemented within twenty-four hours. For other time-limits, see diagram on page 93.)

The thresholds differ for local authorities and other applicants. Local authorities will have to satisfy Sheriffs that they have *reasonable grounds to suspect* that a child is suffering or likely to suffer significant harm. Further, they will have to satisfy the Sheriff that they are making (or are having others make) enquiries so that they can decide whether to take any action to safeguard the child's welfare, and that such enquiries are urgently required yet frustrated by unreasonably denied access to the child. Any other applicant (which can also be a local authority) would have to satisfy a Sheriff that there are *reasonable grounds to believe* a child is or will suffer significant harm, and that an order is necessary. (Section 57)

(3) The highest thresholds lie with the *Exclusion Orders*. (EOs allow for an alleged abuser, the 'named person', to be excluded from a location or from contact with a child. Interim orders are available and a full EO can last for six months. Only local authorities can apply.)

For an interim order, a Sheriff must be satisfied that:

- the child *has* suffered, *is* suffering or *is likely to* suffer significant harm, as a result of the named person's actual or threatened conduct
- the order is necessary to protect the child and better safeguards the child's welfare than removing the child
- a person is capable of taking care of the child and any other member of the family requiring care, and who will reside in the child's family home. (Section 76)

For a full order, numerous other requirements are made about the named person's right to be heard and situations where an order could not be made. A range of living arrangements are listed where a named person could not be excluded (generally because of the home also being the place of the named person's employment).

For anyone involved in this process, the differences between 'reasonable grounds' and 'reasonable cause', suspecting and believing, contribute additional complexities when the most basic term of 'significant harm' is itself legally undefined at the time of writing. What evidence or supporting information will be required in order to meet such thresholds is, as yet, unknown. So many exemptions exist for exclusion orders that they may be difficult for local authorities to obtain in the first place. Their comprehensibility to parents and children, who are unlikely to deal with such issues regularly, will be a test of professionals' communication and expertise.

The changes in child protection procedures have not been met with professional equanimity: 'there are some fears in Scotland that the new provisions of the 1995 Act, in their eagerness to respect formal and legal rights, may work to the disadvantage of children—and possibly of some parents' (Marshall 1996: 263). Whether children will languish or even be further harmed because of the possibly heightened thresholds is not yet tested. (Some protection is provided by Section 61(5), which allows a police constable to remove a child to a place of safety when a CPO can not be applied for and the removal is deemed necessary. The police constable would still have to be satisfied that the conditions for 'any applicant' applying for a CPO were met.) The interface with criminal proceedings is left unaddressed. Given its substantial time delays and low rate of prosecutions, an exclusion order may not provide a satisfactory long-term solution for a child who wishes to remain in his or her home.

Concluding thoughts

Even from this initial and necessarily partial analysis of the Act, areas of opportunity, of potential crisis and of critical decision-making are evident. The Act maintains a degree of flexibility for services to come together in innovative ways to best meet the rights and needs of children and their families through the combination of Section 12 and duties towards 'children in need'. Attempts have been made to encourage inter-agency co-operation and to smooth interactions between different fora (e.g. between children's hearings–adoption–courts). New duties may result in new and/or improved services and support for children with and affected by disabilities, for children who run away, or for children who are otherwise homeless. The wide 'looked after' category, combined with the corporate definition of local authorities, could result in a much wider range of services and recognition of children's rights. Children's rights to participate are given recognition as never before in Scottish children's legislation, and courts, lawyers, children's hearings and services could use these legislative duties to improve their practice considerably.

At the same time, the Act is being implemented at a time of turmoil and financial crisis for local authorities. The very flexibility allowed in public care provision could mean curtailed and stigmatising services. When powers have been laid on local authorities rather than duties, or qualifications made, services or support may never be funded. The Act does not address fundamental questions of resource allocation, employment nor income that lie behind many of the problems faced by children, young people and families today. The Act does not necessarily resolve disputes between agencies and departments, over who will provide a service. The readjustments between welfare and justice approaches may leave some children more vulnerable and the children's hearing system itself seriously weakened.

Changes in terminology, duties and procedures highlight points of critical decision-making. The requirements around orders for child protection, with the new terminology of 'significant harm', will take considerable time to be understood and interpreted. 'Children in need' will require definition from agencies corporately as well as individual service providers. The translation of key principles—children's and parent's right to be heard, the paramountcy of a child's welfare, due regard to religious persuasion, etc., and promoting contact between children and parents—into reality will depend heavily on actual practice and procedures. The Children (Scotland) Act provides a framework, but its implementation will decide how it will actually affect children and their families.

Chapter 6

◆

COMPARISONS ACROSS THE UK

MANY of the critical areas for decision-making raised in the previous chapter—for example, defining 'children in need' or 'significant harm', and operationalising key principles—can be considered in light of experience elsewhere in the UK. Other UK children's legislation contains provisions that are phrased alike and use similar concepts. The legislation for England and Wales, the Children Act 1989, was implemented in October 1991. Scotland can thus learn from over six years of English and Welsh experience. The Northern Ireland Order, the Children (NI) Order 1995, was implemented shortly before the 1995 Act. Thus fewer lessons can be learnt from its implementation as Scotland faces its own, but differences in the legislation and in service structure allow for useful reflection.

At the same time, the differences between the legislation and the context need to be kept in mind. While the Children (Scotland) Act 1995 has been described as Scotland's Children Act 1989, the legislation is not an exact replica and is being implemented in a different legal, structural and cultural context. (For further discussion, see Chapter One.) Far more amendments to Scottish adoption legislation were made by the 1995 Act than were made by the 1995 Order for Northern Ireland's adoption law or by the 1989 Act for adoption legislation in England and Wales. Certain of the Scottish adoption amendments will be mentioned below, but a full comparison of adoption legislation across the UK will not be undertaken.

The discussion below will concentrate on comparisons between the 1995 Act, the 1995 Order and the Children Act 1989. It will raise issues under the now-familiar themes of targeting, working together, children's rights and welfare versus justice. It will not provide a comprehensive comparison, as that would be beyond the scope of this book. While there are exceptions, it will predominantly focus on what the Scottish legislation contains, and then compare it with other UK legislation—thus Northern Ireland's law on child labour or the complaints procedure set up under the 1989 Act will not be discussed here. What this chapter will provide is some comparison and discussion in key areas raised in Chapter Five, concentrating on duties towards 'children in need' and children's services plans, that have considerable information from England and Wales but tend to be covered less frequently in the Scottish arena.

A note on terminology: for the most part, the term 'local authorities' is used in this chapter. Technically, this can only be found in the 1989 and 1995 Acts; the 1995 Order uses the term 'authorities'. This difference is important, as 'authorities' represents the different structure in children's services in Northern Ireland (see Chapter One). The 1995 Order refers to 'articles' rather than 'sections'—thus when the term 'articles' is used, readers will be aware that this refers to provisions with the Northern Ireland Order.

At certain points legal cases in England and Wales are referred to but it is vital to remember that they do not provide conclusive legal interpretation for Scotland. Scotland has its own legal system, and legal cases in England and Wales can only be suggestive of possible judicial interpretations in Scotland.

Children in need

'Children in need' is now a category found across UK children's legislation. As discussed in previous chapters, 'children in need' was first introduced in the Children Act 1989. It was the legislative answer to the Short Report's (House of Commons 1984) call for a revised preventive duty, which went beyond preventing children's reception into care to include 'family support'. The phrasing of the general duty to 'safeguard and promote the welfare of children' occurs almost word-for-word across all three pieces of legislation (Section 17, Children Act 1989; Article 18, Children (NI) Order 1995; Section 22, Children (Scotland) Act 1995). The definition is also largely replicated across the legislation, except for the addition of children 'adversely affected' by disability in the Scottish legislation. Even without this specification, children affected by disability could no doubt be included in the other jurisdictions, due to the generality of other parts of the definition. But the separate category in the 1995 Act likely has more judicial weight because of its specificity. A young carer, for example, would probably have a stronger legal case if s/he was not assessed for services by a local authority in Scotland, than in England, Wales or Northern Ireland.

Other, relatively small differences, are of note because they raise policy issues as well as practical ones. While authorities across the UK have powers to be 'enabling' authorities and commission others to provide legally-required services for them, both the 1989 Act and 1995 Order state that authorities 'shall facilitate the provision by others' of 'children in need' and other services (Section 17(5) and Article 18(5)). This duty is not placed on local authorities within the Scottish section on 'children in need', so that local authorities will have more discretion in who will provide 'children in need' services. An amendment to the Scottish Act included the principle of giving 'due regard to a child's religious persuasion, racial origin and cultural and linguistic background' when local authorities are providing their services for 'children in need' (Section 22(2)). The 1989 Act and the 1995 Order do not contain this principle specifically for their parallel duties. People who receive certain social security benefits (e.g. family credit) cannot be required to repay local authority assistance for 'children in need', in all legislation, but the list of relevant benefits differs.

Of considerable significance are the more detailed requirements for services for 'children in need', in both the 1989 Act and the NI Order, compared to the dearth of detailed requirements in Scotland. Schedule 2 of the 1995 Order and Part I of Schedule 2 in the 1989 Act have lengthy lists of services that local authorities/authorities have the *duty* to provide for 'children in need' (for example, see Figure C for list of services required by the NI Order). The 1995 Act has no such schedule. The government agreed to amend the Bill to put some such specific duties on local authorities: so that Article 19 on day care etc. is basically repeated in Section 27 of the 1995 Act. Scottish local authorities will have to publish information on services and, in fact, on a wider range of 'relevant' services (identified in Section 19, see Chapter Five) than required in either the 1995 Order or the 1989 Act. Overall, though, Scotland has far less specificity in the services that it must provide than other parts of the UK. This allows Scottish local authorities more flexibility, and the possibility of using scarce resources to the best effect. On the other hand, when local authorities are facing such stringent cut-backs, they could choose not only to define 'children in need' quite narrowly, but also to provide a very limited range of services.

Figure C: Duties and powers on authorities due to Schedule 2 of the Children (Northern Ireland) Order 1995

Authorities have a duty to:
- identify the extent of 'children in need' in their areas
- publish information on children's services such as those for 'children in need' and 'looked after' children and seek to ensure those 'who might benefit from the services' receive the relevant information
- open and maintain a register of disabled children
- prevent children in their area from suffering ill-treatment or neglect, and to inform other authorities if a child (who is 'likely to suffer harm') is to live in another area
- provide services so as to minimise the effect of disability on disabled children; to give disabled children the opportunity to lead lives 'which are as normal as possible'
- seek to reduce the need for children to be involved in care, criminal and various other proceedings or to be placed in secure accommodation; seek to discourage children from committing criminal offences
- provide for 'children in need' living with their families: advice, guidance and counselling; occupational, social, cultural or recreational activities; home help; facilities for or assistance with travelling to and from home so as to take advantage of services; assistance so that children and their families can have a holiday
- provide family centres
- help children to live with their families or to promote contact between children and their families
- when making arrangements for day care, or encouraging people to be foster parents, to give regard to different racial groups in the area

Authorities have the power to:
- assist another person, in order to protect a child, by providing that person with accommodation or cash.

Other duties are laid out in Article 19, such as providing day care, after-school care, and holiday care for 'children in need', and the power to provide facilities (such as training, advice, guidance and counselling) for those caring for children or who may accompany them.

Certainly, when the 1989 Act was implemented in England and Wales, many local authorities faced pressures to take both restrictive options. The range of research evidence now available paints a largely depressing picture. From their replies from eighty-two English local authorities in autumn 1992, Aldgate and Tunstill (1995) found that some local authorities were narrowly defining 'in need' priority groups for services, as children at risk of significant harm. The most common pre-determined groups were children local authorities already had responsibility for: children at risk of significant harm (76% of local authorities), at risk of neglect (74%), those in care (73%), those accommodated (72%) and those on remand (70%). Aldgate and Tunstill were concerned about the limited numbers of local authorities that included the following groups of children as predetermined groups for 'children in need':

- children from homeless families (35% of local authorities)
- drug/solvent abusing children (33%)
- children excluded from school (29%)
- children in bed and breakfast accommodation (29%)
- children with a mentally ill carer (28%)
- children in substandard housing (27%)
- children in low income families (27%)
- young people in bed and breakfast accommodation (27%).

Research evidence indicated that such children were at considerable risk of entering care, poor health and low educational attainment—all features of the 'children in need' legislated definition.

Given the limits of identified groups of 'children in need', it was unsurprising that Aldgate and Tunstill found that: 'Family support services are often seen as optional and a luxury rather than as an integral part of Section 17 services…' (41) and concluded that '… too much emphasis is still being given to child protection investigation at the expense of family support services' (41). Despite the legal requirements to provide certain services, Aldgate and Tunstill (1995) found that not all local authorities were providing such services (although they said they were planning to develop them). For example, only 85% of local authorities said they provided help with travel, 80% provided family centres and 54% befriending. More positively, a wide range of services tended to be available in each local authority.

Research evidence from elsewhere had similar findings. Colton et al. (1995) reported on research with eight social service departments (SSDs) in Wales. Colton and colleagues analysed policy documents, and undertook interviews with lead child care managers, social workers, parents and children. The SSDs tended to concentrate their efforts on children at risk of abuse and neglect. Those departments that attempted to define 'children in need' more broadly were being forced to retrench, under the pressures of resource constraints. Bull et al. (1996) undertook research across eighteen local authorities in England, using interviews and case studies. Local authorities in the study were split between those who defined need quite restrictively, and the much smaller group of authorities who used a broader, more inclusive definition. As implementation proceeded, Bull *et al.* found that pressure to define groups more precisely, so as to target services, moved authorities further away from a broad definition. Bull et al. (1996) explained why: 'It reflects local authorities' concern about ensuring that resources meet individual needs, and that need does not outstrip the services available to meet it' (6).

Research from a child protection perspective repeats the same message, with even more fervour. For example, Thoburn (1995) discussed findings from research on 117 child protection conferences, in four localities from 1993 to 1994, and criticised how families accessed services:

> A common pattern is that families and young people who ask for help, especially those who are vulnerable by reason of homelessness, are turned away, only to be pulled into the system, when things deteriorate and protection becomes a serious concern. In some cases it is the other professionals such as health visitors or teachers, and in other cases family members themselves, who feel obliged to exaggerate the risk of abuse in order to receive a service to which they have failed to gain access in other ways. (77)

The use of child protection procedures to access services is problematic, because such access is linked to *parental fault* whereas 'children in need' services are not. While 'children in need' services in themselves can be perceived as stigmatising (Colton et al. 1995), services provided for children at risk can be even more so.

In Scotland, the children's hearing system provides an alternative course of action. A child, who has been thought to be abused or at risk of being abused could be referred to the Reporter, proceed to a children's hearing and come out with a supervision requirement without any formal determination of parental fault. Still, the resulting services could be seen as stigmatising. Further, the children's hearing system was predicated on the belief that, for whatever reason, parenting had failed in some way for a child to be in need (see Chapter Three). While the type of failed parenting may be more vague than when seeking court orders for child protection, the overtones of parental fault may well remain.

English and Welsh local authorities have found it particularly hard to implement their duties towards children with disabilities. Disabled children's place within the definition of 'children in need' itself proved difficult for some local authorities. Although children with disabilities were a sub-category of the definition, 32% of Aldgate and Tunstill's authorities did not list disabled children as a pre-determined group of children (1995). Welsh SSDs found it difficult to identify children with disabilities in their area (Colton et al. 1995). Despite the duty to open and maintain a register of disabled children, none of the Welsh SSDs had done so twelve months after the Act's implementation (Colton et al. 1995). Child care managers were unsure what the purpose of the register was, beyond its statutory requirement, and parents could be unwilling to have their children placed on it for fear of stigmatisation (Colton et al. 1995). A Social Service Inspection (SSI) in May 1993 (SSI 1994) of four local authorities found that further work was needed in services for disabled children: involvement of parents and children; provision of culturally and racially sensitive services; coherent services; and better information. Respite services were considered over-regulated. The SSI did find evidence of good practice in two authorities, where positive relationships had been established with parents, who felt listened to and respected. Specialist staff appointments seemed to help improve services and relationships with disabled children and their families. The Children Act Report 1994 (Secretaries of State for Health and for Wales 1995) particularly noted the lack of progress to improve services for disabled young people aged sixteen to twenty-five. Despite the 'mainstreaming' of disabled children's services, many SSDs were struggling to understand the implications of their new duties for disabled children, let alone deliver helpful services.

Court cases have begun to test social services departments' interpretation of 'children in need'. For example, a High Court decision criticised the London Borough of Tower Hamlets for failing to carry out an individual assessment of a child as a 'child in need'. The child had been verbally abused because of the condition of his disabled mother, and his family had been assaulted and attacked. The family as a whole was assessed, but not the individual child under the Children Act 1989. (Community Care 1997; *R. v Tower Hamlets LBC, Ex p. Bradford*) Another case given even more coverage is an House of Lords ruling against Oldham Social Services Department (*Re C (a minor) (interim care residential assessment)* 1996 HL[1]), which allowed the court to order a particular assessment even though the Department had officially decided against it. The ruling said that 'In exercising its discretion whether to order any particular examination or assessment, the court will take into account the cost of the proposed assessment and the fact that local authorities' resources are notoriously limited' (Lord Browne-Wilkinson), but this assertion has not stopped fears being expressed that courts will have more control in allocating resources and thus throw in disarray local authorities' own prioritisation and planning (Cervi 1997). 'Children in need', particularly once it is defined by a local authority and plans published, may not be as flexible for local authorities as once thought.

Northern Ireland will provide another case study of implementing the category of 'children in need'. It will do so in another administrative context. While Boards have the responsibility primarily to assess health and social care needs and commissioning services, Units of Management, Trusts or the private and voluntary sectors will provide the services. McColgan (1995) feared that: '… child care services may become dependent on financial priorities and individual service processes of trusts rather than on rights of access to services as laid down in the Children (Northern Ireland) Order 1995' (642). Again the question of equity is worrisome. With social services located in joint Health and Social Services Boards, social care may be subservient to medical considerations. Complaints have been made of a 'technocratic' diagnostic approach

---

1 http://www.parliament.the-stationery-office.co.uk/pa/ld199697/ldjudgmt/jd961128/inrec.htm

that works against universal community services (see Aldgate and Hill 1995). Organisationally, the incorporation of personal social services into the health system, complete with the purchaser–provider split, may create problems for operationalising the preventive hope of 'children in need'.

'Children in need' will also be implemented in a different financial context in Northern Ireland. If families' economic status and household size are taken as indicators of social need, Northern Ireland has the lowest average gross and disposable weekly household incomes, and the largest average household size, of any region in the UK. On the other hand, Northern Ireland benefits from major alternatives to central government funding. Northern Ireland has access to European 'Structural Funds' due to its Objective 1 status. The 'Peace Programme' (The European Union Special Support Programme for Peace and Reconciliation in Northern Ireland and the Border Counties of Ireland) provides some £250 million until January 1998. Around £13.66 million has been targeted towards day care, education and family support for children up to the age of twelve. The International Fund for Ireland's Communities in Action Programme, launched in June 1995, provides over £2.5 million a year to community-run projects for children in their early years, young people, and opportunities for women (Smith 1996). Such an infusion of funds has the chance of making remarkable change, particularly as the 1995 Order is implemented during this time. On the other hand, these funds will not be available indefinitely. Care will need to be taken to ensure sustainability of new services and support in the longer-term. Recent publicity casts doubt on the extent of this apparent financial windfall (Downey 1997). Certainly, the funds each have specific remits, which do not cover the full scope of the 1995 Order.

Inter-agency collaboration

The debates around the definition of 'children in need' are made even more confusing because of disagreements or misconceptions *across* agencies. The Audit Commission (1994) reported on the failure of health and social services to create common understandings of need, thus hampering joint working at its most basic stage. Growing attention is focused on the lack of education for many young people who are 'looked after'—including a dramatically higher rate of school exclusions—and the lack of co-ordination between education and social services to meet this gap (Aldgate et al. 1993; Buchanan 1993). Sinclair et al. (1994) wrote about children who were placed in residential schools because of emotional or behavioural difficulties, or who were excluded from school. The children were not given the same services or rights in education as they would have received in social services—even though such children could well fit into the definition of 'children in need'.

A particular flash-point has been inter-agency co-operation for young people who are homeless. Young people who are homeless could presumably, if they were under eighteen, be considered 'children in need' and provided with support and services as a result. They could also potentially be provided with 'accommodation' or 'befriending' under different sections of the children's legislation. These sections in themselves present confusing age-ranges and criteria. For example, Section 20 of the 1989 Act lays out the following powers and duties for local authorities:

- For a 'child in need' (who is thus under age eighteen), a local authority *must* provide accommodation if: no person has parental responsibility for the child; the child is lost or has been abandoned; the person caring for the child is prevented from providing accommodation or care.
- for a child under age eighteen, a local authority *may* provide accommodation if the local authority thinks it will safeguard or promote the child's welfare; for a young person between the ages of sixteen and twenty-one, a local authority *may* provide accommodation in a community home if thought that it would safeguard and promote the young person's welfare.
- for a 'child in need' between the ages of sixteen and eighteen, a local authority *must* provide accommodation for a child if the authority *considers* it likely to *seriously prejudice* the child's welfare if accommodation is not provided.

(The last duty is not found in the 1995 Act.) 'After-care' provisions in Section 24 set out even more powers and duties:

- for a young person who has been 'looked after' (and other forms of accommodation) after reaching the age of sixteen and is less than twenty-one, a local authority *must* advise and befriend the young person and *may* give the young person assistance.

In Scotland, the duty to provide assistance is stronger—it must be provided for eligible young people—but it has a tighter age range—only up to the age of nineteen. No mention is made of 'befriending' in the Scottish legislation.

Research evidence shows that young people leave local authority 'care' at a far earlier age than other young people do from their family homes. In Biehal *et al*'s survey (1996), nearly two-thirds of 'looked after' young people left before the age of eighteen, and a quarter did so at age eighteen. More than one-fifth became homeless at some stage during their first two years of leaving care. Despite the evident problems of youth homelessness, and particularly for young people who have left care, they do not necessarily receive accommodation either under the Children Act 1989 or the Housing Acts. Young people's mobility across local authority boundaries is one problem (Kirby 1994), although provisions are made within the Act for such situations. A major difficulty is caused by the lack of joint agreements between housing and social services departments on how to assess homeless young people and which department has the responsibility to house them. McCluskey (1994) found that only half of surveyed SSDs had joint assessment procedures with housing authorities, while a third had no jointly agreed procedures at all.

In relation to housing, some SSDs have tried to use Section 27 of the 1989 Act, which requires agencies to co-operate when requested (a direct parallel to Section 21 of the 1995 Act, described in Chapter Five). They have taken housing authorities to court when they refused to help provide accommodation for homeless families. These legal cases have not proved particularly successful (Clements 1994; Cowan and Fionda 1994), and have left Section 27 an apparently weak duty indeed.

Inter-agency co-operation and collaboration seem to work better with certain agencies than others. Aldgate and Tunstill (1995) applauded SSDs' success in making positive links with housing, health, and education. Less positive was the failure to link with planning and transport departments, the police and the probation service. A particular gap was found with voluntary agencies. Aldgate and Tunstill were surprised to find the lack of consultation *within* social services, which was only found in 44% of surveyed local authorities. The SSI inspection of four local authorities (1994) was also critical about inter-agency collaboration for disabled children:

> The Act [Children Act 1989] requires social services departments, education and health authorities to work together in the best interests of children and clearly locates the lead responsibility. It was therefore perturbing to find a lack of clarity in some authorities about who held the lead responsibility. The parents interviewed wanted a more coherent, co-ordinated form of services. There appeared to be far greater scope for agencies to identify where work could be jointly funded, staff appointed between agencies and for staff to be jointly trained. (Reported in Secretaries of State for Health and for Wales (SSH and W) (1994): para. 2.32)

To help this continuing confusion over, and failure of, inter-agency collaboration and co-operation, hope was increasingly placed in children's services plans.

Children's services plans

In England and Wales, children's services plans originally had no legislative basis in the Children Act 1989. The Children (Scotland) Act 1995 was in fact the first to legislate for children's services plans. England and Wales soon followed in 1996, where the Children Act 1989 (Amendment) (Children's Service Planning) Order SI 1995 No. 785 put children's services plans on a statutory footing. Previously, children's services plans had been promoted through guidance and had not been mandatory. The Department of Health had produced a Local Authority Circular (92) 18 that provided few specifics and was considered fairly weak. The guidance produced in Wales, following the Local Government etc. (Wales) Act 1994, was considered much stronger and more detailed (Sutton 1995).

The children's services plans produced by English local authorities came under considerable scrutiny in the first half of the 1990s, with the SSI publishing an influential report (1995) and the National Children's Bureau (Sutton 1995) producing theirs. The SSI for Wales published a report *Preparing Children's Services Plans* (1995). Research on 'children in need' also touched on the planning process (e.g. Aldgate and Tunstill

1995; Audit Commission 1994; Bull et al. 1996; Tunstill 1995). The research found a range of deficiencies within the plans:

(1) *Unclear purpose and intention.* Not all plans stated a clear purpose and intention. Following from this, they were often unclear about the audience for their plans.

(2) *Limited ascertainment of need.* While certain local authorities had drawn on a variety of sources (e.g. extensive demographic data, consultation with users), others adopted 'a traditional unimaginative approach dependent on referrals coming into the department' (Tunstill 1995: 659). The indicators of need used were often biased towards identifying urban need rather than rural.

(3) *Limited data collection and analysis.* Most local authorities were collecting data, but not all were collating it. A decentralised approach to data collection (e.g. from area teams) sometimes led to data inconsistency.
Not all local authorities had appropriate computer hardware or software, sufficient research expertise nor staff for data analysis.

(4) *Poor methods for determining priorities.* Many local authorities determined their priority services groups based on definitions of risk from earlier legislation, rather than on empirical data about children who might be in need in their areas. In fact, policy documents were often developed *before* data had been collected. Thus, a *service-led* rather than a *needs-led* approach was often taken.
Various interest groups were at times determining priorities.
One local authority in Aldgate and Tunstill's research (1995) used a tertiary hierarchy of risk and prevention. Aldgate and Tunstill were concerned that this hierarchy would divert resources to the third (high risk) level and the local authority was '...in danger of resurrecting old boundaries such as those between care in the community and accommodation...' (40).

(5) *Mixed achievements in inter-agency collaboration and consultation.* When pre-Act inter-agency relationships were strong, social services had considerable success in collaborating with other agencies. When such relationships had not been strong, collaboration was more superficial or difficult to achieve. Certain agencies were hesitant to engage in collaboration, for fear of financial implications. Most local authorities were very poor at collaborating with voluntary organisations, with notable exceptions. Possible overlaps and confusion between different pieces of legislation were not always addressed. The SSI (1995) felt that inter-agency collaboration was hampered by the absence of: shared definitions of need; databases providing information on the extent of need based on these shared definitions; and systems of meetings and decision-making through which agencies could uniformly analyse need and decide how each agency should respond.
Consultation tended to be stronger for services for disabled children and their families, than for other types of services. Around half of SSDs consulted

with at least four other organisations, the most common being health and education (Aldgate and Tunstill 1995).

(6) *Cursory consultation with service users and elected members.* Service users were seldom involved in initial planning stages, with the exception of the parents of disabled children. Two difficulties were identified: the diversity of local issues and the 'lingering philosophy of service led planning' (Aldgate and Tunstill 1995: 29).

While Sutton (1995) reported on some participation initiatives, consultation with children and parents tended to be low and insubstantial. More promising examples of consulting with young people are reported in a recent publication from the Local Government Information Unit (Willow 1997). Consultation with ethnic minority groups was often poor.

In some local authorities, elected members were not involved in the development of policy documents, but only consulted about the prioritisation of predetermined groups and on budgets and costings.

(7) *Insufficient attention to commissioning services.* Aldgate and Tunstill (1995) tentatively concluded that the 'mixed economy of care' was used to increase the quality of services and to provide services that the statutory agency would not otherwise provide—but not typically to provide traditional 'core' responsibilities.

(8) *Lack of monitoring and evaluating outcomes.* Plans did not always map current services and resources, set key objectives and cost action plans, nor have monitoring and evaluation systems.

(9) *Failure to link, or poor linkages with other plans and reviews.* The SSI (1995) did not find evidence of links with the early years reviews required by the 1989 Act. Combined community care and children's services plans were not evaluated well: they were thought to be less accessible, and have a less clear planning framework for children's services, than plans solely for children's services.

From their investigations, several of these reports put forward ideas about best practice and issues to consider (e.g. Audit Commission 1994; SSI 1995; SSI for Wales 1995; Sutton 1995). A formidable list now exists for those involved in the planning process. Many of these ideas have been incorporated into new guidance.

Following the 1996 Order legislating for children's services plans, considerably more comprehensive guidance was jointly produced from the Department of Health and the Department of Education and Employment and sent out to health authorities and trusts by the NHS Executive. The central government thus sought itself to take a corporate approach, as well as encouraging children's services to do so. The guidance is not prescriptive.

What does not seem to have been researched and/or discussed are other alternatives to using 'pre-determined groups' for planning or emphasising an administrative purpose for planning. For example, Aldgate and Tunstill (1995) criticised many local authorities for being 'service-led', offering 'pre-determined groups' as the 'needs-led' approach. The use of groups is also contrasted with planning on the basis of past, individual, referrals. Training information from the Department of Health, and guidance consistently suggests planning on the basis of groups. Similarly, the possibility of plans being political or community-empowerment tools, rather than administrative, is little explored in influential publications, although it is in other planning literature such as health promotion (see Percy-Smith 1996). While in the end these choices may indeed by the best approaches to planning for children's services, alternatives could be considered more widely to see if they might provide further advantages.

Northern Irish Health and Social Services Boards will also be required to produce children's services plans (Northern Ireland Department of Health and Social Services (NIDHSS) 1996). As the Boards are working within a joint health and social service strategy, targets for 'children in need' are set alongside medical ones. For 'children in need' these are:

> By 2002, of the children assessed by Boards as children in need,
> —those below compulsory school age should receive good quality early years services within their own homes or elsewhere, or a combination of both; and
> —those of school age should receive family support services operating out of school hours.
> By 2002 there should be a 50% reduction in the number of children abused or reabused who are on child protection registers. (NIDHSS 1996: para. 8.12)

When further elaborating on these targets, the NIDHSS document suggests that the DHSS provide guidance on the means of assessing needs of children, so that Boards will have comparable methodologies. Further guidance will be produced on the format and content of children's services plans 'which ensure equity and access to services across the Province' (76). Neither of these points to ensure equity are contained in other UK guidance on children's services plans.

Children's services plans are receiving considerable attention across the UK in terms of research, policy and practice development. For example, the National Children's Bureau have established an unit specifically to provide support and consultation on children's services plans. The 1997 White Paper on Social Services from the Department of Health and the Welsh Office wanted to widen the remit of and consultation on children's services plans:

> If the maximum effect is to be achieved, however, the planning process must be seen as the corporate responsibility of the local authority as a whole and fully involve other statutory services including health, education, probation, other

juvenile justice services and housing. The Government therefore proposes to widen the statutory framework accordingly. (para. 3.9)

Research has been commissioned in Scotland to examine the involvement of voluntary organisations in such plans. Conferences, seminars and training days have been organised for those involved in planning. Children's services plans are being seen not only as a legal requirement, but also an opportunity to address the criticism that is made over and over again: the lack of inter-agency collaboration and co-operation.

Partnership with parents

While parents were not included as *partners* in English and Welsh planning at agency level, 'partnership with parents' was a common preoccupation for policy makers and practitioners when considering an individual child. None of the UK legislation specifically mentions the phrase or even the term 'partnership', but it can be found in key principles within Government guidance.

Commentators on the 1989 Act have concentrated on numerous dimensions of partnership with parents, such as: receiving information, parents' contact with their children, attention to parents' views, and parents' participation in decision-making. These will be briefly considered in turn below, both in comparing legislative requirements and research evidence where available.

Information

In order to be partners, parents need to be informed of what services are available, their rights and what they can expect. A clear requirement for this is the duty, in all UK legislation, to prepare and publish information (see above). Both the 1989 Act and 1995 Order have an additional duty to the Scottish legislation: they must take 'such steps as are reasonably practicable' so that those who might benefit from the services receive relevant information. Such an obligation was not laid on local authorities in the 1995 Act, although the need to distribute the information widely was recognised in guidance (SWSG 1997a).

Aldgate and Tunstill (1995) did not investigate the publication of information extensively, but felt from interviews that publicity efforts were not far advanced. Most publicity was in pamphlet form and written only in English. Publicity was available in standard places: schools, libraries and social services. They noted some exceptions, particularly the use of other agencies to help in dissemination and preparing tapes for people who were visually-impaired.

A national survey by the SSI in 1992 was much more satisfied with efforts made by social services (reported in SSH and W 1993). Popular and effective locations for distributing information included public libraries, GP surgeries, Citizens Advice Bureaux and family centres. Local solicitors, places of worship and borough magazines were methods used by some authorities. But in common with Aldgate and Tunstill, they did find that only sixty of 108 local authorities surveyed published their information in at least one language other than English, and only thirty-four published information in formats suitable for people with certain disabilities. A later SSI inspection of four local authorities in May 1993 was considerably more critical about information on disability services:

> The variety of services needed by disabled children and their families means that good dissemination by local agencies of information about services is particularly important. The overwhelming message from all the parents met during the inspection was that they were not receiving enough information, or the right information at the right time. (SSI 1994: para. 5.6.1)

Because children's services plans were also published, the cross-over with the duty to publish service information has been confusing for some local authorities in England (SSI 1995).

'Voluntary' care and parental contact

Several principles come together—such as prevention, supporting children with their families, and non-intervention—to encourage services to work with parents without state intervention. Thus, the intention is that 'voluntary' care, now called 'accommodation', should increase at the expense of statutory orders or supervision requirements. The proportion of 'looked after' children who are voluntarily 'accommodated' in England and Wales has increased since the Act's implementation, as intended (SSH and W 1995). The 1989 Act and 1995 Order *removed* requirements on parents to give notice completely, and parents can remove children so 'accommodated' at any time (except when there are court orders etc.); Section 25 of the 1995 Act reduced the notice time from twenty-eight to fourteen days (see Chapter Five).

'Accommodated' children are 'looked after' children in all UK legislation (note that the definition of 'looked after' does differ between legislation). Local authorities/authorities have certain duties for children 'looked after' that promote 'partnership with parents'. For example, Article 29 of the 1995 Order requires authorities to promote parental contact (as well as with relatives or friends) and Article 26 requires authorities to seek the views of parents when making a decision. Bilson and Barker (1995) undertook research in England and Wales that covered 80% of young people 'in care' (1991–92). At this early stage of the 1989 Act's implementation, the data on parental contact was disheartening. Nearly two out of five children (37%) had no parental contact, and less than half (47%) had regular contact. Those in residential care were more likely to have contact than those in foster care. One out of four children who had been in care for over five years had regular contact with parents.

When courts make orders, they can specify contact (as can children's hearings in Scotland). A Department of Health study of contact orders (1994) highlighted the complexity of many contact arrangements and the substantial support they required from local authorities. Given that foster carers were on 'the front line' of such arrangements, they often had to adapt their routines quite significantly. They also had to deal with the emotional effects associated with the preparation, transportation and return of children (see Sellick 1996). As demand for foster care increases (SSH and W 1994), foster carers are often having to enact the local authorities' duties to promote partnership and contact with parents.

Partnership in child protection

Can there be 'true partnership' when local authorities can apply to take away parents' children? Can parents be partners in such procedures, given that the state is intervening because of some concern about parental fault? Research by Thoburn and colleagues (Thoburn 1995) found, with some surprise, that such participation could be encouraged:

> there were cases which we had placed in out 'worst' scenario where we considered that it would be highly unlikely that a parent would be engaged in the social work and protection process, but where by the end of the 6-month period a skilled social worker and sensitive procedures had resulted in active participation. There were other cases where it should have been very easy to work in partnership but where either insensitive procedures or practice alienated parents and failed to involve them. (83)

Parents generally preferred to be at all or most of child protection conferences, although they may find attendance painful. Professionals' comments were also generally favourable about parents' attendance. Some would still prefer, however, to have family members excluded from certain parts of conferences. Two studies were carried out, the first with 220 consecutive child protection cases during 1990 and 1991. In this study, 57% of parents and carers said they had understood what was happening in the course of child protection proceedings and 43% felt they contributed. Only 35% said they took part in decision making. Just under half said they had not felt involved in the proceedings. Importantly, Thoburn reported no evidence that working in partnership ever made things 'turn out badly' for children or parents.

The second study covered information from 117 consecutive initial or incident child protection conferences held in two county authorities and two London Boroughs in 1993–94. When parents were in conflict with local authorities and their children were away from home, Thoburn reported that the parents tended to receive 'a very poor service' (83) and were seldom involved. One reason could be the different expectations of parents and social workers. While social workers did tend to offer parents counselling to 'come to terms with their loss', parents at that time wanted negotiation and advocacy to maintain relationships with their children. They wished to know about plans for their children. Thoburn noted that the only times when partnership with parents seemed inappropriate, happened when different workers were not allocated for the child who had been abused and for the abusing parent. When this was rectified, the service for the child was improved. (85)

Initially, the numbers of care and emergency child protection orders were far lower than pre-1989 Act Place of Safety Orders. Such statistics could represent improved preventive work with children and their families, and/or improved partnerships. Alternatively, this statistical drop could have been due to: unfamiliarity with the legislation; anxiety and uncertainty about the provisions; and/or uncertainty about the meaning of 'significant harm' (Fox Harding 1993). Whatever the reasons, this decrease has not been maintained. Similarly, while there was an initial decrease in the numbers of children placed on child protection registers after the 1989 Act came into force, registrations are now back to pre-Act levels (SSH and W 1995).

Few applications, however, have been made for child assessment orders (Children Act Advisory Committee (CAAC) 1992–95). Reasons could be the uncertainty about these new orders, but also that professionals may not wish to antagonise parents with whom they may well need to work with in the future (Dickens 1993). The small number of applications could represent the 'non-intervention' principle working in practice. It is also possible that knowing local authorities can apply to courts to obtain such orders can itself 'encourage' parents to co-operate.

Parental responsibilities, rights and partnerships

The concept of parental responsibilities underlies that of 'partnership with parents'. Parents are seen as originally and primarily responsible for the welfare and upbringing of their children. Parents may be supported in their parental responsibilities, but the state should not intervene unless the child's welfare is at risk (and on clearly stated grounds). Such a *laissez-faire* philosophy (Fox Harding 1991b) is not without contradictions within UK children's legislation, but is clearly evident.

Section 2 in the 1989 Act addresses parental responsibilities, and Section 3 provides a minimalist definition for the Act: 'all the rights, duties, powers, responsibilities and authority which by law a parent of a child has in relation to the child and his property' (which is also largely replicated in Article 6 of the 1995 Order). Commentators have been far more impressed by the specifics set out in Section 1 of the Children (Scotland) Act 1995:

- to safeguard and promote the child's health, development and welfare;
- to provide, in a manner appropriate to the stage and development of the child (i) direction and (ii) guidance
- if the child is not living with the parent, to maintain personal relations and direct contact with the child on a regular basis
- to act as the child's legal representative.

These responsibilities only apply as far as is practicable and in the child's interests. The parental responsibilities are further specified by age: only guidance extends until the child is eighteen, whereas the other responsibilities cease when the child is sixteen. Parental responsibilities are so foundational to the 1995 Act that it is the *first* section within it, before even a mention of children's rights. Because parents first and foremost have the responsibility for their children, local authorities should thus work in partnership with them as far as possible, unless the child's welfare is at risk.

Just as Scottish law differs from elsewhere on the UK in specifying parental responsibilities, so does the specification of parental rights. Thus Section 2 of the 1995 Act defines rights that would require co-ordination between those with parental responsibilities (should there be more than one). These rights are exact corollaries of parental responsibilities so that, for example, parents have the right to control, direct or guide their children and to maintain personal relations and direct contact with them. Although for the most part they can act independently of each other, parents must consult each other on 'major decisions' (see Chapter Five). Further, if one parent dies and a guardian is appointed, parents in Scotland will have to be 'partners' in their parental responsibilities and rights with the guardian. In contrast, under the 1989 Act guardians appointed by parents only take on that role when the surviving parent dies. This rule, however, does not apply if the appointing parent had a residence order. Similarly, a court can only appoint a guardian if the child has no one with parental responsibility or the dead parent (or guardian) had a residence order.

While unmarried fathers did not gain automatic parental responsibilities as recommended by the Scottish Law Commission (1992a), they now have the option of 'parental responsibilities agreements' like other unmarried fathers in the UK. The take-up of such agreements in England and Wales, though, has been slight. Only 4% of unmarried fathers in England who registered as the father when the child was born have obtained such an agreement (Grant 1997).

All UK legislation uses the revised 'residence' and 'contact' orders rather than the former 'custody' and 'access'. Numerically, applications are continuing to rise in England and Wales. During 1995, 7% more orders were made for 'residence', while 12% more were made for 'contact' than the year before (CAAC 1995). Whether 'joint parenting' in fact existed before such orders were made or continues is under-researched. Walker (1996), however, suggested that some highly participative fathers 'disengage' from their children because they cannot cope with the emotional stress of losing their role or as a result of conflict with the ex-partner. In a study of Exeter families, children said they needed to see both parents freely and to have flexible contact arrangements (Cockett and Tripp 1996). What surprised observers in England and Wales was the relatively large number of private law applications from grandparents seeking contact with their grandchildren (Booth 1995).

Children's views

Just as Scottish legislation is the only UK legislation to require parents to consult each other over 'major decisions', so the 1995 Act is the only one to require parents to consult their children. Worry has been expressed in England that children's views are not sought in uncontested agreements between parents (Bell 1993; Houghton-James 1995; National Commission of Inquiry into the Prevention of Child Abuse (NIPC) 1996).

Procedurally, UK legislation sets up a variety of ways and fora in which young people's views can be heard. Formally, children have various rights and possibilities to be involved or to have party status in court proceedings. Under the 1989 Act:

- Children are automatically parties to care proceedings, and can have a solicitor appointed to represent them.
- Children are not parties to private law proceedings, and must apply to court for leave to make an application to become a party. In private law proceedings, a Court Welfare Officer's report would contain details of the child's views (if the child was able or wished to state views).

The right of children to be heard in care proceedings is somewhat complicated as various people can be appointed to represent them and their interests. Section 41 of the 1989 Act (Article 60 of the 1995 Order) establishes a presumption that a guardian ad litem (GAL) will be appointed for a child, in a wide range of proceedings, 'unless satisfied that it is not necessary to do so in order to safeguard his interests.' The role of a GAL is to safeguard the child's best interests and thus is not the same as a legal representative who represents a child's wishes in court. The court does not have to appoint a GAL if the child is of sufficient understanding to instruct a solicitor. At this point, representation becomes further complicated. Rules establish that a GAL may appoint a solicitor to help represent the child's wishes in court, or the court can do so. Because of the costs of care proceedings, the majority of children are represented by the solicitor instructed by the GAL and separate representation is only undertaken if there is a quite clear conflict between the GAL and the child. If solicitors find they are receiving conflicting instructions from children and their GALs, solicitors should follow the GAL's instructions unless the child is of sufficient understanding to instruct the solicitors directly. Clearly, a great deal rests on whether a child is considered of 'sufficient understanding'. Further, certain court decisions have weighed the need to protect children more highly then their rights to be heard (see Cleland 1996).

In its first inspection of the GAL service since the 1989 Act's implementation, the SSI found that GALs were following Department of Health advice, and were separately recording the wishes and feelings of children when making court reports. GALs felt it was most difficult to work with the six- to ten-year-old age group, and worried that the views of children within this age group could be inappropriately discounted. The SSI concluded that, while for the most part there was positive practice of consulting with children, GALs did need to develop their skills further in communicating with children (reported in P. Smith 1996).

Scottish care proceedings are confusing because of the potential overlap of roles and appointments between safeguarders and curators ad litem. Curators ad litem can be appointed by the court, under common law, in any proceedings to represent the child's interests. Curators could be appointed, for example, in family law actions where particularly difficult issues such as emotional abuse are involved. Curators have a statutory role in adoption proceedings, which is specified by regulations. With safeguarders' role in statute for care proceedings, it might make sense that curators were not appointed in care proceedings; however, as exemplified in the Orkney child protection events in the early 1990s (see Chapter Two), curators are sometimes appointed in such proceedings.

Both safeguarders and curators ad litem have a similar remit: to safeguard children's best interests in proceedings. They represent children's views only so far as that fits into their safeguarding responsibility. This does leave the question of who does represent children's views, if their safeguarders or curators ad litem disagree with them. Legal aid is available for a child to apply to vary/recall CPOs or attached directions. But within children's hearings, for example, children have no right to have someone representing their views, as a legal representative. (For discussion, see Chapters Five and Seven.) The 1989 Act, and parallel provisions in the 1995 Order, clearly go further than Scotland in establishing a specific person to represent a child's wishes, in care proceedings.

All children's applications to become party to private law proceedings in England and Wales must now go to the High Court (Booth 1995). A child can instruct a solicitor to make such an application, as the rules were changed to allow solicitors to judge 'sufficient understanding' initially. However, the final arbiter remains the court. The court can remove a 'next friend' or a GAL if it considers the child of sufficient understanding. The reactions of courts have been mixed. While some courts have supported children's participation, others have sought to limit children's presence in court and to limit interviewing children directly (Cleland 1996). Court decisions have established that an assessment of a child's understanding should be in the context of the proceedings (Houghton-James 1995). Lord Justice Butler-Sloss made it clear in her decision on *Re W (minors) (residence Order)* [1992] FCR 461 that the child's wishes were informative but *not* determinative: the welfare principle was paramount.

In Scotland, a child is not automatically party to private law proceedings but may be able to instruct a solicitor to make an application to become a party. As mentioned above, curators ad litem can be appointed in such proceedings. Court rules do provide for any person with 'an interest in the proceedings' (which can include children) who is not a party to receive 'intimation' of any family action. It has been debated whether intimation must be the *full* set of papers about the cases, which could include detailed allegations against a parent, or can be one particular form (since resolved in favour of a single form). Attempts have been made under the revised rules to improve this process for children. Rules also establish processes by which children's views should be garnered for courts. In an amendment to the Age of Legal Capacity (Scotland) Act 1991, the Children (Scotland) Act underlines the legal capacity of a young person, under the age of sixteen, to instruct a solicitor on civil matters—'where that person has a general understanding of what it means to do so' (Schedule 4, para. 53 (3)). What this proviso does not make clear is *what* a 'general understanding' consists of, *how* it can or should be judged, nor *who* should make such a judgement in the first instance.

Children's competency to make decisions about medical examinations and treatments has had considerable judicial testing in England and Wales, since the famous Gillick case (see Chapter Two). This landmark ruling, however, was later confused by court decisions that suggested that children could not necessarily *refuse* treatment. Courts were the ultimate arbiter over a child's refusals (Cleland 1996; NIPC 1996). The right of a child (who is 'capable of understanding') to refuse medical examination and treatment is more clearly stated in law, in Scotland, but has not been tested in court.

The debates around children's representation and legal/medical competency have been well-rehearsed in England and Wales, and to a lesser extent in Scotland. They bring with them fundamental questions about children's participation, which can also be extended to other, non-judicial proceedings. For example:

- How does one know if a child is competent? Does it depend on the context or is it a more general characteristic?
- Who is able to ascertain a child's competency? Who decides if a child is competent?
- Even if a child is considered competent, can a decision be made to override the child's views?
- If a child is made party to proceedings, should the child be treated the same as other parties—even if this seems to be against a child's best interests?
- Why can children direct solicitors in certain proceedings but not in other types of litigation?
- What about the views of children who are not considered competent— what weight should be given to them?

Children's right to have their views heard is also extended in the UK children's legislation in other fora: for example, when local authorities make decisions about children 'looked after'. While research reports that most young people come to perceive their move to foster or residential care as positive (Kufeldt et al. 1996; Triseliotis et al. 1995), many young people have felt they had little choice about *where* they would go. Some wanted more choice about placements, although others recognised that there were usually few or no alternatives (Buchanan et al. 1993; Triseliotis et al. 1995). Children are now routinely involved in their care reviews. The majority of young people asked about reviews have expressed satisfaction with them and feel they were listened to. Some young people have voiced deep resentment about adults discussing their personal lives and making crucial decisions as if the young people were not there (Fletcher 1993). The Children's Rights Development Unit (1994) quoted children's disappointment at the tokenism of their care reviews:

> They held a meeting and pretended to involve me by calling me in at the end and saying, 'We think it would be best for you to go to a secure unit. What do you think?' but I wasn't prepared, so I didn't really say much. But it was a farce anyway, because they had a social service minibus parked outside with a driver waiting for me to be taken there. (Eighteen-year-old quoted in CRDU 1994: 37)

> All I ask for in my reviews is to see my brothers and sisters to see if they are OK, but nothing ever gets done about it. (Quoted in CRDU 1994: 37)

More choice about who attends their care reviews was desired by many young people, so as to lessen the number of people involved and include only those known to the young people (Triseliotis et al. 1995; Freeman et al. 1996).

In research described above, Thoburn and colleagues (1995) found that children were most likely to be involved in decisions about how the child protection investigation was to be conducted. Children over ten were more likely than parents to participate in decisions about whether care or accommodation would be used, and about the services to be offered.

In order to participate, children require information. Just as parents do not always receive information about services, young people also often do not receive the information they need. A young person who was 'looked after' was quoted in Buchanan's article (1993): 'Nobody tells me anything' (35). The Department of Health had published over 1.5 million leaflets for young people, but Buchanan (1993) found that few of these had reached young people. Information not only needs to be available, it must reach young people at the time they require it. Complaints procedures have been set up in local authorities, for all social services. Young people, however, may require support in order to go through what can appear a daunting task against the power of the state and bureaucracy.

A growing research base investigates children's participation in various aspects of their lives. While instances of good practice are recognised, the literature points to the variety of situations that actively work against children's participation, let alone promote it. Even when there is considerable belief within the particular agency or by professionals that children have the right to participate, people can find it difficult to turn this right into reality (Hart 1992; Hill and Tisdall 1997).

Uniquely across the UK, adoption orders for a child aged twelve or over cannot be granted in Scotland unless the child consents. Such a measure has been suggested for England and Wales as well, but not yet implemented. CRDU (1994) mentions the arbitrariness of the age of twelve, as was discussed in Chapters Three and Five. What Scottish legislation does extend for all children, 'subject to their age and maturity' and 'as far as is practicable', is the right to have their views considered when a court or adoption agency are reaching any decision relating to the children's adoption. In Northern Ireland, a child's wishes and feelings must also be ascertained and given due consideration, when deciding on any course related to a child's adoption. The 1995

Act also extends downwards the age at which young people can gain access to their adoption records—from the age of seventeen to the age of sixteen (Sch. 2, para. 22). In England, Wales and Northern Ireland, people must be eighteen before they have such a right. Thus *some* children in Scotland have the right to know their birth identity.

Children's rights to identity

Scottish legislation is the first to promote due regard to a child's religious persuasion, racial origin and cultural and linguistic background within adoption law. While not articulated in other UK adoption legislation, this right is given considerable policy and practice attention elsewhere (Stubbs 1987; Tizard and Phoenix 1993). Although Scotland may be the first to have this principle applied to adoption legislation, it can be found in both the 1989 Act and the 1995 Order in different areas. All three pieces of legislation apply the principle to local authorities making decisions about 'looked after' children.

The 1989 Act goes even further in Section 33 (6), so that a local authority cannot 'cause the child to be brought up in any religious persuasion other than that in which he would have been brought up in if the order had not been made' when a child is under a care order—although notably this only applies to religion and not other aspects of a child's culture and background. Given the sectarianism in Northern Ireland, it is of little surprise that the same provision can be found in Article 52 (6) of the 1995 Order. While a similar provision had been in previous Scottish law, it was not repeated in the 1995 Act.

Both the 1995 Order and the 1989 Act contain specific strictures in Schedules 2. Paragraph 12, for example, requires authorities in Northern Ireland to have regard to 'the different racial groups to which children within the authority's area who are in need belong' when making arrangements for day care or encouraging people to act as foster parents. Scotland, without its specific schedules, does not have this requirement. It does, however, apply this principle to local authorities providing services for 'children in need' (Section 22 (2)).

Research has long suggested that young people from certain ethnic minority backgrounds—i.e., those categorised as of 'mixed parentage'—have been disproportionately looked after by English and Welsh local authorities compared to other young people (Rowe et al. 1989; Banks 1995). Banks (1995) postulated that this research may have over-estimated the proportion, because the total population of children of mixed parentage may have not have been included in the calculations. People from Asian backgrounds are disproportionately *not* looked after by local authorities (CRDU 1994). Whatever the statistical situation, qualitatively some young people from certain ethnic minority backgrounds have not had a positive experience of local authority care. Active discrimination of white carers against young people from different ethnic backgrounds has been reported (CRDU 1994). Worry has been expressed about young people's problems with identity, particularly if they are not white but are brought up in an environment where virtually all other people are white. Research undertaken by Tizard and Phoenix (1993), however, did not find the much-discussed linkages between same-race placement for adopted children of mixed parentage, a positive racial identity and high self-esteem.

A useful consideration by several writers (e.g. Banks 1995) pointed to the individuality of children's backgrounds. Although children can be grouped as 'black', their families may have come from very different parts of the world, they may have different religions, and they may have different languages. Children from 'mixed parentage' can have a wide variety of parental backgrounds. Fully matching a child's background to that of carers can be a tall task indeed. Poor matching has been reported: for example, a 'black' child—who was actually of mixed UK white–Hong Kong Chinese parentage—was placed with African-Caribbean foster parents, with disastrous results (Lau 1991). The lesson seems to be that culture, religion, language and ethnic origins need to be recognised as separate, but related, issues.

Families from different cultures can have different child-rearing practices and family formations, which may not be appreciated by white workers. For example, lone parent families are often seen as an undesirable, if not actively negative, family formation by workers, while in certain cultures lone parent families are well-accepted (Banks 1995; Lau 1991; Thanki 1994). Professional practice can be based on unexamined, eurocentric values. Health provision, for example, may be assessing children's developmental progress based on white ethnocentric models of child development and cultural norms (Thanki 1994). As was criticised in some of the child protection inquiries in the 1980s, practitioners can be reluctant to intervene and delay intervention until problems reach crisis proportions. For example, when Farmer and Owen (1995) undertook research on child protection procedures, they found that more of the cases involving minority ethnic families ended up in uncertainty, than for other families, and thus the ensuing intervention had a diffuse focus. Many black families ended up without much needed services, partially because of the lack of ethnically appropriate resources.

Most of the authors mentioned above offer a range of advice to social services. Seden (1995) wrote of the need for sensitive and aware assessments, which included attention to religious persuasion, good review procedures, an active policy of recruiting a diverse range of foster carers who then received training, information and resources. Lau (1991) made a list, encouraging consideration of: the families' authority and decision-making structures; belief systems and value orientations; and the life cycle of the family. Banks (1995) ended his article with practice and policy issues, including the need for professionals to review how they used notions of 'race' or 'culture', the dearth of national statistics, the need to match closely a child's background in placements, and to consider prevention.

Candappa (1994) examined the place of young people from ethnic minority backgrounds in 'children in need'. Six of the twenty-six local authorities surveyed in England and Wales specifically referred to young people from ethnic minority backgrounds in their 'children in need' categories. Reviews of early years services found that local authorities had major problems in consulting ethnic minority communities. There was a low take-up of services. Candappa considered the danger of separating out children into a potentially stigmatising 'in need' category, versus the disadvantages faced by many children from certain ethnic minority backgrounds.

The research from England and Wales thus shows the difficulties and sensitivities required in fulfilling the duties of the 1989 Act to giving 'due regard' to a child's religious persuasion, racial origin and cultural and linguistic background. England and Wales do have a different ethnic make-up from Scotland, particularly as fewer African-Caribbeans live in Scotland. Scotland has its own difficulties, particularly because in many areas the population is quite homogeneous—and few families can be found from minority ethnic groups. In such areas, local authorities will have to given even more attention to how they can meet their duties.

Meeting children's rights across services and proceedings

Across UK children's legislation, the paramountcy of the child's welfare is established for decision-making in a range of proceedings: private law orders, public care, children who are 'looked after'. The 1995 Act order differs, however, from both the 1989 Act and the 1995 Order in that it does not contain a 'welfare checklist'. At the beginning of the 1989 Act, numerous areas are laid out that courts must have regard to:

(a) the ascertainable wishes and feelings of the child concerned (considered in the light of his age and understanding);

(b) his physical, emotional and educational needs;

(c) the likely effect on him of any change in his circumstances;

(d) his age, sex, background and any characteristics of which the court considers relevant;

(e) any harm which he has suffered or is at risk of suffering;

(f) how capable each of his parents, and any other person in relation to whom the court considers the question to be relevant, is of meeting his needs;

(g) the range of powers available to the court under this Act in the proceedings in question. (Section 1 (3))

The Scottish Law Commission (SLC) had considered such a checklist in its Family Law Report (1992a). The potential advantages were rehearsed: it would ensure commonalty across a wide range of professionals; it would help those lacking experience; and it might aid parents and children in understanding how judicial decisions are arrived at and perhaps help in reaching agreement. While most of those consulted by the SLC supported such a checklist for Scotland, legal opinion was largely and strongly opposed. A statutory checklist could not be complete. It might divert attention away from other factors that should be considered and make decision-making mechanical. The SLC concluded that a welfare checklist should not be made in Scottish law, but that the right of children to express their views was so important as to be separated out from the general principle of the paramountcy of children's welfare.

All UK children's legislation contains exceptions to the principles of children's rights. For example, the paramountcy of children's welfare, children's (and parents') right to express their views, due regard to a child's religious persuasion, racial origin and cultural and linguistic background can *all* be ignored when a local authority thinks it necessary for a 'looked after' child, for the purposes of 'public safety'. The 1995 Act goes even further than other children's legislation, in extending such exceptions to the paramountry of a child's welfare to both courts and children's hearings in a range of their decision-making.

Some differences can be found in the wording of these exceptions which may have practical significance. Section 22 (6) of the 1989 Act bases the exception on 'serious injury' as does Section 26 (4) of the 1995 Order. In the Scottish legislation, the provisions are potentially wider due to the use of 'serious harm (whether or not physical harm)'. As Chapter Five discussed, there is no legal definition of 'serious harm' given in the Act or clearly defined yet in case law. However, Norrie (1996) suggested it would contain emotional as well as physical injury, and harm to property as well as people. Scotland may not only have more fora where children's rights can be ignored, but these fora may also be able to do so in a wider range of circumstances. The 1995 Act did escape the extension of such powers to the Secretary of State. Both the 1995 Order and the 1989 Act allow the Secretary of State to give directions to the local authority. This provision was deleted from the Children (Scotland) Bill as it went through Parliament.

To date, a systematic evaluation of how this provision has been used in England and Wales does not appear to have been undertaken. Alarming signals can be found in the decision on *Re M (a minor) (secure accommodation order)* [1995] All E.R. 407. Despite the welfare checklist laid out in Section 1 of the 1989 Act, and the paramountcy of children's welfare stated there, the Court of Appeal found that such overarching principles did not pertain to sections later on in the Act—namely, those for secure accommodation: 'In my judgement s 1 was not designed to be applied to Pt III of the Act. To that extent I would disagree with vols 1 and 4 of the *Children Act 1989 Guidance and Regulations*, although I do agree that the welfare of the child is an important consideration' (Lord Butler-Sloss: 413). Indeed, local authorities do not have a duty to treat a child's welfare as paramount, in its Section 22 on 'looked after' children, unlike Scotland. The potential advantages of Scotland's section-by-section approach to children's rights appear higher than first thought (see Chapter Five).

A principle left largely unarticulated in Scottish legislation has been more specifically spelt out in other UK legislation: the need to minimise time delays. Indeed, Section 1 of the 1989 Act places the need to prevent prejudicial time delays right after the subsection asserting the paramountcy of a child's welfare. Unfortunately, however, evidence finds that time delays are largely now back to pre-1989 Act levels (CAAC 1995). The situation was considered so bad that the Lord Chancellor's Department commissioned a study of time delays in public and private law by Dame Margaret Booth. In 1995, disposal times had increased across all levels of court, to an average of 52 weeks for the High Court, 43 weeks for the county court, and 27.5 weeks for the family proceedings court (CAAC 1995). From her findings, Booth made numerous suggestions, for example:

- ensuring judges have appropriate time to read the papers
- better case management training for district judges
- proactive judges
- pre-trial reviews.

Several points have particular salience for Scotland. For example, Booth identified the problems caused by 'inadequately prepared barristers and the involvement of solicitors not on the Law Society's Children Panel with insufficient family experience' (CAAC 1995: 18). The panel for England and Wales only accepts those lawyers who have sufficient knowledge and expertise to work with children and their legal issues. The Law Society of Scotland has recently introduced a child law specialism, but as of yet has not established such a panel of vetted lawyers. The use of experts sometimes caused unnecessary duplications of assessment and considerable time delays. For example, Booth (CAAC 1995) reported on unnecessary duplication of expert assessments. Booth suggested a clearer definition of experts' roles and earlier agreements between parties on the use of experts. Such simplification may limit unnecessary intervention in the lives of children and their families.

While generally the principle of avoiding time delays is well-supported, a few dissenting views have been expressed in certain situations. For example, Sone (1997) worried that social workers' wish to avoid delay in placing a child could result in inappropriate placements being made, and thus a child might face more moves than were necessary. The 1989 Act does qualify its principle, stating that it is a 'general principle' and that any delay is 'likely' to prejudice the welfare of the child. Sometimes, however, the principle may be applied inappropriately.

Welfare versus justice?

The differences between the Scottish children's hearing system and the court-based system elsewhere in the UK have been well-discussed (e.g. Morris and Giller 1987; Allen 1996). Generally, Scotland is depicted as having a 'welfare' approach to young people who offend—although it has notable exceptions for children who commit very serious crimes. Scotland continues to have the lowest age of criminal responsibility in Europe (age eight). The encroachment of 'punishment' agendas continue to batter children's hearings, such as the suggestion (since refused) to extend 'tagging' as an option for children's hearing supervision requirements.

Packman (1993) described the place of young people who offend in the 1989 Act:

Only the young delinquents hover somewhat ambiguously on the fringe of the Act; no longer eligible for committal to care (though supervision with a condition of residence is a new option)—yet destined to be remanded to local authorities' facilities once their incarceration in adult remand centres is finally phased out. But the most recent alarms over grave and persistent juvenile offenders seem to threaten even these tenuous links with the care system. (193)

Before the 1989 Act, children 'at risk' and children who offended could receive supervision orders from both criminal and in care proceedings, under the Children and Young Persons Act 1969. The 1989 Act leaves children who offend under the 1969 Act, but takes with it children in need of care and protection. Local authorities do have duties, under the listing of services in Schedule 2, to reduce the need for criminal proceedings against children and must encourage them not to commit offences. The Audit Commission's much-publicised report, *Misspent Youth* (1996), declared that far too little was done by services to prevent young people from offending. In Scotland, children who receive supervision requirements (whether residential or home supervision) from a children's hearing are considered 'looked after'; these children may have been referred to the hearings on offence grounds. Local authorities have duties to *all* 'looked after' children, such as taking the child's welfare as paramount and after-care. Scotland thus maintains a welfare approach to young offenders not only in official proceedings, but also in the services offered to them after proceedings.

Child protection

Scottish and Northern Irish emergency and child assessment orders were modelled on those in the 1989 Act. The Scottish emergency orders (CPOs) have a different timetable due to their interaction with the children's hearing system, but across the UK the emergency orders have tight time-limits. They use the same terminology of 'significant harm' (discussed below) and have similar thresholds. They do have numerous differences, however, which may or may not result in significant differences in practice.

For example, the legislation differs in its allocation of parental responsibilities. Section 44 (4)(c) of the 1989 Act and Article 63 (4)(c) of the 1995 Order give the applicant parental responsibilities *automatically* on the granting of an emergency order; Section 58 of the 1995 Act allows the Sheriff to give directions on the exercise or fulfilment of parental responsibilities or rights, but they are not given automatically to the applicant. The 1989 Act and 1995 Order are qualified, however, so that applicants are required to only take such actions in meeting their parental responsibilities as 'is reasonably required to safeguard or promote the welfare of the child' (Section 44 (5) (b) and Article 63 (5) (b)).

While Scotland legislated first for an 'exclusion of an alleged abuser order', amendments to the 1989 Act through the Family Law Act 1996 have introduced similarly provisions for England and Wales. On paper, several differences are evident. The differences emerge primarily because the exclusion requirements are integrated into emergency protection and interim care orders for England and Wales, whereas the 1995 Act created a separate exclusion order altogether. It would be possible to forbid contact between a child and an alleged abuser with a Scottish CPO, but presumably not to exclude an alleged abuser from his or her home.

While *only local authorities* can apply for such orders in Scotland, in England and Wales *any person* can apply for an exclusion requirement in an EPO (Emergency Protection Order). Scottish exclusion orders can last up to six months; EPOs can only last up to eight days, and exclusion requirements placed on interim care orders can last up to eight weeks. Because the provisions for England and Wales are tied to EPOs, the threshold may be lower than Scotland's. That is, any applicant for an EPO must satisfy the court of *reasonable cause to believe* a child is likely to suffer significant harm, and a local authority that it has *reasonable cause to suspect* a child is or is likely to suffer such harm. A Sheriff in Scotland has to be satisfied that a child 'has suffered, is suffering, or is likely to suffer, significant harm' (Section 76 (2) (a))—thus a difference between 'fact' in Scotland and 'reasonable cause' in England and Wales. Scotland also appears to have more grounds for an alleged abuser not to be excluded (e.g. based on the dwelling being used as employment) written into legislation than the 1989 Act as amended.

If a local authority applies for a CAO in Scotland, a Sheriff can decide to grant a CPO. This choice is also available in other UK legislation. Early problems with EPOs, where parents sought to use them because they were unable to gain an ex-parte (i.e. without the other party being present) residence order under private law provisions, have been solved by allowing ex-parte applications in private law.

An overall analysis of the child protection system in England and Wales has some salience for Scotland. Parton (1991) wrote of the shift of approach: 'If in the past child abuse has been seen as essentially a medico-social problem, where the expertise of the doctor has been seen as focal, increasingly it has been seen as a socio-legal problem, where legal expertise takes pre-eminence' (18). Just as in Scotland, Parton (1991) noted that not all child protection policies and practices were directly accountable to the courts. He described the 'grey areas' outside the gaze of the court and legalistic principles:

> where the more voluntaristic, indirect and universal child care services have been remodelled and refashioned so as to meet the needs of the child protection system which emphasises much more the targeting of provisions and concentrates on the direct observations and regulation of behaviour. (207)

When social workers have insufficient knowledge to show that a family is 'safe', systems of monitoring, observation and surveillance gain in significance (206).

The anxiety about assessing risk and agonising over registration can take over other considerations, to the extent that child protection conferences have been observed to leave the actual child protection plan to the end of meetings and take, on average, no more than nine minutes to make the plan (DoH 1995: 29). If a child was registered, then Brandon et al. (1996) found that the categorisation often failed to reflect the conferences' concerns accurately about the likely reason for any future significant harm:

in 30 of the [105] cases future emotional harm features as the primary concern. Only a minority of them (just under a third) were children at risk of serious physical injury, life threatening neglect or of sexual assault for whom a repeated assault might be avoided as a result of registration. Yet most protection plans concentrated on preventing physical or sexual harm and very few coherently addressed ways of preventing emotional harm. (19)

The actual allocation of services was not based on assessments of children's potentially impaired development, but on whether parents were judged as likely to be responsible for such impairment or harm. 'Children in need' services were thus allocated on the basis of perceived parental fault or deficiencies, rather than a child's potential and/or impaired development. Thus, children who are abused by strangers, or children deeply affected by marital breakdown, receive far less attention than children who are seen as 'at risk' from their parents (DoH 1995).

The thresholds for intervention have been the subject of much study (e.g. Adcock et al. 1991; DoH 1995). The Department of Health publication (1995) asserted that any potentially abusive incident had to be seen in context, before assessments and interventions were made. The potential outcomes, or likely effects of maltreatment on the child, had to be considered in that context. Studies found that a single abusive event often did not cause long-term difficulties for children (unless it was a severe assault or sexual maltreatment). Long-term difficulties were more likely a consequence of an unfavourable living environment, especially one of low warmth and high criticism (DoH 1995). Notably, only the 1995 Act specifically mentions 'neglect' within its criteria for orders on child protection.

Legally, certain court cases have established important parameters for the key criterion of 'significant harm', at least for England and Wales. For example, the House of Lords firmly (re)established the balance of probabilities as the standard of proof when granting a care order, in *Re H and Others (Minors) (sexual abuse: standard of proof)* 1995] 1 E.R. 1. The term 'likely' within the criteria (i.e. 'likely to suffer significant harm') indicated a '... real possibility [of harm], a possibility that cannot sensibly be ignored having regard to the nature and gravity of the feared harm in the particular case' (Lord Nicholls: 15–16). Evidence must be the basis of any court decisions, and '... the more serious the allegations the less likely it is that the event occurred and, hence, the stronger should be the evidence before the court concludes that the allegation is established on the balance of probability' (Lord Nicholls: 16). A legal commentary by Rodgers (1996) was unconcerned about that heightened requirement for evidence in potentially more serious cases—but might this encourage local authorities to emphasise lesser instances of harm, so that they can get an order, if they are worried they cannot substantiate more serious abuse?

The House of Lords' decision on *Re M (a minor) (care order: threshold conditions)* [1994] 3 All E.R. 298, [1994] 2 AC 424 established the relevant time for deciding on harm. This would be the date of the care order application or, if there were temporary protective arrangements continuously in place before that date, the date when such temporary arrangements were initiated. *Re O (a minor) (care proceedings: education)* [1992] 4 All E.R. 905 helped with the interpretation of 'harm', requiring it to be a 'comparison with a child of equivalent intellectual and social development... and not merely an average child' (906).

The Children Act 1989 was always more specific than the 1995 Act in defining 'harm'. In Section 31 (9) of the 1989 Act (which refers to care and supervision orders), 'harm' is defined as 'ill-treatment or the impairment of health or development'. 'Development' is then defined as meaning physical, intellectual, emotional, social or behaviour development. 'Health' is defined as meaning both physical or mental health. 'Ill-treatment' includes sexual abuse and non-physical forms of ill-treatment.

Safe refuges

While Scotland may have led in legislation for an exclusion of an alleged abuser in child protection, England and Wales was first to legislate for 'safe refuges'. A critical difference, however, lies with time limits for children's stay in such refuges. Time limits are set out in legislation in Scotland, stating a maximum of seven days, apart for 'exceptional circumstances' as the Secretary of State will determine, where the maximum is fourteen days. In England and Wales, no statutory time limits are set out in the Children Act 1989. Regulations specify a maximum of fourteen days and no more than twenty-one days in any period of three months. Even with these extended time limits, there remains some discretion. Certainly, there are fears in Scotland that the time limits in Scotland will be too short actually to help address the situation leading a child to run away, based on the English and Welsh experience. Very few safe refuges have actually been established in England and Wales, which begs the question of whether they will be in Scotland.

Implementation

As the above chapter has traced, the UK legislation has both important differences and similarities in its specific provisions. The comparisons are extremely informative, particularly when they point to potential pitfalls which could be avoided or practice that could be assimilated. At the same time, each piece of legislation must be seen within its own context.

An important context is the implementation process in each region, which has differed considerably. First, the 1989 Act received some of the most comprehensive guidance ever produced for legislation. With its twelve volumes, social workers have a considerable amount of prescription and suggestions. Further guidance is available in such areas as child protection and children's services plans. This amount of guidance provides a large information base for professionals. It may, however, create an 'information overload' (NIPC 1996: 271) for some professionals and considerable anxiety, at least when the Act was initially implemented. The Scottish Office deliberately decided not to issue the same quantity of guidance, issuing three volumes with an accompanying bibliography and index. While the guidance has been issued very close to the implementation date of the 1995 Act, which itself caused anxiety, its smaller amount helps professionals digest it. It will allow greater flexibility for local authorities and others in services and supports. It also could mean greater inequity across Scotland, with its thirty-two local authorities.

Secondly, implementation dates and training were somewhat more extended in England and Wales. The implementation time was slightly longer in England and Wales (twenty-three months) than in Scotland (for full implementation, twenty-one months) or Northern Ireland (nineteen months, including a month's delay). The implementation in Scotland was staggered, so that most of the family law was implemented in November 1996, giving a fifteen month lead in time. The Scottish Office did not give out all its tenders for training, so that out of three tenders the one commissioned was for training materials (British Agencies for Adoption and Fostering (BAAF) 1996). The actual delivery of this training was not funded, nor subsidised, directly by The Scottish Office. The Scottish Office consider children's services plans so important, that they have held three seminars across Scotland on the topic in early 1997. Local authorities were invited to attend, bringing along six people of their choice. The 1995 Order was implemented in Northern Ireland without all of the guidance available. While it is an issue for further research, it may be that implementation and training were more rushed in Northern Ireland and Scotland than in England and Wales. At the same time, lengthy delays between the passing of an Act and its implementation can lead to its provisions being out-dated and sometimes never in fact implemented.

Thirdly, the 1995 Act includes no requirement for The Scottish Office to monitor the Act and report to Parliament. In contrast, the 1989 Act allows local authorities and the Secretary of State to conduct research, and can require local authorities to produce information for the Secretary of State. Every year, the Secretary of State must submit a report on the 1989 Act to Parliament. (Section 83) Article 181 of the 1995 Order similarly requires the NIDHSS to submit an annual report before the Assembly. The Government has promised a programme of research and monitoring on the 1995 Act for Scotland, but concern is raised about its potential thoroughness to cover *all* aspects of the Act, and how frequently various provisions would be researched.

Scotland can learn a great deal from the past experience in England and Wales, and the possibilities for the Northern Ireland Order. These will be further addressed in the following chapter.

Chapter 7

◆

THOUGHTS ON THE FUTURE

THE effects of a particular piece of legislation are difficult to foretell. Issues that may have seemed critical when analysing a White Paper or constructing amendments for a Bill may cease to be so central in the light of practice. Political, ideological and structural contexts change, so that implementation can take place in a very different situation from when the legislation was actually planned. Judicial decisions and interpretation will add definition to terminology, duties and powers. One piece of legislation can be affected by another, so that new criminal justice, education or adoption legislation, for example, can not only amend previous legislation but also alter the relationships between services and the panoply of policies that may affect any one child or young person.

The most important influences on implementation usually lie in the policies, procedures and practices that emerge as a result of the legislation. Various national bodies, like the Scottish Rules Council and The Scottish Office, issue their own regulations, guidance and/or procedures. Local bodies, such as local authorities, further interpret national guidelines and requirements, with their own policies and procedures. Training can lead to certain areas being highlighted, certain view points encouraged, and certain practices embedded. Managers and front-line service providers must make day-to-day decisions on how the legislation translates into practice, taking choices that may either circumvent the intentions of the legislation or enhance them. Legislation only provides a framework: it is the resulting practice that makes the most difference.

The Children (Scotland) Act 1995 was greeted with considerable warmth by many, as the long awaited up-date of Scottish children's legislation. It did not engender the overwhelming approbation received by the equivalent legislation for England and Wales, the Children Act 1989. A number of reasons could explain this. Scotland waited over six years after England and Wales received its new legislation, yet some of the lessons learnt from the 1989 Act's implementation do not seem to have been applied to the 1995 Act. Categories and concepts foreign to Scotland were imported, even though they had not proved particularly successful in England and Wales. Even though Scotland may not have had new legislation, some of the good practice developed in England and Wales as a result of the 1989 Act had already been applied in Scotland before the 1995 Act. Scotland has its own traditions, culture and practice, so that some of the provisions or principles so well-appreciated in England and Wales were already well-established ones in Scotland. Certain provisions actually may be perceived as backward steps for Scotland, whereas they may have been seen as forward ones for England and Wales. The Children Act 1989 was implemented at a time of considerable stress for English and Welsh authorities, as they were also implementing community care legislation. The stress may be even higher in Scotland, with the 'double whammy' of a relatively unpopular local government reform and huge resource constraints on many of the local authorities.

Scotland does have certain disadvantages in implementing the 1995 Act, particularly in terms of public law. Local government reform has created an immense turmoil in local authorities, taking place in a short amount of time and with many redundancies. Many of the local authorities are considerably smaller in size than their Regional predecessors, with resulting losses in economies of scale and budgets for services such as education and social work. Duties and powers predicated on different sizes of local authorities have remained virtually unchanged. Some authorities have lost their wealthier areas from Regional days, so that authorities who have communities in the greatest need (at least by urban indicators) may have smaller tax bases from which to raise the cash to meet need. Initially after implementation, many local authorities found it politically distasteful to co-operate with adjourning local authorities (even though possible under the Local Government (Scotland) Act 1994), so that opportunities to create economies of scale by joint commissioning and/or planning have not yet been fully exploited.

The changes in local authorities had corresponding alterations in personnel and structures. Inter-agency collaboration between both individuals and services was often disrupted, with time needed to build up new working arrangements and, hopefully, relationships of trust and co-operation. Not only have social work services for children altered, but numerous changes have affected other services dramatically in recent years—education being a prime example. Individual service providers, who may well feel insecure and stressed by reform, may also feel overburdened by the constant amount of change in their professional lives and work.

Along with structural change has been a widespread panic about resources in local authorities. The Children (Scotland) Bill itself laid out a very minimalist, and arguably unrealistic, assessment of resources that would be needed to implement the final Act. Local authorities, facing drastic budget cuts and pressures from all sides, are implementing the Children (Scotland) Act at a time of considerable financial crisis for many authorities. Local government reform has also affected other types of providers. Many Scottish voluntary organisations have suffered financially as a result of the reform. The fall in local authority funding comes at a time when many organisations are also negatively affected by falling charitable donations, due to the introduction of the National Lottery. A number of Scottish voluntary organisations have benefited considerably from National Lottery distributions. But the distributions are not divided amongst all Scottish voluntaries, and thus do not replace some organisations' losses.

Further, National Lottery grants explicitly are not intended to cover core-funding of organisations, and there can be no expectation of grant renewals. Other sources of funding, such as (what was formerly termed) Urban Aid, has been removed from certain areas. Many voluntary organisations are now floundering, perhaps particularly those smaller and user-led ones and those that formerly worked on a regional basis, and many face closure or have closed. The voluntary sector may lose organisations, with their accumulated expertise and profiles within their communities, which will not be easily replaced.

The list of disadvantages is somewhat daunting. However, at least in the short term, these are the realities for children's services. The needs and rights of children and their families remain. Thus, attention must be drawn to the potential advantages that are the converse of every disadvantage. For example, local government reform has been immensely painful for many authorities, professionals, voluntary organisations and, unfortunately, for many of their service users. Yet, structural change has benefits. Unhelpful service empires can be demolished, with an influx of new people with new ideas. In times of change, new structures and policies can be constructed, which better meet services' aims and people's needs. With the new structures can come new and innovative ways of planning and working. Opportunities exist for previous bad relationships with other agencies or other individuals to become redundant and new, more positive ones to be established. Local governments and services were not without their critics and their deficits in the past; new ones provide the opportunities actually to address these and improve.

Even though the voluntary sector may have been decimated by local government reform and other financial losses, it was from a position of considerable and growing strength. Hope must lie with the organisations that survive, that indeed may be stronger for doing so and may be more streamlined and effective. Those that can work nationally and/or who can work very locally may become the most predominant. National ones can provide the support and expertise to deliver sensitive and well-run services, be excellent employers, and ensure that any volunteers are well-supported and trained. Very local organisations can encourage services to stay close to community needs and may find themselves user-led. Voluntary organisations may have more opportunities in gaining contracts for services, as local authorities find themselves unable to provide specialist services and with the official encouragement of the 'mixed economy'. Moray Council, for example, is contracting out most of its children's services to two large voluntary organisations: NCH Action for Children Scotland and the Aberlour Child Care Trust.

The Children (Scotland) Act 1995 may have been created without sufficient attention to the interface between it and the new local authorities. It may have been created without adequately considering and learning from experiences in England and Wales. But that does not mean it has to be implemented with these lacunae. New local authorities had a year to determine their new structures and begin to look towards the Act's implementation. Research from England and Wales is emerging with increasing abundance in professional, academic and official government literature. Those with experience of England and Wales have moved up to work in Scotland, in both policy and service provider positions. Various organisations have sought to disseminate not only Scottish good practice, but also that of England, Wales and Northern Ireland.

Further, the mistake should never be made that the 1995 Act is merely a Scottish equivalent to the Children Act 1989 or the Children (Northern Ireland) Order 1995. Scotland has its own legal and service tradition, which may help maintain and promote aspects of the Children (Scotland) Act 1995. Scotland does not have to follow the path of England and Wales, and in many areas it will not. Local authorities now have over twenty years experience of working with the Social Work (Scotland) Act 1968 and the general welfare duty of Section 12. While somewhat pruned, the duty still remains and certainly its preventive ethos can prevail. Agencies have developed their own collaborative and co-operative patterns, with good strong relationships continuing in many areas. Being smaller, Scotland has often had closer connections than England between its national policy makers and practitioners, and organisations representing service users. The loyalty to the children's hearing system is extremely high amongst its practitioners and, from the evidence of when the Bill went through Parliament, in The Scottish Office. The Scottish Office has largely withstood, admittedly with some wavering and some breaches, the punitive approach to young people who offend so prevalent in England and Wales. In many ways, Scottish people relish in being different from and better than England and Wales; this in itself can help maintain the preventive and welfare approach of Scottish children's services and foster further innovations.

What, then, might be considered the future for the Children (Scotland) Act 1995? More importantly, what will be the future for the children, young people and their families who are affected by it? Some of the issues emerging from the previous chapters will be brought together below, often raising more questions than they do answers at this stage of implementation.

Children in need: an opportunity for preventive work?

Previous chapters have explored the new duties towards 'children in need' in considerable detail. Certain problems have been identified, in both Chapters Five and Six. Research evidence from England and Wales suggests that the preventive aim of the 'children in need' category has generally not been realised. Scarce resources and historical continuity have led to a focus on those children for whom local authorities already had a responsibility, particularly those children perceived of as 'at risk of significant harm'. Children with certain characteristics, such as being homeless or being excluded from school, were included within some local authorities' definitions of need but not those of other local authorities. Children could be receiving a very different service—or indeed, no service at all—depending on where they lived.

While Scotland has long had a more preventive approach to children's services than most of England and Wales, many of these problems could well happen in Scotland. Scottish social services could lose what they have of a community approach, with an increasing focus on the individual child or the individual family. The SWSG guidance on 'children in need' (1997a) indeed is written primarily from an individualist perspective, with frequent references to assessment and case management. Scottish social work services often suffered from stigma pre-1995 Act implementation, but this may worsen in the future if 'children in need' services become even more residual and even more individualistic. The integrative duties for children with and affected by disabilities, i.e., to minimise the effects of the disability and help the children live 'as normal a life as possible', are a welcome counter to potentially segregating tendencies. But the extent to which these rather vague duties will be implemented, given resource constraints, is a potential problem.

Scotland, though, does have this traditionally more preventive approach to children's services. Social work services in Scotland have never been offered under a fully open-door policy, or on demand. To that extent, there has long been some degree of assessment, which can remain the same for those who did not require a more intensive one. The new category of 'children in need' is indeed very flexible, it particularly provides for those children with or affected by disabilities, and has some welcome associated provisions, such as day care and due regard to children's religious persuasion, racial origin and cultural and linguistic background. While the new duty emphasises that children should be supported in their families as much as is appropriate, it has the advantage of focusing on the child—a child-centred philosophy, which recognises that, at times, a child must be seen as separate from the family unit because their rights and needs are not always the same. 'Children in need' could help, by that very phrase, to promote *needs-led* services rather than service-led ones (although it does not provide any such guarantee). Coupled with the corporate definition of local authorities, decisions could be made to deliver services to 'children in need' and others through a combination of various departments. There has been an emphasis on multi-disciplinary training, pushed by the SWSG and promoted in much of the initial 1995 Act training (e.g., British Agencies for Adoption and Fostering 1996). Thus, perhaps, the potential of schools and recreation for children's welfare could be fully exploited; the connections between the housing, educational, environmental, recreational and welfare needs of children could be better recognised and addressed. 'Children in need', by its very definition, is so vague as to mean largely what a local authority and service providers make of it.

So whether or not 'children in need' exemplifies increased service targeting is a question that awaits monitoring over the Act's implementation. The question is posed when the Audit Commission's (1994) report still resonates, with its suggestion that social services in England and Wales become less residual while health services become more targeted:

health agencies will need to focus more of their scarce resources, while local authorities will need to broaden their remit to promote a wider range of initiatives that provide families with support. (3)

The balances have not yet been finalised between the traditionally universal services of education and health, for families and children, and the traditionally targeted social work services.

Working together

The Children (Scotland) Act 1995 does raise many areas where the balances between services, and their interactions, will have to be reassessed and reformulated. For one, potential conflicts between different pieces of Scottish legislation will need to be resolved, either deliberately or by default. Such resolution is not new, as legislation effecting children before the 1995 Act already had considerable overlap and conflicts— for example, education and community care legislation for young disabled people. The 1995 Act only provides some new and some very familiar examples (see Chapter Five). But with the corporate definition of local authorities, hopefully at least some of these will be resolved purposefully and to good effect.

A local authority could take a concerted approach to young people who are homeless, to avoid the young people being shuttled back and forth between services without them in fact receiving useful services, or even a service at all. It could combine housing and social work service resources to provide for the basic housing needs of the young person and any accompanying social needs as appropriate. Local authorities could take a co-ordinated approach to young people who are excluded, or are at risk of being excluded, from school. Education and social work services could come together, again to provide for the basic educational needs of the young person and any accompanying social needs as appropriate. They could thus ensure that children do not 'fall through the cracks' between systems:

> I left care and went home and as soon as that happened, social services wanted nothing to do with me and education wanted nothing to do with me. The pair of them thought: good he's off our hands, pass the buck to someone else. It was brilliant living at home again and I wanted to go to a normal school again but once you have got the reputation of being chucked out of school a lot of schools won't accept you. (Fourteen-year-old, quoted in CRDU 1994: 153)

Given that a high number of young people who are 'looked after' are excluded from school (Borland et al. 1997), the local authority as 'parents' or 'carers' could work to ensure that the young people are in environments where they can take the best advantage of educational opportunities. As mentioned in Chapter One, some local authorities have decided structurally to amalgamate services, with housing and social work services some of the most common to combine. Fife Council decided to organise itself around 'strategies' rather than traditional departments. A co-ordinated approach is likely to be more preventive, more effective and ultimately the most helpful for children, young people and their families. The calls for inter-agency working have been so frequent over the years, and seemingly without resolution. Might the duty for children's services plans, the corporate definition of local authorities and the duty to co-operate actually result in considerably more effective co-operation between services and service providers?

When children's services are discussed, education, health and social work form a trinity of services often mentioned in the same breath. In the area of child protection, other services such as police and personnel within the children's hearing system are frequently added. Housing is sometimes recognised, particularly in situations of domestic violence and for young people who are homeless or leaving local authority care. Indeed, these services are perhaps the most central to children, young people and their families. However, when the 'whole child' is considered, it becomes apparent that other services should not be side-lined. Recreation may provide services that actually make the most improvements in the lives of certain children and their families. Local Enterprise Companies may impact on young people as they face (un)employment, or foster day care for employed parents. Promoting the role of voluntary organisations and the independent sector can be glimpsed in some of the SWSG guidance, but not consistently.

With decentralisation, fragmentation and the purchaser–provider split, it may be difficult to know exactly *who* or *what agency* one is supposed to co-operate with. A Health Board may be involved in planning for children's needs, but GP fundholders and private patients can also buy services. Providers are now spread out with the 'mixed economy', in the public, private and voluntary sectors. With devolved school management introduced in April 1996, headteachers could hold increased power (although the extent of this has been disputed by Midwinter and McGarvey (1994)). Scotland has generally followed such fragmentary policies more reluctantly than England, but the potential exists for a multiplicity of agencies and individuals with whom co-ordination and co-operation might be necessary.

As Hallett and Birchall (1992) described, co-ordination is generally characterised as essential and beneficial. But co-operation and collaboration are not inevitably positive aims, and some criticise them roundly. Collaboration in particular can stifle innovation, as all services are yoked to the same agenda. It can lead to increased bureaucracy, as meetings must be organised for inter-agency work, as papers must be exchanged to ensure inter-agency agreement and so all those in collaboration can be kept informed of developments. An example is given by Thoburn (1995), who wrote of practitioners lurching from meeting to meeting, in child protection cases, as they strove to adhere to procedures and maintain inter-agency collaboration. Collaboration is not without financial implications. The amassing of various professionals for a single meeting can be calculated as a considerable cost, if all the individual salaries per hour of the professionals were totalled. The organisation of such meetings can cause delay. For children, young people and families, a sea of professionals at a meeting can be intimidating and lessen their participation (Thoburn 1995; Tisdall 1996). The focus on inter-agency collaboration in decision-making can subtract from the resources and energy put towards ensuring opportunities are available, the delivery of services, or following up plans. The focus can be on 'managing the problem' rather than substantially challenging it. Thus, while the failures of the lack of inter-agency co-operation and collaboration are well-documented and criticised, such co-operation and collaboration does have its potential costs and disadvantages. A way to minimise such disadvantages could be to take Sutton's (1995) advice: to map the overlap of services, to consider the areas where services should co-operate and collaborate, and where they have separate spheres.

Particular worries have been expressed for voluntary agencies, as they increasingly become caught up in the 'contract culture', delivering services for local authorities. Voluntary agencies and outside commentators have worried about agencies losing their independence, and thus their ability to innovate, to disagree with local authorities, or to advocate for people they may represent. Driven by the need to survive financially, their services could become tailored to official requirements rather than following the needs of their service users. Voluntary organisations could find themselves constrained by their contracts, having to fulfil quotas and regulations that may not be purposeful or meet the needs of service users. The competition for some contracts could lead to voluntary agencies becoming increasingly cut-throat, lessening co-operation between voluntary agencies and encouraging secrecy. If voluntary organisations are offering services via volunteers, they can be asking volunteers to take on roles previously filled by employed professionals, and sometimes without sufficient support and training. Charitable funds and volunteers' in-kind donations can be siphoned into supporting state services, which were previously funded from local authorities and central government. The contract culture may favour those voluntary organisations that are run like businesses, which may go against some organisations formed on the basic ethos of being user-led—and an inclusive, participative method of working may not be conducive to a highly competitive business ethic. The administrative and bureaucratic burdens of small organisations participating in the contract culture can be high, and take away from the actual provision of services. Just as local authority services have been accused of being 'service-led' and not 'needs-led', the contract culture can lead voluntary agencies to be led by service requirements rather than the needs of their actual or potential service users (Bemrose and MacKeith 1996; Douglas 1997; Solomon 1995).

Changes within the voluntary sector may not be completely recognised by policy makers and SWSG guidance. For example, Children in Scotland commented on the draft SWSG guidance for 'children in need' that: 'The guidance should also recognise that in the late 1990s voluntary sector provision does not different very significantly from public sector provision: the voluntary sector is increasingly involved in the delivery of statutory provision' (1996b: para 3.14.2). Voluntary agencies themselves do not have to be passive in their relationships, although local authorities do have considerable power. For example, Francis (1995) reported of voluntary agencies who refused to meet the too tight time-limits set by local authorities to sign contracts, or said no to unfavourable contractual conditions, and only benefited from their stance. Many groups have managed to retain their campaigning stance and independence, keeping key services such as advocacy. While little utilised, Francis (1995) suggested that larger voluntary organisations could enter into partnerships with smaller groups to help them deliver services—giving the example of specialist services such as user-led organisations for people with disabilities, who are also from ethnic minority backgrounds.

Social work in particular is facing a reconsideration of its role, with local government reform, pressures from a variety of requirements and stresses such as community care and child protection. Social work professionals could become defensive, with the corporate definition of authority under the Children (Scotland) Act 1995 and a corresponding fear of losing power. Social work professionals might well wonder what their roles will be as services change. Parton in 1985 already worried about the increasing stress on child protection work, at the expense of prevention and alleviating the socio-economic problems facing certain children and their families. Child protection has also strengthened management and procedures rather than professional discretion. From a different perspective, the Fife Inquiry's Report ('Kearney Report' 1992) worried about social workers losing their professional discretion as they sought to meet local authority policy requirements. Social workers may be forced towards being accountants, managers and/or auditors rather than having a 'deep approach' based on counselling and relationships with individuals and communities (Howe 1996). Voluntary services may take over the 'deep approach':

> Therapeutic and nurturing services were being delivered by voluntary agencies and other caring professionals, and investigations and monitoring were dominating more and more in the work of the statutory child-care worker. (Solomon 1995: 117)

Within the SWSG guidance for 'children in need' (1997a), for example, much is described about social workers' role as assessors and case managers. Far less is spoken about their role in service delivery. Such tendencies have evident problems: social work professionals might be unhappy with such roles; bureaucrats may not be the best ways to manage, support and deliver services; bureaucratic procedures often deal badly with individuals who do not fit neatly into categories; bureaucracy usually does best with static situations and tends to have trouble with change. Bureaucracy generally requires close monitoring in identified categories, but many useful aspects of social work may not be quantifiable or otherwise counted. Once again, the combined possibilities of local government reform and the 1995 Act's implementation provide opportunities for a re-evaluation and a re-alignment of social workers' roles, the purposes of social work, as well as the combined purposes of children's services. The progress towards strict bureaucracy is not inevitable; management and monitoring do not have to be at the expense of a 'deep approach'.

Partnership with parents

A focus on 'partnership with parents' presents a possibly counter-balance to bureaucracy, in that it can be interpreted as emphasising relationships. The need to take into account parents' views in numerous situations, and to try and encourage contact, is already established good practice and the Act's duties are likely to emphasise this. The focus can provide tensions for professionals, as they may feel caught between their duties towards children's best interests and towards parents. As children become increasingly independent in their views, professionals can feel caught between a child's views and those of the parents. Partnership can take time, effort and information from all parties. Partnership requires regularly maintenance and, with changes as children develop and families alter, may have to be re-formulated regularly.

Few would dispute the benefits for many children of professionals working positively with their parents. But putting forward the notion of 'partnership' is much more doubted, because it can postulate a relationship of equality, choice and agreement that is simply not reality. When state representatives have the power to intervene in families against their choice, whether they are in the process of doing so or their power is evidently ready to be used, parents are the likely weaker 'partners' in the relationship. King (1995) described with particular fervour the potentially exploitative use of 'partnership' *against* parents, due to legal intervention in child protection:

> In law's coding of the situation, 'partnership failure' becomes a significant event by precluding arguments that the parents can be trusted to work in unison with social workers concerned for the child's future safety. It becomes, in effect, a pre-coding for law, avoiding the necessity of undertaking the complex and lengthy task of examining the intelligence, integrity and personalities of the parents. Partnership failure speaks for itself. (150)

For example, the use of home supervision contracts for children's hearings has many possible advantages in terms of clarity and monitoring. They do, however, have the potential of suggesting 'partnership' exists when it may not. This risk is evident from the original suggestion in the White Paper (SWSG 1993a), which notably did not include what the social work department would do in the contract, although both parents' and children's commitments were listed. Howe (1996) railed against the use of 'partnership' at all in social work, calling it a 'ubiquitous and endlessly promiscuous concept' (84), bringing in market rhetoric and presuming a rationality between partners that may well not exist. Woodhouse (1995) caricatured the assumptions behind 'partnership with parents' in child protection work:

- the rational parent

- the social worker within infinite time and patience
- the sharing of control and power
- a coincident understanding shared by parent and social worker (of what the problems are and what the solutions to them might be) (136)

Woodhouse found that such assumptions were not always realised. Despite its positive and friendly associations, perhaps 'partnership' is a misleading concept to apply to situations where equality between partners is unlikely. More realistic and accurate concepts might be those more commonly used for relationships between agencies, such as co-operation, collaboration and consultation—which have varying degrees of presumed commonality and relationships (see Chapter Five).

Indeed, why are there different phrases used for different people with whom social work services and professionals deal? A multitude of words are used to describe relationships between agencies, with those used above and other descriptions such as 'inter-agency' or 'multi-disciplinary' and 'working together'. Yet in policy papers surrounding children's legislation, the phrase 'partnership with parents' is commonly found. For children, legal phrases suggest 'due regard to a child's view', and more informal guidance uses phrases like 'consultation with children' or 'listening to children'. While not attempting an extensive discourse analysis here, the usage may suggest different ways of thinking and practice. The divide between the phrases suggest that the relationships are different. For example, parents are not part of the 'inter-disciplinary team', although they are valued as 'partners'; the relationship of partnership is primarily between the parents and the social workers and not between parents and the others on the 'inter-disciplinary team'. Children are not typically considered 'partners' even though they are, or at least should be, the central people in children's services (with some exceptions—e.g. SWSG 1997a: 6). Little distinction is made between children who may be too young to state their views (i.e. infants), who arguably could not be 'partners', to young people who are at least as able to be partners as their parents. 'Listening to children' connotes a very different relationship that 'partnership with parents': while listening in itself is positive, it does not require any agreement or action that the term partnership does suggest. The distinctive discourse between parents and children does denote, once again, a separation between the two.

The different discourses can be interpreted either negatively or positively. They could be seen to diminish the impact of children's views compared to parents' or other professionals' views. They could be seen to exclude parents from 'working together' in a team, with other professionals. The discourses do recognise that relationships need to be established with children, parents, and other agencies. They indicate that children cannot necessarily be subsumed into the family unit. Whatever their evaluation, the discourses do set up clear distinctions across the relationships between professional–professional, professional–parent, and professional–child—with the professional purposefully described first in that dyad, as the professional typically has the power to define, or at least instigate, the relationship.

Children's rights

The emphasis on listening to children should not be discounted, for its frequent mention in policy documents and the 1995 Act itself is a considerable step forward in recognising children's rights to participate. Indeed, UK children's legislation was held up in the UK's submission to the United Nations (UN) Committee on the Rights of the Child (1994) as major steps towards implementing the UN Convention on the Rights of the Child.

To what extent can the UK Government's assertion be justified? Certainly, many of its articles are supported by the legislation, but many gaps can still be found. A brief survey is given below:

Article 1 (a child is defined as below the age of eighteen, unless by law majority is attained at an earlier age):
The age of eighteen is applied to most of the public law sections, including services for 'children in need'. However, children over the age of sixteen are not necessarily dealt with by the children's hearing system and, if they offend, may well find themselves in court. Further, the age of criminal responsibility is eight in Scotland, so technically children at that age or above can also be caught up in criminal court proceedings (a situation strongly criticised by the UN Committee (1995)). The private law is also inconsistent at times with Article 1, for parental responsibilities are not universally extended up to a child's eighteenth birthday. This could be seen as respecting a child's independence, for they may well not appreciate being 'directed' by their parent or wish to maintain contact with their parent. None the less, such inconsistencies do not fulfil Article 1.

Article 3 (in all actions concerning children, the best interests of the child shall be a primary consideration)
The Children (Scotland) Act 1995 in fact creates a higher requirement, so that a child's welfare must be the *paramount* consideration in a wide range of court and children's hearing proceedings under the Act, as well as decisions for 'looked after' and in adoption. Yet courts, children's hearings and local authorities can ignore even a (looked after) child's interests as a primary consideration when the public is judged at risk of 'serious harm' (see Chapters Five and Six).

Article 8 (preservation of identity)
Adoption could be considered 'lawful interference' and thus could be allowed to infringe a child's right to preserve his or her identity. Arguments are made, however, against 'closed' adoption prevalent in the UK since the late 1940s, where a child's relationships with their birth or former parents and family are cut off (e.g. see Ryburn 1995). The 1995 Act makes little change to this 'closed' adoption, although recognising the reality of step-families in step-adoptions. While restricting access to adoption court records and the adoption register to

those of age 16 or older may be in a child's best interests, the age limit is inconsistent with Article 1.

Article 12 (in all matters affecting the child, the child has a right to express his/her views and to have them given due weight)
As mentioned above, the 1995 Act explicitly legislated for this right of children not only in formal court proceedings, but also in service delivery for children who are 'looked after' and for parents making major decisions on their parental responsibilities. However, numerous gaps can be found in the Act. For example, the principle is not applied to children's hearings' consideration of who should be excluded, or on lifting a prohibition on publication of children's hearing proceedings. Third parties administrating children's property do not have to consider children's views. While the legal presumption of children over the age of twelve being of 'sufficient age and maturity to form a view' may be much appreciated by lawyers, it may have repercussions in non-legal situations where it is read as presuming younger children do *not* have such capacity (see Chapter Five). Given the difficulties of turning such principles into reality, considerable work may be needed to ensure the principle that all children's views should be considered, if the children wish to state their views, is realised.

Article 19 (protection from abuse and neglect)
The UN Committee (1995) specifically criticised the UK for failing to ban corporal punishment of children by all.

Article 28 (adequate standard of living)
The 1995 Act does not deal with the fundamental problems facing many children and their families in Scotland today: for example, youth and adult unemployment; poverty; and poor housing.

Article 30 (the right of children of minority communities and indigenous people to enjoy their own culture and to practice their own religion and language)
While not consistently applied throughout the legislation, the Act should be commended for including some notice of a child's religious persuasion, racial origin, and cultural and linguistic background. The principle is vaguely worded and qualified. Yet hopefully it will provide a powerful incentive to local authorities, who may indeed have to think hard as to how to operationalise it in the context of small authorities and small populations (see Chapters Five and Six).

While considerable worry has been expressed about the implementation of public law, given resource constraints in the state and voluntary sectors, the private law provisions may make a substantial difference in recognising the rights of children. The ability of children to be represented legally, in a number of different proceedings, has been met with considerable enthusiasm by members of the legal profession and judiciary. The new rules and procedures could truly ensure that children's views are taking into account in contested cases. If parents and children know of a parent's duty to consult their children on 'major decisions', this could have a substantial effect on family life and substantially improve children's rights. The new Act provides considerable challenges for the legal profession, the judiciary and parents: it will be important that all have the necessary information to foster and recognise the rights of children.

The UN Convention itself has not been free from criticism (see Chapter Two), and several of its disadvantages are replicated in the 1995 Act. For example, both the Convention and the Act are written in terms of an individual child. Beyond the discourse problem that the Act therefore regularly refers to a child as 'he', this individualism has problems dealing with conflicts between a child and others. Whose rights 'win' if one child's rights conflict with anothers? Sometimes such supposed conflicts are resolvable be redefining each child's rights, but ultimately some conflicts cannot be semantically solved. The UN Convention does not deal with such problems; the Act does so by allowing itself an exception so wide as potentially to be draconian (i.e. Sections 16 (5) and 17 (5)).

Services can have difficulty with such individualism. For example, state education's primary legislative duty is to provide adequate and efficient education to *all* children in their areas. The 1995 Act does not address this potential conflict, which emerges all too obviously when a large proportion of 'looked after' young people are excluded from school. This individualism can also cause problems when more than one child is in question in a particular situation. For example, if a sibling wishes to tell something to a children's hearing, the hearing would have no right to exclude the parents because the sibling is not the child in question. A further problem with individualism is less applicable to the UN Convention but very much to the Act. Community care experience has demonstrated the difficulties and choices that must be made between working on the basis of individual need or community need (Percy-Smith 1996b). The Act's individualism is reflected, for example, in SWSG guidance for 'children in need' (1997a). The overwhelming impression from the draft guidance is that of 'gate-keeping' and assessment. Next to no mention is made of meeting the needs of communities nor the possible advantages of open-door services in providing truly preventive and non-stigmatising approaches. The focus tends to be on individual pathology, rather that community services and development. Individualism thus leaves certain issues unresolved or unaddressed. Yet it has its advantages, in seeing each child as having his/her own history, own needs and own rights. Are there possibilities to take the best from both approaches?

Another conflict left unresolved is between children's and parents' rights. For example, Article 30 promotes recognition of children's backgrounds while Article 14 states a child's right to freedom of thought, conscience and religion. Similarly, the 1995 Act promotes due regard to a children's background and respecting parental views, while also having duties to consider children's views. Because these duties are qualified, service professionals will be able to resolve them within the law. But they do pose important practice considerations. As Seden (1995) articulated: 'At what age does a child have the right to make his or her own decision? What is appropriate parental involvement in arranging a child's marriage or preventing them from joining a sect' (12)?

The UN Convention is predominantly drafted to describe the relationships between adults and children, whether the adults be gathered collectively as 'the state' or addressed individually as parents. The UN Convention is less attentive to rights of children in relation to other children. For example, the Convention does not contain requirements to respect and support children's own friendships and support networks (Ennew 1995). The Convention itself was drafted without any considerable involvement of children. Similarly, the 1995 Act predominantly describes the relationship between the state–parents–child, the parents–child and, to some extent, the state–child. It pays little attention to the rights of children in relation to each other. For example, the explicit right of children to sibling contact is not made, only to parental contact. Commendably, considerations of sibling contact can be made within court orders and can be part of local authorities' decision-making. Yet, it is not given specific legislative backing. Nothing is said about supporting children's peer networks (although again it is possible for it to be covered in the interpretation of duties). As described in Chapter Four, the policy-making and particularly the parliamentary process actively worked against the involvement of children and young people, as well as their families. One considerable improvement was made by the evidence-taking within the Bill procedures. But other children, such as children with physical disabilities or children in independent schools, could have had a great deal to say to the Special Standing Committee, but they had no organisation as well-organised and supportive as Who Cares? Scotland to facilitate their participation. The SWSG can be commended for its funding of *Speaking Out* consultation, when a variety of young people were consulted for the White Paper (SWSG 1994). Unfortunately, such funding was not repeated to respond to consultative guidance and policies issued from the SWSG in 1996-97. Almost all adult agencies are not fulfilling the obligation to take account of children's views in 'all matters that affect them'.

While the 1995 Act is described as children's legislation, what the Act addresses is a largely state-run and adult-led system, organised not from a child's perceptive but from historical and traditional ones. Thus, the worlds of child care services and education are kept separated, although to a child there can seem little difference between day care provided by education or by social work, or a residential school place funded by either service. The 1995 Act, as well as its counterparts elsewhere in the UK, may indeed go far in meeting the requirements of the UN Convention. But it does not cover all aspects that affect children, which is what the UN Convention requires. Educational legislation and policy is a clear contrast, where there is no legal requirement for education to promote a child's welfare nor listen to a child's views.

Education legislation specifies *parents'* rights—e.g. to choose their children's schools, to make appeals concerning records of special educational needs or in relation to school exclusions—but not rights for children under the age of sixteen. Technically, educational services would have to give due regard to 'looked after' children's views and welfare but not other children in the classroom.

As indicated above, the 1995 Act seems as much about parenting as it does about children. The Act does begin, for example, with a section on parental responsibilities and not on children's rights. Indeed, the potential tensions between the two have become a flash point in England and Wales, where the 1989 Act faced a rash of criticism. Local authorities were being accused of putting children's rights before those of parents, and the very right of children to express their views was attacked. (Department of Health and the Welsh Office 1997; Valios 1997b). The criticisms of the 1989 Act seem somewhat ironic when, in Scotland, its parallel legislation is being implemented. Hopefully, though, Scotland can find a satisfactory balance between parental and children's rights, which does not retreat to the now historical approach of treating children as 'objects of concern'.

Children's hearings and emergency child protection: which rights and whose rights?

The children's hearing system provides one forum where it has long been accepted that children have the right to participate and indeed, in children's panels, informality is encouraged to facilitate young people's comfort. The children's hearings system may provide a bulwark against the furore in England and Wales.

Yet children's rights, including their welfare, are still balanced against the rights of parents. While parents can be excluded, they still must be told the substance of what has been said. If a child says something before a hearing or writes a report, as they will be encouraged to do by professionals, parents have the right to receive all reports before the hearing just as professionals do. Yet children have not been extended this right to receive children's hearing reports, even with qualification. Parents' rights in this case seem to address 'due process', but children are excluded from such procedural justice and possibly from the tools for participation.

The Children (Scotland) Act 1995 has made several re-balances between welfare and justice, hearings and the courts. It has altered the process and procedures initiated by an emergency order (i.e. from the former Place of Safety Orders to the new Child Protection Orders), so that children and parents have opportunities to appeal at virtually every step. A new power has been given to the courts, to make a welfare decision when a disposal has been appealed from a children's hearing. The government has explained these changes as attempts to protect the children's hearing system from adverse rulings from the European Court of Human Rights. These changes, intentionally, are not meant fundamentally to change the system, but to make enough changes to meet the European Convention on Human Rights' requirements. Whether these changes do any more than clutter and confuse system, rather than safeguard the hearings, can only be answered by future rulings. Certainly some feel that the Sheriff's new power may signal the demise of a foundational principle of the children's hearing system: the general division between welfare decisions being made by the children's hearing system and justice decisions being made by the courts (see Chapter Five).

The Scottish Office believes it can lift its reservation to Article 39 (d) in the UN Convention (that is, children's right to have prompt access to legal and other appropriate assistance), because of these alterations (Campbell 1997). The 1995 Act has not, however, changed the stance on children's representation *in* children's hearings. Legal aid is not available for lawyers legally to represent children within a hearing. The debates for and against such representation remain strong, but the role of a safeguarder— as well as a safeguarder's training, management, support and pay—needs urgent resolution. The Scottish Child Law Centre lobbied for a child advocate to be introduced into such proceedings at the time of the Orkney Inquiry (see Chapter Three). Children can already bring along a 'representative' to a hearing, although many do not know about this right (Hansard 6.2.95). There are those who would worry that the introduction of an advocate would cause a numerical overload for a children's hearing, which would intimidate children and work against its principle of informality and discussion. Others would argue that while everyone else is there in a child's best interests, a child has no one there who explicitly and only is there to help the child express his or her views.

Welfare and justice has not been re-balanced by the Act so as to address substantive, versus procedural, justice for children. The hearings continue to focus on individual children, with no real and powerful means to amass systematically the issues for individual children into a concerted change to children's opportunities and needs. None of the child protection changes fundamentally alter the focus on parental fault, thus failing to address other abuse of children or indeed underlying reasons why parents might abuse, whether psychological or social. The hearings have gained some new powers, which could help them deal with the diversity of children that now attend. They can appoint a safeguarder in a wider set of circumstances, which could help them in difficult child protection cases. They can set a time for a review, to ensure that the supervision requirement matches the (changing) needs of children and their families. They may be able to access a wider range of resources, due to the corporate definition of local authority. Home supervision contracts are being promoted through guidance, to tighten up on home supervision requirements. Whether these changes will help children's hearings deal with young people who persistently offend is questionable. Perhaps the answer lies more in substantive justice, however, and the availability of both preventive and rehabilitative services, than in the children's hearings themselves.

The increasing attention to justice issues—i.e. procedural rights, and particularly those of parents—has caused worry in England and Wales, as well as in Scotland, that children's welfare may be sidelined. This worry has been expressed for the new thresholds of significant harm and associated child protection procedures. King (1995) wrote provocatively of how the 1989 Act limits public responsibility for children:

> This delegation of responsibility by politics to law allows judicial reasoning and government policy to claim in unison that the limits of public responsibility are defined by the criterion of proof. If there is inadequate evidence to prosecute or to take care proceedings, then for the law the act is not recognizable as unlawful, while politically it remains within the private sphere and so cannot be controlled through direct intervention. Furthermore, this delegation also permits governments to hide behind law's immunity from responsibility for future consequences. (146–147)

Worry has also been expressed over child care priorities versus those of the criminal justice system. The statistics remain dramatically low for successful prosecutions of alleged abusers (NIPC 1996). The length of time taken for a criminal prosecution goes far beyond most children's best interests. The actual experience of a criminal trial has been accused of abusing the child yet again. Marshall (1996) summarised the conflict between the systems:

> The desired outcomes in child protection proceedings is clearly defined in terms of the interest of the child. In criminal proceedings it is defined in terms of the interest of society. It is undoubtedly true that conviction of a child abuser can be protective of other children by triggering vetting processes which reduce his potential for access to commit further offences. ... The child victim may now be safe, and it may be considered that involvement in criminal proceedings may not serve the child's interests and may even be damaging. Is it legitimate to force a child to participate for the sake of others? (257)

Even though Lord Clyde stated that children's interests must be paramount (see Chapter Three), the Act makes no attempt to resolve such tensions.

The 1995 Act, and later the Family Law Act 1996 that applies to England and Wales, have created a new re-balancing that heightens attention to children's welfare and their civil liberties. Both introduce new possibilities to exclude an alleged abuser from contacting, and/or living with, a child. But the new orders have severely constricted criteria. Even while fundamentally underlining the priority of the child's welfare, the Scottish exclusion order provisions allow for many exceptions to be argued on behalf of the alleged abuser, largely seeking to protect the alleged abuser's livelihood. These could preclude the granting of an order. Even more surety of a child's risk seems to be needed to gain an exclusion order, than an order to remove a child from his or her home. With the Family Law Act's amendments to the Children Act 1989, it appears that the choice between emergency orders to remove a child or to exclude an alleged abuser is more equal (although still with more criteria for an exclusion requirement). But the English and Welsh version are more time-constrained than the Scottish one (see

Chapter Six). How these provisions work out in practice will actually determine what the re-balancing will be, for local authorities may or may not choose to apply for such orders, and courts may or may not agree to grant them.

Choices for the future

Local authorities face many choices in their implementation of the Children (Scotland) Act 1995. They will need to make vitally important decisions about how they will define 'children in need', how they will work together 'corporately', and how they will collaborate with other agencies. Children's services plans could provide an opportunity to transform services, creating a consultative and collaborative environment not only with other agencies but also with children, parents and communities. Many of the principles within the Act, for both children's and parents' rights, will only have meaning in practice. Local authorities have choices to make in many areas of service delivery. How many of their powers will they use: will they set up or fund safe refuges? will they provide day care for children who are not officially 'in need'? How will they implement their duties for after-care? How will they interpret 'due regard to a child's religious persuasion, racial origin and cultural and linguistic background'?

Parents individually will have choices in terms of promoting joint parenting and listening to children's views. They will have choices to make should they become involved in children's services planning, request services for their children or become involved in unwelcomed state intervention. Parents, at least initially, will have to decide what is a 'major decision', for which they should consult another parent(s) and the child. Courts will have the considerable responsibility of producing legal interpretations on many areas of the Act, which could have profound impact on practice and children's lives. Further, procedurally, court personnel are required themselves to listen to children's views and can choose to make courts more child-friendly and child-oriented fora than most have been in the past. Lawyers will have an important role in facilitating children's access to their legal rights.

Children may also have choices. Their rights to participate have had some additional emphasis, due to the Act. According to legislation and associated rules, they should have the option to state their views—or not—in a variety of proceedings. They could become involved in planning for children's services. They could become more informed participants, if local authorities provide them with the required information. Children may be able to access 'safe refuges', a service to be initiated by their own actions.

Few would say the Children (Scotland) Act is perfect legislation. Specific areas of amendment can already be suggested, ranging from a consistent inclusion of children's rights, to creating a sounder basis for respite services. The Act must be systematically monitored, to suggest such future amendments but also to ensure that children, young people and their families are receiving services that they need, to provide a national overview to guard against gross inequities, and to gather together examples of good practice.

The Children (Scotland) Act 1995 is an evolution, rather than a revolution, in children's policy. While many elements of Scottish children's services are highly commendable, certain criticisms seem likely to continue:

- the difficulties of inter-agency collaboration;
- the lack of coherence between different types of legislation (for example, while social security legislation may encourage all parents to work, single mothers are unable to access affordable day care in order to take up employment);
- the lack of coherence between different fora (e.g. between private law proceedings on parental responsibilities, and adoption and child care proceedings in public law);
- the failure to provide adequate preventive services, so that the barest minimum of children require active protective intervention; and
- the failure to provide an adequate standard of living so that children have the best chance to fulfil their potential.

What might a more radical approach look like? Attention could be given to examining a coherent policy for children. The inclusion of all children's services in one piece of legislation is unrealistic, for it would be far too unwieldy. But it would be possible to ensure that common principles are included in all legislation that affect children; it would be possible, for example, to have 'children in need' definitions included across legislation for health and education services. If not only legislation, but policies, were systematically co-ordinated for children, a 'whole child' approach could actually be created. A co-ordinated and coherent children's policy could both recognise that children usually do live in families and that children are also people in their own right. An alternative or complement to integrating and completely co-ordinating children's policy could be to increase the 'vetting' of all legislation and policy, and not just those overtly concerned with children, through the use of 'child impact' statements.

Marshall (1996) explored three ways in which the UN Convention could be further incorporated into UK law:

- a short interpretative Act creating a presumption that all UK law is to be interpreted in a way that accords so far as possible with the UN Convention;
- insertion of interpretation sections into specific Acts creating this presumption; or
- encouraging a practice of deliberate Ministerial statements in Parliament that the legislation is designed to comply with the UN Convention. (259)

Marshall appeared to favour the first choice. Presently, an existing rule of statutory operation could create such a presumption but Marshall stated that the boundaries of this rule are not clear. An Act would put the issue beyond doubt for the UN

Convention, heighten the Convention's profile and ensure that principles are applied to all law. It would even likely allow administrative action to be reviewed judicially, in light of the Convention.

Greater attention could be drawn to children's issues through structural changes in national government. A recent committee report on effective government structures (Hodgkin and Newell 1996) advocated a:

- Minister of State for Children (a Minister for Children's Issues and a Minister for Children were appointed in 1997 in Scotland and Wales respectively)
- Senior Cabinet member with a responsibility for children
- Cabinet Office Children's Unit
- Cabinet Committee, or Sub-Committee, for Children or a Standing Inter-Ministerial Group on Children
- House of Commons Select Committee on Children.

The report also recommended establishing a Children's Commissioner as an independent body influential on, but outside, central government. Considerable attention has been given in the UK to the necessary characteristics of a Children's Commissioner (see also Rosenbaum and Newell 1991).

A Commissioner's relationship to children would be fundamental—a Commissioner must have ways to ensure that children's views influence the Commissioner's agenda, priorities and conclusions. Different ways to access children's views have been developed in other countries. For example, Denmark's National Council on Children's Rights obtains children's views through: direct consultation with children; affiliated school classes and one day care institution; a further network of children's groups across the country; and a free telephone service where children can record their views and identify issues (Cohen and Hagen 1997). Although Chapter Three alluded to the *Review of Scottish Child Care Law'* s recommendation that further consideration be given to a Scottish Child Welfare Commission, which could have similar functions to the Children's Commissioner described above, no such official attention has yet been given to it by the Scottish Office.

Whatever the system, true attention to Article 12 of the UN Convention on the Rights of the Child requires considerable more involvement of children in making policy and planning services. Scotland has had its own initiatives in creating youth fora to influence local authorities and fostering children's rights. Willow (1997) described numerous examples across England and Wales, and Europe. Munich has set up 'children's advisers' to its mayor. Slovenia has a Children's Parliament where child representatives question high-ranking ministers annually, although this Parliament has no power over budgets or to make policy (Pavlovic 1996). Street children in India undertook a poster campaign, and collected 950 usable responses as a basis for a government report. Too few means are presently available in Scotland for children to make an organised and powerful contribution to policies that affect them.

Reasons for including children's views in policies and practice have been well-rehearsed. The benefits of user involvement in the design and delivery of services have been listed as greater effectiveness and satisfaction. Children are users of children's services; thus their participation in defining, designing and monitoring their services is likely to create similar benefits. Children cannot automatically be expected to take on adult responsibilities when they reach legal majority, if they have been prevented from developing and practising these skills before then. Thus, in the desire to create 'better citizens' and to foster children's sense of responsibility, self-esteem, self-competence and capabilities, children's participation in decision-making is advocated (Ashworth 1995). Even an economic reason can be given: the skills required in decision-making (e.g., taking on responsibility, negotiation, working as a team, creative thinking, independence) are what employers want and will need in their employees (Pearce 1997). Fundamentally, if children are considered as people, then their basic rights to be listened to and to participate should be recognised—irrespective of the fact that they may become future adults. A thorough analysis of the implementation of the Children (Scotland) Act 1995 from children's perspectives would be a worthwhile and informative task indeed.

Whether radical or evolutionary, the focus of children's services must remain clear. Children's services should not be, at their most basic, about government structures, professional hierarchies, or fulfilling bureaucratic requirements. Their obligations to meet the needs and rights of children and young people must always be paramount, and the needs and rights of families when they help support those of children and young people. Historical analyses show that the creation of certain services was grounded in controlling children and families, as much as helping them or providing children with opportunities (see Hill and Tisdall 1997). Social policy analyses show the immense pressures on services from other interests, of procedures that get established, of professionals and services seeking to protect, maintain and promote themselves, about the methods service providers use to constrain and organise their work.

Keeping children and young people at the centre of children's services is consistently difficult against these pressures. It must never be considered redundant or repetitive to return to the basic premise: children's services should exist to meet the needs and rights of children and young people.

REFERENCES

Adcock, M., White, R. and Hollows, A. (eds) (1991), *Significant Harm: its Management and Outcome*, Croydon: Significant Publications.

Aldgate, J. and Hill, M. (1995), 'Child Welfare in the United Kingdom', *Children and Youth Services Review*, 17 (5/6): 575–598.

Aldgate, J. and Tunstill, J. (1995), *Making Sense of Section 17: Implementing Services for Children in Need within the 1989 Children Act*, London: HMSO.

Aldgate, J., Heath, A., Colton, M. and Simm, M. (1993), 'Social work and the education of children in foster care', *Adoption & Fostering*, 17 (3): 25–34.

Allen, R. (1996), *Children and Crime: Taking Responsibility*, London: IPPR.

Armstrong, B. (ed) (1989), *A People without Prejudice? The Experience of Racism in Scotland*, London: Runnymede Trust.

Armstrong, D. K., Galloway, D. and Tomlinson, S. (1993), 'Assessing Special Educational Needs: the child's contribution', *British Educational Research Journal* 19 (2): 121–131.

Ashworth, L. (1995), *Children's Voices in School Matters*, London: Advisory Centre for Education.

Audit Commission (1994), *Seen but not Heard. Co-ordinating Community Child Health and Social Services for Children in Need*, London: HMSO.

Audit Commission (1996), *Misspent Youth: Young People and Crime*, London: Audit Commission.

Banks, N. (1995), 'Children of Black mixed parentage and their placement needs', *Adoption & Fostering*, 19 (2): 19–24.

Bell, V. (1993), 'Governing childhood: neo-liberalism and the law', *Economy and Society*, 22 (3): 390–407.

Bemrose, C. and MacKeith, J. (1996), *Partnerships for Progress. Good Practice in the Relationship between Local Government and Voluntary Organisations*, Bristol: The Policy Press.

Biehal, N., Clayden, J., Stein, M. and Wade, J. (1996), 'Moving on. Young people and leaving care schemes', paper given at *British Youth Research: The New Agenda*, 26–28 January 1996, Glasgow.

Bilson, A. and Barker, R. (1995), 'Parental contact with children fostered and in residential care after the Children Act 1989', *British Journal of Social Work*, 25: 367–381.

Booth, Dame Margaret Justice (1995), 'The Children Act 1989—the proof of the pudding', *Statute Law Review*, 16 (1): 13–20.

Borland, M., Pearson, C., Bloomfield, I., Hill, M. and Tisdall, K. (1997), *Education and Looked After Children Away from Home*, Literature Review for the Scottish Office, Glasgow: Centre for the Child & Society.

Bradshaw, J. (1972), 'The concept of social need', *New Society*, 19: 640–643.

Brandon, M., Lewis, A. and Thoburn, J. (1996), 'The Children Act definition of 'significant harm'—interpretations in practice', *Health and Social Care in the Community*, 4 (1): 11–20.

British Agencies for Adoption and Fostering (BAAF) (1996), *The Children (Scotland) Act 1995. A Training Programme*, London: BAAF.

Browne, M. (1996), 'Needs assessment and community care', in Percy-Smith, J. (ed.), *Needs Assessment in Public Policy*, Buckingham: Open University Press, pp. 49–66.

Bruce, N. (1975), 'Children's hearings: a retrospect', *British Journal of Criminology*, 15 (4): 333–344.

Bruce, N. (1982), 'Historical background', in Martin, F. M. and Murray, K. (eds.), *The Scottish Juvenile Justice System*, Edinburgh: Scottish Academic Press, pp. 3–12.

Bruce, N., and Spencer, J. (1976), *Face to Face with Families*, Loanhead: Macdonald Publishers.

Buchanan, A. (1993), 'Life under the Children Act 1989', *Adoption & Fostering*, 17 (3): 35–38.

Buchanan, A., Wheal, A. and Coker, R. (1993), *Answering Back*, (Dolphin Project), University of Southampton: Department of Social Work Studies.

Bull, J., Cameron, C. and Moss, P. (1996), 'The 1989 Children Act: welfare, day care and early years provision', *Health and Social Care in the Community*, 4 (1): 3–10.

Butler-Sloss, Rt. Hon Justice E. (1988), *Report of the Inquiry into Child Abuse in Cleveland 1987*. Cm. 412, London: HMSO.

Campbell, N. (1997), 'National perspective' *Scotland's Children and Young People: Making a reality of children's rights and tackling the wrongs*. Conference, Stirling, 14th February.

Campbell, T. D. (1992), 'The rights of the minor: as person, as child, as juvenile, as future adult', *International Journal of Law and the Family*, 6: 1–23.

Campbell, T. H. (1977), 'Punishment in Juvenile Justice', *British Journal of Law and Society,* 4: 76–86.

Candappa, M. (1994), 'Equal opportunities and ethnicity in the early years: implementing the Children Act', *Children & Society*, 8 (3): 218–231.

Cervi, B. (1997), 'Playing God', *Community Care*, 23–29 January: 20–21.

Children Act Advisory Committee (CAAC) (1994), *Annual Report 1992/93*, London: Lord Chancellor's Department.

Children Act Advisory Committee (CAAC) (1995), *Annual Report 1993/94*, London: Lord Chancellor's Department.

Children Act Advisory Committee (CAAC) (1996), *Annual Report 1994/95*, London: Lord Chancellor's Department.

Children in Need Working Group (1995), *Defining, Managing and Monitoring Services for Children in Need in Wales*, Wales: SSI (Wales).

Children in Scotland (1995), *Children (Scotland) Act (1995) A Guide*, Glasgow: Scottish Local Government Information Unit.

Children in Scotland (1996a), *Scotland's Children. Children (Scotland) Act 1995 Implementation Newsletter.* October 1996, No. 3.

Children in Scotland (1996b), *Response. Draft Guidance on Children and Their Needs—Supporting Children and Families*, Edinburgh: Children in Scotland.

Children in Scotland (1996c), *Children (Scotland) Act (1995) Information Pack*, Edinburgh: Children in Scotland.

Children's Rights Development Unit (CRDU) (1994), *UK Agenda for Children*, London: CRDU.

Cleland, A. (1996), 'The Child's Right to be Heard and Represented in Legal Proceedings', in A. Cleland and E. Sutherland (eds) *Children's Rights in Scotland,* Edinburgh: W. Green, pp. 21–34.

Cleland, A. and Sutherland, E. (eds) (1996), *Children's Rights in Scotland*, Edinburgh: W. Green.

Clements, L. (1994), 'House Hunting', *Community Care*, 28 July–3 August.

'Clyde Report' (1993), *The Report of the Inquiry into the Removal of Children from Orkney in February 1991.* Return to an Address of the Honourable the House of Commons, 27 October 1992, chaired by Lord Clyde. Edinburgh: HMSO.

Cockett, M. and Tripp, J. (1996), 'Divorce, mediation and the rights of the child', in M. John (ed.), *Children in Our Charge: The Child's Right to Resources*, London: Jessica Kingsley.

Cohen, B. and Hagen, U. (1997), *Children's Services: Shaping Up for the Millennium*, Edinburgh: HMSO.

Colton, M., Drury, C. and Williams, M. (1995), 'Children in Need; Definition, Identification and Support', *Social Work*, 25: 711–728.

Community Care (1997a), 'Tower Hamlets loses assessment case in High Court', 16–22 January.

Cooper, J. (1983), 'Scotland—the management of change', in *The Creation of the British Social Services 1962–74*, London: Heinemann, pp. 33–53.

CoSLA, NALGO, NUPE, TGWU, and GMB (1992), *Caring for the Future: Report of the inquiry into staff employed in residential care*, Glasgow: CoSLA.

Cowan, D. S. and Fionda, J. (1994), 'Meeting the need. The response of local authorities' housing departments to the housing of ex-offenders', *British Journal of Criminology*, 34 (4): 444–458.

Department of Health (1991), *The Children Act 1989: Guidance and Regulations*, London: HMSO.

Department of Health (1992), *Choosing with Care*, London: HMSO.

Department of Health (1994), *The Children Act 1989. Contact Orders Study*, London: HMSO.

Department of Health (1995), *Child Protection. Messages from Research*, London: HMSO.

Department of Health and Social Security (DHSS) (1985), *Social Work Decisions in Child Care—Recent Research Findings and their Implications*, London: HMSO.

Department of Health and Social Security (DHSS) (1985a), *Review of Child Care Law and Family Services*, London: HMSO.

Department of Health and Social Security (DHSS) (1987), *The Law on Child Care and Family Services*, Cmnd 62, London: HMSO.

Department of Health and the Welsh Office (1997), *Social Services: Achievement and Challenge*, CM 3588, London: The Stationery Office.

Dickens, J. (1993), 'Assessment and the control of social work: an analysis of the reasons for the non-use of the Child Assessment Order', *Journal of Social Welfare and Family Law*, volume 3: 88–100.

Douglas, A. (1997), 'Shift of power', *Community Care*, 9–15 January.

Downey, R. (1997), 'Cash shortfall on Children Order', *Community Care*, 6–12 February, 5.

Doyal, L, and Gough, I. (1991), *A Theory of Human Need*, London: Macmillan.

Education Committee, House of Commons (1996), *Special Educational Needs: The Working of The Code of Practice and The Tribunal*, Second Report, No. 205, London: HMSO.

Eekelaar, J. (1994), 'The interests of the child and the child's wishes: the role of dynamic self-determinism', *International Journal of Law and the Family*, 8: 42–61.

Ennew, J. (1995), 'Outside childhood: street children's rights' in B. Franklin (ed.), *The Handbook of Children's Rights. Comparative Policy and Practice*, London: Routledge, pp. 201–214.

Erickson, P. G. (1982), 'The client's perspective', in F. M. Martin and K. Murray (eds.), *The Scottish Juvenile Justice System*, Edinburgh: Scottish Academic Press, pp. 93–104.

Farmer, E. and Owen, M. (1995), 'Child protection practice: private risks and public remedies. Decision making, intervention and outcome in child protection work', in *Child Protection: Messages from Research*, Department of Health, London: HMSO, pp. 61–64.

Finlayson, A. (1992), *Reporters to Children's Panels. Their Role, Function and Accountability*, Edinburgh: Scottish Office.

Fletcher, B. (1993), *Not Just a Name: The Views of Young People in Foster and Residential Care*, London: National Consumer Council/Who Cares? Trust.

Foreman, A. (1996), 'Health needs assessment', in Percy-Smith, J. (ed.), *Needs Assessment in Public Policy*, Buckingham: Open University Press, pp. 66–81.

Fox Harding, L. (1991a), *Perspectives in Child Care Policy*, London: Longman.

Fox Harding, L. (1991b), 'The Children Act 1989 in context: four perspectives in child care law and policy (I)', *Journal of Social Welfare and Family Law*, 2: 179–193.

Fox Harding, L. (1993), 'The Children Act in practice: underlying themes revisited', *Justice of the Peace* 157 (39): 600–602 and 616–618.

Francis, J. (1995), 'Culture Club', *Community Care*, June 30–July 5.

Freeman, I., Morrison, A., Lockhart, F. and Swanson, M. (1996), 'Consulting service users: the views of young people' in M. Hill and J. Aldgate (eds), *Child Welfare Services: Developments in Law, Policy Practice and Research*, London: Jessica Kingsley Publishers, pp. 227–239.

Gordon, A. (1996), 'The role of the state' in Cleland, A. and Sutherland, E. (eds.), *Children's Rights in Scotland*, Edinburgh: W. Green, pp. 95–120.

Grant, M. (1997), 'Benefit to unmarried fathers of new parental rights', *Scotsman*, 23. 1. 97.

Hallett, C. and Birchall, E. (1992), *Coordination and Child Protection: A Review of the Literature*, Edinburgh: HMSO.

Hansard, House of Commons Official Report (1988), *Parliamentary Debates*, 6th December, Westminster. London: HMSO.

Hansard, House of Commons Official Report (1994), *Scottish Grand Committee*. 5th December, Edinburgh. London: HMSO.

Hansard, House of Commons Official Report (1995), *Parliamentary Debates*, 1st May 1995, Westminster. London: HMSO.

Hansard, House of Commons Official Report (1995), *Special Standing Committee. Children (Scotland) Bill.* Eighth Sitting, 28th February, Afternoon Part II, Westminster. London: HMSO.

Hansard, House of Commons Official Report (1995), *Special Standing Committee. Children (Scotland) Bill.* Fifth Sitting, 21st February, Afternoon, Edinburgh. London: HMSO.

Hansard, House of Commons Official Report (1995), *Special Standing Committee. Children (Scotland) Bill.* Second Sitting, 6th February, Morning, Glasgow. London: HMSO.

Hansard, House of Commons Official Report (1995), *Special Standing Committee. Children (Scotland) Bill.* Thirteenth Sitting, 14th March, Morning, Westminster. London: HMSO.

Hansard, House of Lords Official Report (1995), *Committee of the Whole House off the Floor of the House. Children (Scotland) Bill.* First Sitting, 6th June, Westminster. London: HMSO.

Hansard, House of Lords Official Report (1995), *Parliamentary Debates* 5th July, Westminster. London: HMSO.

Hansard, House of Lords Official Report (1995), *Parliamentary Debates* 12th July, Westminster. London: HMSO.

Hart, R. A. (1992), *Children's Participation. From Tokenism to Citizenship*, Innocenti Essays, No. 4. Florence: UNICEF International Child Development Centre.

Hawtin, M. (1996), 'Assessing housing needs', in Percy-Smith, J. (ed.), *Needs Assessment in Public Policy*, Buckingham: Open University Press, pp. 98–116.

Hewitt, M. (1992), *Welfare, Ideology and Need*, Hemel Hempstead: Harvester Wheatsheaf.

Hill, M. (1990), 'The Manifest and Latent Lessons of Child Abuse Inquiries', *British Journal of Social Work* 20: 197–213.

Hill, M. and Tisdall, K. (1997), *Children & Society*, Essex: Longman.

Hodgkin, R. and Newell, P. (1996), *Effective Government Structures for Children. Report of a Gulbenkian Foundation Inquiry*, London: Calouste Gulbenkian Foundation.

Houghton-James, H. (1995), 'Children divorcing their parents', *Journal of Social Welfare and Family Law*, 17: 185–199.

House of Commons 'Short Report' (1984), *Children in Care: Second Report from the Social Services Committee,* London: HMSO.

Howe, D. (1996), 'Surface and depth in social-work practice' in Parton, N. (ed), *Social Theory, Social Change and Social Work*, London: Routledge, pp. 77–97.

Howe, E. (1992), *The Quality of Care: Report of the Residential Staff's* Inquiry. London: Local Government Management Board.

Hughes, W. H. (1985), *Report of the Committee of Inquiry into Children's Homes and Hostels*, Belfast: HMSO.

Jackson, L. and Meade, G. (1996), 'Boy wins right to challenge smacking' *Scotsman*, 10. 9. 96.

Kearney, B. (1987), *Children's Hearings and the Sheriff Court*, Edinburgh: Butterworths.

'Kearney Report' (1992), *The Report of the Inquiry in Child Care Policies in Fife*. Return to an Address of the Honourable the House of Commons, 27 October 1992, chaired by Sheriff Kearney. Edinburgh: HMSO.

Kearney, B. (1996), 'The Children (Scotland) Act 1995: provisions anent children's hearings and child protection—the relevance for sheriffs', *Legal Services Agency Seminar*, November 1996.

Kelly, A. (1996), *Introduction to the Scottish Children's Panel,* Winchester: Waterside Press.

King, M. (1995), 'Partnership in politics and law: a new deal for parents?' in Kaganas, F., King, M. and Piper, C. (eds), *Legislating for Harmony. Partnership under the Children Act 1989,* London: Jessica Kingsley Publishers, pp. 143–153.

King, M. and Piper, C. (1990), *How the Law Thinks About Children,* Aldershot: Gower.

Kirby, P. (1994), *A Word From the Street . . . Young people who leave care and become homeless,* London: Community Care.

Kufeldt, K., Armstrong, J. and Dorosh, M. (1996), 'Connection and continuity in foster care', *Adoption & Fostering,* 20 (2): 14–20.

Lambert, L. (1990), *Freeing children for adoption : summary of main findings,* Edinburgh: Scottish Office.

Lau, A. (1991), 'Cultural and ethnic perspectives on significant harm: its assessment and treatment', in Adcock, M., White, R. and Hollows, A. (eds), *Significant Harm: Its Management and Outcome,* Croydon: Significant Publications, pp. 101–113.

Law Commission (1988), *Review of Child Law, Guardianship and Custody,* 172, London: HMSO.

Levy, A. and Kahan, B. (1991), *The Pindown Experience and the Protection of Children,* Stafford: Staffordshire County Council.

Lishman, J. (ed) (1983), *Collaboration and Conflict,* Aberdeen: Aberdeen University Press.

MacAskill, E (1994) 'Criminal Justice Bill will feature in Queen's speech' *The Scotsman,* 1.7.94.

MacAskill, E (1994) 'Scottish children's bill is shelved' *The Scotsman,* 7.7.94.

McCluskey, J. (1994), *Acting in Isolation: An Evaluation of the Effectiveness of the Children Act for Young Homeless People,* London: CHAR.

McColgan, M. (1995), 'The Children (Northern Ireland) Order 1995: considerations of the legislative, economic and political, organisational and social policy contexts', *Children and Youth Services Review,* 17 (5/6): 637–649.

McEwen, A. and Salters, M. (1995), 'Public policy and education in Northern Ireland', *Research Papers in Education* 10 (1): 131–141.

Marshall, K. (1996), 'The Scottish legal system' *Childhood Matters, Report of the National Commission of Inquiry into the Prevention of Child Abuse,* Vol. 1, London: The Stationery Office, pp. 239–261.

Marshall, K. (1997), *Children's Rights in the Balance. Reconciling Views and Interests,* Edinburgh: The Stationery Office. Forthcoming.

Martin, F. M., Fox, S. J., and Murray, K. with Erickson, P., Kelly, B. and Myers, M. (1981), '*Children Out of Court,* Edinburgh: Scottish Academic Press.

Midwinter, A. and McGarvey, N. (1994), 'The restructuring of Scotland's education authorities: does size matter?', *Scottish Educational Review,* 26 (2): 110–117.

Mitchell, J. K. (1997), 'Children's hearing system and the Children (Scotland) Act 1995', *SCOLAG Journal,* Jan/Feb: 9–17.

Moir, J. A. P. (1995), *Opinion of Counsel in respect of Children (Scotland) Bill for the Consortium for the Children (Scotland) Bill,* Edinburgh and Glasgow: Children in Scotland and the SCLC.

Morris, A. (1974), 'Scottish juvenile justice: a critique' in R. Hood (ed.), *Crime, Criminology and Public Policy,* London: Heinemann. pp. 347–374.

Morris, A. and Giller, H. (1987), *Understanding Juvenile Justice,* London: Croom Helm.

Murray, G. and Rowe, A. (1993) 'Children's Panels: Implications for the Future', *Policy & Politics,* 1(4): 327–340.

Murray, K. and Hill, M. (1992) 'The recent history of Scottish child welfare', *Children & Society,* 5 (3): pp. 266–281.

National Commission of Inquiry into the Prevention of Child Abuse (NIPC) (1996), *Childhood Matters,* Volume 1, London: The Stationery Office.

Norrie, K (1996), *Children (Scotland) Act 1995,* Edinburgh: W. Green

Norrie, K. McK. (1997) *Children's Hearings in Scotland.* Edinburgh: W. Green.

Northern Ireland Department of Health and Social Services (NIDHSS) (1996), *Health & Wellbeing: into the next millennium,* Belfast: NIDHSS.

Oliver, M. (1990), *The Politics of Disablement,* London: Macmillan.

Osborne, R. D., Cormack, R. J. and Miller, R. L. (1987), *Education and Policy in Northern Ireland*, Belfast: Policy Research Unit.

Packman, J. (1993), 'From prevention to partnership: child welfare services across three decades', *Children & Society*, 7 (2): 183–195.

Parton, N. (1985), *The Politics of Child Abuse*. London: Macmillan.

Parton, N. (1991), *Governing the Family. Child Care, Child Protection and the State*. London: Macmillan.

Pavolvic, Z. (1996), 'Children's parliament in Slovenia', in John, M. (ed.), *The Child's Right to a Fair Hearing*, London: Jessica Kingsley Publishers, pp. 93–107.

Pearce, I. (1997), 'Equipping children for the world of work: the importance of competence in decision-making', *Children's Participation in Decision-Making*, Conference, London, 28th January.

Percy-Smith, J. (1996a), 'Introduction: assessing needs. Theory and practice', in Percy-Smith, J. (ed.), *Needs Assessments in Public Policy*, Buckingham: Open University Press, pp. 3–10.

Percy-Smith, J. (1996), 'Assessing community needs', in Percy-Smith, J. (ed.), *Needs Assessment in Public Policy*, Buckingham: Open University Press, pp. 82–97.

Petch, A. (1988), 'Answering Back: parental perspectives on the children's hearings system', *British Journal of Social Work*. Vol. 18, pp. 1–24.

Piper, C. (1995), 'Partnership between parents', in Kaganas, F., King, M. and Piper, C. (eds), *Legislating for Harmony: Partnership Under the Children Act 1989*, London: Jessica Kingsley Publishers, pp. 35–52.

Porteus, D. (1996), 'Methodologies for needs assessment', in Percy-Smith, J. (ed.), *Needs Assessment in Public Policy*, Buckingham: Open University Press, pp. 32–46.

Reppucci, N. D. and Crosby, C. A. (1993), 'Law, Psychology and Children. Overarching Issues', *Law and Human Behaviour*, 17 (1): 1–10.

Roberts, H., Smith, S. J. and Bryce, C. (1995), *Children at Risk? Safety as a Social Value*, Milton Keynes: Open University Press.

Rodgers, M. E. (1996), 'Standard of proof in care order applications under the Children Act 1989', *Web Journal of Current Legal Issues*, 1996 [2], http://www.ncl.ac.uk/~nlawwww/1996/issue2/rodgers2.html

Rosenbaum, M. and Newell, P. (1991), *Taking Children Seriously*, London: Calouste Gulbenkian Foundation.

Ross, S. and Bilson, A. (1989), *Social Work Management and Practice. Systems Principles*, London: Jessica Kingsley.

Rowe, J., Cain, H., Hundebly, M. and Keane, A. (1989), *Child Care Now*, London: BAAF.

Ryan, M. (1994), *The Children Act 1989: Putting it into Practice*, Aldershot: Ashgate Publishing.

Ryburn, M. (1995), 'Secrecy and openness in adoption: a historical perspective', *Social Policy & Administration*, 29 (2): 150–168.

SCAFA (1990), Young Runaways, A Scottish Review, Brenda Morgan-Klein, Edinburgh: HMSO.

Scott, J. (1989), 'Child care law review—an opportunity for Scotland', *Adoption & Fostering* 13 (2): 43–48.

Scott, P. D. (1975), 'Children's hearings: a commentary', *British Journal of Criminology*, 15 (4): 344–347.

Scottish Child Law Centre (SCLC) (1995), *Guide to the Children (Scotland) Act 1995*, Glasgow: SCLC. 0141. 226. 3434

Scottish Child Law Centre (1997), *You Matter*, EdinburghL The Stationery Office.

Scottish Education Department and the Scottish Home and Health Department 'Kilbrandon Report' (1966), *Social Work and the Community: Proposals for Reorganising Local Authority Services in Scotland*. Presented to Parliament by the Secretary of State for Scotland by Command of Her Majesty, October 1966. Cmnd. 3065. Edinburgh: HMSO.

Scottish Home and Health Department and the Scottish Education Department (1994), *Children and Young Persons in Scotland, Scotland: report by the Committee appointed by the Secretary of State for Scotland*. Presenmted to Parliament April 1964, Cmd. 2306, Edinburgh: HMSO.

Scottish Law Commission (SLC) (1992a), *Report on Family Law,* No. 135, Edinburgh: HMSO.

Scottish Law Commission (SLC) (1992b), *The Scottish Law Commission's Report on Family Law. Summary,* No. 135, Edinburgh: SLC.

Scottish Office (1991), *Review of Child Care Law in Scotland,* Report of a review group appointed by the Secretary of State, chaired by J. W. Sinclair. Edinburgh: HMSO.

Scottish Office (1993), *Scotland in the Union: a partnership for good,* Cmnd. 2225 Edinburgh: HMSO.

Scottish Office (1994a), *Working Together: The Scottish Office, Volunteers and Voluntary Organisations,* Edinburgh: The Scottish Office.

Scottish Office (1995a), *Scotland's Children: A Brief Guide to the Children (Scotland) Act 1995,* Edinburgh: The Stationery Office.

Scottish Office (1995b), *The Parents' Charter in Scotland,* Edinburgh: The Scottish Office Education Department.

Scottish Office (1995c), *Provision for Pre-School Children,* Statistical Bulletin, Education Series, Edn/A2/1995/16, June, Edinburgh: HMSO.

Scottish Office (1995d), *Local Government in Scotland. Decentralisation—A Guide,* Edinburgh: Scottish Office.

Scottish Office (1995e), *Provision of Education for Pupils with Special Educational Needs,* Statistical Bulletin, Education Series, Edn/D2/1995/5, Edinburgh: HMSO.

Scottish Office (1996), *You Matter,* Edinburgh: The Stationery Office.

Scottish Office Education and Industry Department (SOEID) (1996), *Children and Young Persons with Special Educational Needs. Assessment and Recording,* Circular 4/96, Edinburgh: The SOEID.

Secretaries of State for Health and for Wales (1993), *Children Act Report 1992.* Presented to Parliament by command of Her Majesty. Cm 2144. London: HMSO.

Secretaries of State for Health and for Wales (1994), *Children Act Report 1993.* Presented to Parliament by command of Her Majesty. Cm 2584. London: HMSO.

Secretaries of State for Health and for Wales (1995), *Children Act Report 1994.* Presented to Parliament by command of Her Majesty. Cm 2878. London: HMSO.

Secretary of State for Social Services (1974), *Report of the Committee of Inquiry into the Care and Supervision Provided in Relation to Maria Colwell,* London: HMSO.

Seden, J. (1995), 'Religious Persuasion and the Children Act', *Adoption & Fostering,* 19 (2): 7–15.

Sellick, C. (1996), 'Short-term foster care', in Hill, M. and Aldgate, J. (eds), *Child Welfare Services: Developments in Law, Policy, Practice and Research,* London: Jessica Kingsley Publishers, pp. 160–169.

Sinclair, R., Grimshaw, R. and Garnett, L. (1994), 'The education of children in need: the impact of the Education Reform Act 1988, The Education Act 1993 and the Children Act 1989', *Oxford Review of Education,* 20 (3): 281–292.

Smith, B. (1996), 'The European Childhood Fund', *Child Care in Practice: Northern Ireland Journal of Multi-Disciplinary Child Care Practice,* Special Children Order Edition: 10–15.

Smith, G. (1980), *Social Need: Policy, Practice and Research,* London: Routledge & Kegan Paul.

Social Services Inspectorate (SSI) (1994), *Services to Disabled Children and Their Families. Report of the national inspection of services to disabled children and their families, January 1994.* London: HMSO.

Social Services Inspectorate (SSI) (1995), *Children's Services Plans. An Analysis of Children's Services Plans 1993/4,* Wetherby: Department of Health.

Social Services Inspectorate (SSI) for Wales (1995), *Preparing Children's Services Plans.* Cardiff: SSI for Wales.

Social Work Services Group (SWSG) (1993a), *Scotland's Children: Proposals for Child Care Policy and Law.* Cm 2286. Edinburgh: HMSO.

Social Work Services Group (SWSG) (1993b), *The Future of Adoption Law in Scotland,* Edinburgh: SWSG.

Social Work Services Group (SWSG) (1994), *Scotland's Children: Speaking Out. Young People's Views on Child Care Law in Scotland*, Edinburgh: The Scottish Office.

Social Work Services Group (SWSG) (1997a), *Scotland's Children. The Children (Scotland) Act 1995 Regulations and Guidance,* Volume 1: Support and Protection for Children and their Families, Edinburgh: The Stationery Office.

Social Work Services Group (SWSG) (1997b), *Scotland's Children. The Children (Scotland) Act 1995 Regulations and Guidance,* Volume 2: Children Looked After by Local Authorities, Edinburgh: The Stationery Office.

Social Work Services Group (SWSG) (1997c), *Scotland's Children. The Children (Scotland) Act 1995 Regulations and Guidance,* Volume 3: Adoption and Parental Responsibilities Orders, Edinburgh: The Stationery Office.

Social Work Services Inspectorate 'Skinner Report' (SWSI) (1992), *Another Kind of Home: a review of residential child care*, Edinburgh: HMSO.

Solomon, R. (1995), 'Tri-partnership: statutory, voluntary and private partnerships', in F. Kaganas, M. King and C. Piper (eds), *Legislating for Harmony: Partnership Under the Children Act 1989*, London: Jessica Kingsley Publishers, pp. 102–121.

Sone, K. (1997), 'Moving Stories', *Community Care,* 30 January–5 February 1997: 20–21.

Statham, J. and Cameron, C. (1994), 'Young Children in Rural Areas: Implementing the Children Act', *Children & Society*, 8 (1): 17–30.

Stubbs, P. (1987), 'Professionalism and the adoption of Black children', *British Journal of Social Work*, 17: 473–492.

Sutton, P. (1995), *Crossing the Boundaries. A Discussion of Children's Services Plans*, London: National Children's Bureau.

Taylor, R. and Ford, J. (1989), *Social Work and Health Care*, London: Jessica Kingsley.

Thanki, V. (1994), 'Ethnic diversity and child protection', *Children & Society*, 8 (3): 232–244.

Thoburn, J. (1995), 'Social work and families: lessons from research', in F. Kaganas, M. King and C. Piper (eds), *Legislating for Harmony: Partnership Under the Children Act 1989*, London: Jessica Kingsley Publishers, pp. 73–87.

Tisdall, E. K. M. (1996), 'Are young disabled people being sufficiently involved in their post-school planning? Case Studies of Scotland's Future Needs Assessment and Ontario's Educational-Vocational Meetings', *European Journal of Special Educational Needs*, 11 (1): 17–31.

Tisdall, E. K. M. (1997), "Transition to what?' How planning meetings for young disabled people leaving school conceptualise transition' *Youth & Policy* Issue 55: 1–13.

Tizard, B. (1977), *Adoption. A Second Chance*, London: Open Books.

Tizard, B. and Phoenix, A. (1993), *Black, White or Mixed Race?* London: Routledge.

Triseliotis, J., Borland, M., Hill, M. and Lambert, L. (1995), *Teenagers and the Social Work Services*, London: HMSO.

Tunstill, J. (1995), 'The Concept of Children In Need: The Answer or the Problem for Family Support?', *Children and Youth Services Review* 17 (5/6): 651–664.

United Kingdom Government (1994), *The UN Convention on the Rights of the Child. The UK's First Report to the UN Committee on the Rights of the Child*, London: HMSO.

United Nations Committee on the Rights of the Child (1995), 'Concluding observations of the Committee on the Rights of the Child: United Kingdom of Great Britain and Northern Ireland' *Consideration of Reports Submitted by State Parties under Article 44 of the Convention*, Eighth Session. CRC/C/15/Add. 34.

Utting, W. (1991), *Children in Public Care: A review of residential child care*, London: HMSO.

Valios, N. (1997a) 'Law Lords give green light to slash services', *Community Care*, 27 March–2 April: 1.

Valios, N. (1997b), 'Government to review 'misinterpreted' Act', *Community Care*, 9–16 January: 1.

Veerman, P. E. (1992), *The Rights of the Child and the Changing Image of Childhood*, Dordrecht: Martinus Nijhoff.

Wagner, G. (1988), *Residential Care: A positive choice*, Report of the Independent Review of Residential Child Care, London: HMSO.

Walker, J. (1996), 'Re-negotiating fatherhood', in De'Ath, E. (ed.) *Families in Transition*, London: Stepfamily Publications, London.

Weatherley, R. and Lipsky, M. (1977), 'Street-level bureaucrats and institutional innovation: implementing special-education reform', *Harvard Educational Review*, 47 (2): 171–197.

Wilkinson, A. B. and Norrie, K. (1993) *The law relating to parent and child in Scotland*, Edinburgh: W. Green.

Williams, C. (1995), 'Policy review. the impact of local government reorganisation in Wales', *Children & Society*, 9 (4): 94–99.

Willow, C. (1997), *Hear! Hear! Promoting Children and Young People's Democratic Participation in Local Government*, London: Local Government Information Unit.

Woodhouse, S. (1995), 'Child protection and working in partnership with parents', in Kaganas, F., King, M. and Piper, C. (eds), *Legislating for Harmony: Partnership Under the Children Act 1989*, London: Jessica Kingsley Publishers, pp. 132–142.

Younghusband, E. (1978) *Social Work in Britain: 1950–1975*, London: George Allen and Unwin.

APPENDIX 1

THE UNITED NATIONS CONVENTION ON THE RIGHTS OF THE CHILD

Adopted by the General Assembly of the United Nations on 20 November 1989

Text

Unofficial summary of main provisions

PREAMBLE

PREAMBLE

The States Parties to the present Convention.

Considering that in accordance with the principles proclaimed in the Charter of the United Nations, recognition of the inherent dignity and of the equal and inalienable rights of all members of the human family is the foundation of freedom, justice and peace in the world,

Bearing in mind that the peoples of the United Nations have, in the Charter, reaffirmed their faith in fundamental human rights and in the dignity and worth of the human person, and have determined to promote social progress and better standards of life in larger freedom,

Recognizing that the United Nations has, in the Universal Declaration of Human Rights and in the International Covenants on Human Rights, proclaimed and agreed that everyone is entitled to all the rights and freedoms set forth therein, without distinction of any kind, such as race, colour, sex, language, religion, political or other opinion, national or social origin, property, birth or other status,

Recalling that, in the Universal Declaration of Human Rights, the United Nations has proclaimed that childhood is entitled to special care and assistance,

Convinced that the family, as the fundamental group of society and the natural environment for the growth and well-being of all its members and particularly children, should be afforded the necessary protection and assistance so that it can fully assume its responsibilities within the community,

Recognizing that the child, for the full and harmonious development of his or her personality, should grow up in a family environment, in an atmosphere of happiness, love and understanding,

Considering that the child should be fully prepared to live an individual life in society, and brought up in the

The preamble: recalls the basic principles of the United Nations and specific provisions of certain relevant human rights treaties and proclamations; reaffirms the fact that children, because of their vulnerability, need special care and protection; and places special emphasis on the primary caring and protective responsibility of the family, the need for legal and other protection of the child before and after birth, the importance of respect for the cultural values of the child's community, and the vital role of international co-operation in achieving the realization of children's rights.

spirit of the ideals proclaimed in the Charter of the United Nations, and in particular in the spirit of peace, dignity, tolerance, freedom, equality and solidarity,

Bearing in mind that the need for extending particular care to the child has been stated in the Geneva Declaration on the Rights of the Child of 1924 and in the Declaration of the Rights of the Child adopted by the United Nations in 1959 and recognized in the Universal Declaration of Human Rights, in the International Covenant on Civil and Political Rights (in particular in articles 23 and 24), in the International Covenant on Economic, Social and Cultural Rights (in particular in its article 10) and in the statutes and relevant instruments of specialized agencies and international organizations concerned with the welfare of children.

Bearing in mind that, as indicated in the Declaration of the Rights of the Child adopted by the General Assembly of the United Nations on 20 November 1959, 'the child by reason of his physical and mental immaturity, needs special safeguards and care, including appropriate legal protection, before as well as after birth',

Recalling the provisions of the Declaration on Social and Legal Principles relating to the Protection and Welfare of Children with Special Reference to Foster Placement and Adoption Nationally and Internationally (General Assembly Resolution 41/85 of 3 December 1986); the United Nations Standard Minimum Rules for the Administration of Juvenile justice ('The Beijing Rules') (General Assembly Resolution 40/33 of 29 November 1985); and the Declaration on the Protection of Women and Children in Emergency and Armed Conflict (General Assembly Resolution 3318 (XXIX) of 14 December 1974),

Recognizing that in all countries in the world there are children living in exceptionally difficult conditions, and that such children need special consideration,

Taking due account of the importance of the traditions and cultural values of each people for the protection and harmonious development of the child,

Recognizing the importance of international co-operation for improving the living conditions of children in every country, in particular the developing countries,

Have agreed as follows:

PART 1

Article 1

For the purposes of the present Convention a child means every human being below the age of 18 years unless, under the law applicable to the child, majority is attained earlier.

Article 2

1. The States Parties to the present Convention shall respect and ensure the rights set forth in this Convention to each child within their jurisdiction without discrimination of any kind, irrespective of the child's or his or her parent's or legal guardian's race, colour, sex, language, religion, political or other opinion, national, ethnic or social origin, property, disability, birth or other status.

2. States Parties shall take all appropriate measures to ensure that the child is protected against all forms of discrimination or punishment on the basis of the status, activities, expressed opinions, or beliefs of the child's parents, legal guardians, or family members.

Article 3

1. In all actions concerning children, whether undertaken by public or private social welfare institutions, courts of law, administrative authorities or legislative bodies, the best interests of the child shall be a primary consideration.

2. States Parties undertake to ensure the child such protection and care as is necessary for his or her well-being, taking into account the rights and duties of his or her parents, legal guardians, or other individuals legally responsible for him or her, and, to this end, shall take all appropriate legislative and administrative measures.

3. States Parties shall ensure that the institutions, services and facilities responsible for the care or protection of children shall conform with the standards established by competent authorities, particularly in the areas of safety, health, in the number and suitability of their staff as well as competent supervision.

Article 4

States Parties shall undertake all appropriate legislative, administrative, and other measures, for the implementation of the rights recognized in this Convention. In regard to economic, social and cultural rights, States Parties shall undertake such measures to the maximum extent of their available resources and, where needed, within the framework of international co-operation.

Definition of a child

All persons under 18, unless by law majority is attained at an earlier age.

Non-discrimination

The principle that all rights apply to all children without exception, and the State's obligation to protect children from any form of discrimination. The State must not violate any right and must take positive action to promote them all.

Best interests of the child

All actions concerning the child should take full account of his or her best interests. The State is to provide adequate care when parents or others responsible fail to do so.

Implementation of rights

The State's obligation to translate the rights in the Convention into reality.

Article 5

State Parties shall respect the responsibilities, rights, and duties of parents or, where applicable, the members of the extended family or community as provided for by the local custom, legal guardians or other persons legally responsible for the child, to provide, in a manner consistent with the evolving capacities of the child, appropriate direction and guidance in the exercise by the child of the rights recognized in the present Convention.

Parental guidance and the child's evolving capabilities

The State's duty to respect the rights and responsibilities of parents and the wider family to provide guidance appropriate to the child's evolving capacities.

Article 6

1. States Parties recognize that every child has the inherent right to life.

2. States Parties shall ensure to the maximum extent possible the survival and development of the child.

Survival and development

The inherent right to life, and the State's obligation to ensure the child's survival and development.

Article 7

1. The child shall be registered immediately after birth and shall have the right from birth to a name, the right to acquire a nationality, and, as far as possible, the right to know and be cared for by his or her parents.

2. States Parties shall ensure the implementation of these rights in accordance with their national law and their obligations under the relevant international instruments in this field, in particular where the child would otherwise be stateless.

Name and nationality

The right to have a name from birth and to be granted a nationality.

Article 8

1. States Parties undertake to respect the right of the child to preserve his or her identity, including nationality name and family relations as recognized by law without unlawful interference.

2. Where a child is illegally deprived of some or all of the elements of his or her identity, States Parties shall provide appropriate assistance and protection, with a view to speedily re-establishing his or her identity.

Preservation of identity

The State's obligation to protect and, if necessary re-establish the basic aspects of a child's identity (name, nationality and family ties,

Article 9

1. States Parties shall ensure that a child shall not be separated from his or her parents against their will, except when competent authorities subject to judicial review determine, in accordance with applicable law and procedures, that such separation is necessary for the best interests of the child. Such determination may be necessary in a particular case such as one involving abuse or neglect of the child by the parents, or one where the parents are living separately and a decision must he made as to the child's place of residence.

Separation from parents

The child's right to live with his/her parents unless this is deemed incompatible with his/her best interests; the right to maintain contact with both parents if separated from one or both; the duties of States in cases where such separation results from State action.

2. In any proceedings pursuant to paragraph 1, all interested parties shall be given an opportunity to participate in the proceedings and make their views known.

3. States Parties shall respect the right of the child who is separated from one or both parents to maintain personal relations and direct contact with both parents on a regular basis, except if it is contrary to the child's best interests.

4. Where such separation results from any action initiated by a State Party, such as the detention, imprisonment, exile, deportation or death (including death arising from any cause while the person is in the custody of the State) of one or both parents or of the child, that State Party shall, upon request, provide the parents, the child or, if appropriate, another member of the family with the essential information concerning the whereabouts of the absent member(s) of the family unless the provision of the information would be detrimental to the well-being of the child. States Parties shall further ensure that the submission of such a request shall of itself entail no adverse consequences for the person(s) concerned.

Article 10

Family reunification

1. In accordance with the obligation of States Parties under article 9, paragraph 1, applications by a child or his or her parents to enter or leave a State Party for the purpose of family reunification shall be dealt with by States Parties in a positive, humane, and expeditious manner. States Parties shall further ensure that the submission of such a request shall entail no adverse consequences for the applicants and for the members of their family.

The right of children and their parents to leave any country and to enter their own in order to be reunited or to maintain the child–parent relationship.

2. A child whose parents reside in different States shall have the right to maintain on a regular basis save in exceptional circumstances personal relations and direct contacts with both parents. Towards that end and in accordance with the obligation of States Parties under article 9, paragraph 2, States Parties shall respect the right of the child and his or her parents to leave any country, including their own, and to enter their own country, The right to leave any country shall be subject only to such restrictions as are prescribed by law and which are necessary to protect the national security, public order *(ordre public),* public health or morals or the rights and freedoms of others and are consistent with the other rights recognized in the present Convention.

Article 11

Illicit transfer and non-return

1. States Parties shall take measures to combat the illicit transfer and non-return of children abroad.

The State's obligation to try to prevent and remedy the kidnapping or retention of children abroad by a parent or third party.

2. To this end, States Parties shall promote the conclusion of bilateral or multilateral agreements or accession to existing agreements.

Article 12

1. States Parties shall assure to the child who is capable of forming his or her own views the right to express those views freely in all matters affecting the child, the views of the child being given due weight in accordance with the age and maturity of the child.

2. For this purpose, the child shall in particular be provided the opportunity to be heard in any judicial and administrative proceedings affecting the child, either directly, or through a representative or an appropriate body, in a manner consistent with the procedural rules of national law.

The child's opinion

The child's right to express an opinion, and to have that opinion taken into account, in any matter or procedure affecting the child.

Article 13

1. The child shall have the right to freedom of expression: this right shall include freedom to seek, receive and impart information and ideas of all kinds, regardless of frontiers, either orally, in writing or in print, in the form of art, or through any other media of the child's choice.

2. The exercise of this right may be subject to certain restrictions, but these shall only be such as are provided by law and are necessary:

a) for respect of the rights or reputations of others: or

b) for the protection of national security or of public order *(ordre public)*, or of public health or morals.

Freedom of expression

The child's right to obtain and make known information, and to express his or her views, unless this would violate the rights of others.

Article 14

1. States Parties shall respect the right of the child to freedom of thought, conscience and religion.

2. States Parties shall respect the rights and duties of the parents and, when applicable, legal guardians, to provide direction to the child in the exercise of his or her right in a manner consistent with the evolving capacities of the child.

3. Freedom to manifest one's religion or beliefs may be subject only to such limitations as are prescribed by law and are necessary to protect public safety, order, health, or morals or the fundamental rights and freedoms of others.

Freedom of thought, conscience and religion

The child's right to freedom of thought, conscience and religion, subject to appropriate parental guidance and national law.

Article 15

1. States Parties recognize the rights of the child to freedom of association and to freedom of peaceful assembly.

2. No restrictions may be placed on the exercises of these rights other than those imposed in conformity with the law and which are necessary in a democratic society in the interest of national security or public safety, public order *(ordre public)*, the protection of public health or morals or the protection of the rights and freedoms of others.

Freedom of association

The right of children to meet with others and to join or set up associations, unless the fact of doing so violates the rights of others.

Article 16

1. No child shall be subjected to arbitrary or unlawful interference with his or her privacy, family, home or correspondence, nor to unlawful attacks on his or her honour and reputation.

2. The child has the right to the protection of the law against such interference or attacks.

Protection of privacy

The right to protection from interference with privacy, family, home and correspondence, and from libel/slander.

See also Article 37 and young offender's institutions.

Article 17

States Parties recognise the important function performed by the mass media and shall ensure that the child has access to information and material from a diversity of national and international sources, especially those aimed at the promotion of his or her social, spiritual and moral well-being and physical and mental health. To this end, States Parties shall:

a) Encourage the mass media to disseminate inform and material of social and cultural benefit to the child and in accordance with the spirit of article 29;

b) Encourage international co-operation in the production, exchange and dissemination of such information and material from a diversity of cultural, national and international sources;

c) Encourage the production and dissemination of children's books;

d) Encourage the mass media to have particular regard to the linguistic needs of the child who belongs to a minority group or who is indigenous;

e) Encourage the development of appropriate guidelines for the protection of the child from information and material injurious to his or her well-being bearing in mind the provisions of articles 13 and 18.

Access to appropriate information

The role of the media in disseminating information to children that is consistent with moral well-being and knowledge and understanding among peoples, and respects the child's cultural background. The State is to take measures to encourage this and to protect children from harmful materials.

Article 18

1. States Parties shall use their best efforts to ensure recognition of the principle that both parents have common responsibilities for the upbringing and development of the child. Parents or, as the case may be, legal guardians, have the primary responsibility for the upbringing and development of the child. The best interests of the child will be their basic concern.

2. For the purpose of guaranteeing and promoting the rights set forth in this Convention, States Parties shall render appropriate assistance to parents and legal guardians in the performance of their child-rearing responsibilities and shall ensure the development of institutions, facilities and services for the care of children.

3. States Parties shall take all appropriate measures to ensure that children of working parents have the right to benefit from child care services and facilities for which they are eligible.

Parental responsibilities

The principle that both parents have joint primary responsibility for bringing up their children, and that the State should support them in this task.

Article 19

1. States Parties shall take all appropriate legislative, administrative, social and educational measures to protect the child from all forms of physical or mental violence, injury or abuse, neglect or negligent treatment, maltreatment or exploitation including sexual abuse, while in the care of parent(s), legal guardian(s) or any other person who has the care of the child.

2. Such protective measures should, as appropriate, include effective procedures for the establishment of social programmes to provide necessary support for the child and for those who have the care of the child, as well as for other forms of prevention and for identification, reporting, referral, investigation, treatment, and follow-up of instances of child maltreatment described heretofore, and, as appropriate, for judicial involvement.

Protection from abuse and neglect

The State's obligation to protect children from all forms of maltreatment perpetrated by parents or others responsible for their care, and to undertake preventive and treatment programmes in this regard.

Article 20

1. A child temporarily or permanently deprived of his or her family environment or in whose own best interests cannot be allowed to remain in that environment, shall be entitled to special protection and assistance provided by the State.

2. State Parties shall in accordance with their national laws ensure alternative care for such a child.

3. Such care should include, *inter alia,* foster placement, Kafala of Islamic law, adoption, or if necessary placement in suitable institutions for the care of children. When considering solutions, due regard shall be paid to the desirability of continuity in a child's upbringing and to the child's ethnic, religious, cultural and linguistic background.

Protection of children without families

The State's obligation to provide special protection for children deprived of their family environment and to ensure that appropriate alternative family care or institutional placement is made available to them, taking into account the child's cultural background.

Article 21

States Parties which recognize and/or permit the system of adoption shall ensure that the best interests of the child shall be the paramount consideration and they shall:

a) ensure that the adoption of a child is authorized only by competent authorities who determine, in accordance with applicable law and procedures and on the basis of all pertinent and reliable information, that the adoption is permissible in view of the child's status concerning parents, relatives and legal guardians and that, if required, the persons concerned have given their informed consent to the adoption on the basis of such counselling as may be necessary;

b) recognize that intercountry adoption may be considered as an alternative means of child's care, if the child cannot be placed in a foster or an adoptive family or cannot in any suitable manner be cared for in the child's country of origin;

Adoption

In countries where adoption is recognized and/or allowed, it shall only be carried out in the best interests of the child, with all necessary safeguards for a given child and authorization by the competent authorities.

c) ensure that the child concerned by intercountry adoption enjoys safeguards and standards equivalent to those existing in the case of national adoption;

d) take all appropriate measures to ensure that, in intercountry adoption, the placement does not result in improper financial gain for those involved in it;

e) promote, where appropriate, the objectives of this article by concluding bilateral or multilateral arrangements or agreements, and endeavour, within this framework, to ensure that the placement of the child in another country is carried out by competent authorities or organs.

Article 22

1. States Parties shall take appropriate measures to ensure that a child who is seeking refugee status or who is considered a refugee in accordance with applicable international or domestic law and procedures shall, whether unaccompanied or accompanied by his or her parents or by any other person, receive appropriate protection and humanitarian assistance in the enjoyment of applicable rights set forth in this Convention and in other international human rights or humanitarian instruments to which the said States are Parties.

2. For this purpose, States Parties shall provide, as they consider appropriate, co-operation in any efforts by the United Nations and other competent intergovernmental organizations or non-governmental organizations co-operating with the United Nations to protect and assist such a child to trace the parents or other members of the family of any refugee child in order to obtain information necessary for reunification with his or her family. In cases where no parents or other members of the family can be found, the child shall be accorded the same protection as any other child permanently or temporarily deprived of his or her family environment for any reason, as set forth in the present Convention.

Refugee children

Special protection to be granted to children who are refugees or seeking refugee status, and the State's obligation to co-operate with competent organizations providing such protection and assistance.

Article 23

1. States Parties recognize that a mentally or physically disabled child should enjoy a full and decent life, in conditions which ensure dignity, promote self-reliance, and facilitate the child's active participation in the community.

2. States Parties recognize the right of the disabled child to special care and shall encourage and ensure the extension, subject to available resources, to the eligible child and those responsible for his or her care, of assistance for which application is made and which is appropriate to the child's condition and to the circumstances of the parents or others caring for the child.

3. Recognizing the special needs of a disabled child, assistance extended in according with paragraph 2 shall

Handicapped children

The right of handicapped children to special care, education and training designed to help them to achieve greatest possible self-reliance and to lead a full and active life in society.

be provided free of charge, whenever possible, taking into account the financial resources of the parents or others caring for the child, and shall be designed to ensure that the disabled child has effective access to and receives education, training, health care services, rehabilitation services, preparation for employment and recreation opportunities in a manner conducive to the child's achieving the fullest possible social integration and individual development, including his or her cultural and spiritual development.

4. States Parties shall promote in the spirit of international co-operation the exchange of appropriate information in the field of preventive health care and of medical, psychological and functional treatment of disabled children, including dissemination of and access to information concerning methods of rehabilitation education and vocational services, with the aim of enabling States Parties to improve their capabilities and skills and to widen their experience in these areas. In this regard, particular account shall be taken of the needs of developing countries.

Article 24

1. States Parties recognize the right of the child to the enjoyment of the highest attainable standard of health and to facilities for the treatment of illness and rehabilitation of health. States Parties shall strive to ensure that no child is deprived of his or her right of access to such health care services.

2. States Parties shall pursue full implementation of this right and, in particular, shall take appropriate measures:

a) to diminish infant and child mortality;

b) to ensure the provision of necessary medical assistance and health care to all children with emphasis on the development of primary health care;

c) to combat disease and malnutrition including within the framework of primary health care, through *inter alia* the application of readily available technology and through the provision of adequate nutritious foods and clean drinking water, taking into consideration the dangers and risks of environmental pollution;

d) to ensure appropriate pre- and post-natal care for mothers;

e) to ensure that all segments of society, in particular parents and children, are informed, have access to education and are supported in the use of, basic knowledge of child health and nutrition, the advantages of breast-feeding, hygiene and environmental sanitation and the prevention of accidents;

f) to develop preventive health care, guidance for parents, and family planning education and services.

3. States Parties shall take all effective and appropriate measures with a view to abolishing traditional practices prejudicial to the health of children.

Health and health services

The right to the highest level of health possible and to access to health and medical services, with special emphasis on primary and preventive health care, public health education and the diminution of infant mortality. The State's obligation to work towards the abolition of harmful traditional practices. Emphasis is laid on the need for international co-operation to ensure this right.

4. States Parties undertake to promote and encourage international co-operation with a view to achieving progressively the full realization of the right recognized in this article. In this regard, particular account shall be taken of the needs of developing countries.

Article 25

States Parties recognize the right of a child who has been placed by the competent authorities for the purposes of care, protection, or treatment of his or her physical or mental health, to a periodic review of the treatment provided to the child and all other circumstances relevant to his or her placement.

Periodic review of placement

The right of children placed by the State for reasons of care, protection or treatment to have all aspects of that placement evaluated regularly.

Article 26

1. States Parties shall recognize for every child the right to benefit from social security, including social insurance, and shall take the necessary measures to achieve the full realization of this right in accordance with their national law.

2. The benefits should, where appropriate, be granted taking into account the resources and the circumstances of the child and persons having responsibility for the maintenance of the child as well as any other consideration relevant to an application for benefits made by or on behalf of the child.

Social security

The right of children to benefit from social security.

Article 27

1. States Parties recognize the right of every child to a standard of living adequate for the child's physical, mental, spiritual, moral and social development.

2. The parent(s) or others responsible for the child have the primary responsibility to secure, within their abilities and financial capacities, the conditions of living necessary for the child's development.

3. States Parties in accordance with national conditions and within their means shall take appropriate measures to assist parents and others responsible for the child to implement this right and shall in case of need provide material assistance and support programmes, particularly with regard to nutrition, clothing and housing.

4. States Parties shall take all appropriate measures to secure the recovery of maintenance for the child from the parents or other persons having financial responsibility for the child, both within the State Party and from abroad. In particular, where the person having financial responsibility for the child lives in a State different from that of the child. States Parties shall promote the accession to international agreements or the conclusion of such agreements as well as the making of other appropriate arrangements.

Standard of living

The right of children to benefit from an adequate standard of living, the primary responsibility of parents to provide this and the State's duty to ensure that this responsibility is first fulfillable and then fulfilled, where necessary through the recovery of maintenance.

Article 28

1. State Parties recognize the right of the child to education, and with a view to achieving this right progressively and on the basis of equal opportunity, they shall, in particular:

a) make primary education compulsory and available free to all;

b) encourage the development of different forms of secondary education, including general and vocational education, make them available and accessible to every child, and take appropriate measures such as the introduction of free education and offering financial assistance in case of need;

c) make higher education accessible to all on the basis of capacity by every appropriate means;

d) make educational and vocational information and guidance available and accessible to all children;

e) take measures to encourage regular attendance at schools and the reduction of drop-out rates.

2. States Parties shall take all appropriate measures to ensure that school discipline is administered in a manner consistent with the child's human dignity and in conformity with the present Convention.

3. States Parties shall promote and encourage international co-operation in matters relating to education, in particular with a view to contributing to the elimination of ignorance and illiteracy throughout the world and facilitating access to scientific and technical knowledge and modern teaching methods. In this regard, particular account shall be taken of the needs of developing countries.

Education

The child's right to education, and the State's duty to ensure that primary education at least is made free and compulsory. Administration of school discipline is to reflect the child's human dignity. Emphasis is laid on the need for international co-operation to ensure this right.

Article 29

1. States Parties agree that the education of the child shall be directed to:

a) the development of the child's personality, talents and mental and physical abilities to their fullest potential;

b) the development of respect for human rights and fundamental freedoms, and for the principles enshrined in the Charter of the United Nations;

c) the development of respect for the child's parents, his or her own cultural identity, language and values, for the national values of the country in which the child is living, the country from which he or she may originate, and for civilizations different from his or her own;

d) the preparation of the child for responsible life in a free society, in the spirit of understanding, peace, tolerance, equality of sexes, and friendship among all peoples, ethnic, national and religious groups, and persons of indigenous origin;

Aims of education

The State's recognition that education should be directed at developing the child's personality and talents, preparing the child for active life as an adult, fostering respect for basic human rights and developing respect for the child's own cultural and national values and those of others.

e) the development of respect for the natural environment.

2. No part of this article or article 28 shall be constructed so as to interfere with the liberty of individuals and bodies to establish and direct educational institutions, subject always to the observance of the principles set forth in paragraph 1 of this article and to the requirements that the education given in such institutions shall conform to such minimum standards as may be laid down by the State.

Article 30

In those States in which ethnic, religious or linguistic minorities or persons of indigenous origin exist, a child belonging to such a minority or who is indigenous shall not be denied the right, in community with other members of his or her group, to enjoy his or her own culture, to profess and practice his or her own religion, or to use his or her own language.

Children of minorities or indigenous populations

The right of children of minority communities and indigenous populations to enjoy their own culture and to practice their own religion and language.

Article 31

1. States Parties recognize the right of the child to rest and leisure, to engage in play and recreational activities appropriate to the age of the child and to participate freely in cultural life and the arts.

2. States Parties shall respect and promote the right of the child to fully participate in cultural and artistic life and shall encourage the provision of appropriate and equal opportunities for cultural, artistic, recreational and leisure activity.

Leisure, recreation and cultural activities

The right of children to leisure, play and participation in cultural and artistic activities.

Article 32

1. States Parties recognize the right of the child to be protected from economic exploitation and from performing any work that is likely to be hazardous or to interfere with the child's education, or to be harmful to the child's health or physical, mental, spiritual, moral or social development.

2. States Parties shall take legislative, administrative, social and educational measures to ensure the implementation of this article. To this end, and having regard to the relevant provisions of other international instruments, States Parties shall in particular:

a) provide for a minimum age or minimum ages for admissions to employment;

b) provide for appropriate regulation of the hours and conditions of employment; and

c) provide for appropriate penalties or other sanctions to ensure the effective enforcement of this article.

Child labour

The State's obligation to protect children from engaging in work that constitutes a threat to their health, education or development, to set minimum ages for employment, and to regulate conditions of employment.

Article 33

States Parties shall take all appropriate measures, including legislative, administrative, social and educational measures, to protect children from the illicit use of narcotic drugs and psychotropic substances as defined in the relevant international treaties, and to prevent the use of children in the illicit production and trafficking of such substances.

Drug abuse

The child's right to protection from the use of narcotic and psychotropic drugs and from being involved in their production or distribution.

Article 34

States Parties undertake to protect the child from all forms of sexual exploitation and sexual abuse. For these purposes States Parties shall in particular take all appropriate national, bilateral and multilateral measures to prevent:

a) the inducement or coercion of a child to engage in any unlawful sexual activity;

b) the exploitative use of children in prostitution or other unlawful sexual practices;

c) the exploitative use of children in pornographic performances and materials.

Sexual exploitation

The child's right to protection from sexual exploitation and abuse, including prostitution and involvement in pornography.

Article 35

States Parties shall take all appropriate national, bilateral and multilateral measures to prevent the abduction, the sale of or traffic in children for any purpose or in any form.

Sale, trafficking and abduction

The State's obligation to make every effort to prevent the sale, trafficking and abduction of children.

Article 36

States Parties shall protect the child against all other forms of exploitation prejudicial to any aspects of the child's welfare.

Other forms of exploitation

The child's right to protection from all other forms of exploitation not covered in articles 32, 33, 34 and 35.

Article 37

States Parties shall ensure that:

a) No child shall be subjected to torture or other cruel, inhuman or degrading treatment or punishment. Neither capital punishment nor life imprisonment without possibility of release shall be imposed for offences committed by persons below 18 years of age;

b) No child shall be deprived of his or her liberty unlawfully or arbitrarily. The arrest, detention or imprisonment of a child shall be in conformity with the law and shall be used only as a measure of last resort and for the shortest appropriate period of time;

c) Every child deprived of liberty shall be treated with humanity and respect for the inherent dignity of the human person, and in a manner which takes into account the needs of persons of their age. In particular every child deprived of liberty shall be separated from adults unless it is considered in the child's best interest not to do so and shall have the right to maintain contact with is or her family through correspondence and visits, and save in exceptional circumstances;

Torture and deprivation of liberty

The prohibition of torture, cruel treatment or punishment, capital punishment, life imprisonment, and unlawful arrest or deprivation of liberty. The principles of appropriate treatment, separation from detained adults, contact with family and access to legal and other assistance.

d) Every child deprived of his or her liberty shall have the right to prompt access to legal and other appropriate assistance as well as the right to challenge the legality of the deprivation of his or her liberty, before a court or other competent, independent and impartial authority and to a prompt decision on any such action.

Article 38

1. States Parties undertake to respect and to ensure respect for rules of international humanitarian law applicable to them in armed conflicts which are relevant to the child.

2. States Parties shall take all feasible measures to ensure that persons who have not attained the age of 15 years do not take a direct part in hostilities.

3. States Parties shall refrain from recruiting any person who has not attained the age of 15 years into their armed forces. In recruiting among those persons who have attained the age of 15 years but who have not attained the age of 18 years, States Parties shall endeavour to give priority to those who are oldest.

4. In accordance with their obligations under international humanitarian law to protect the civilian population in armed conflicts, States Parties shall take all feasible measures to ensure protection and care of children who are affected by an armed conflict.

Armed conflicts

The obligation of States to respect and ensure respect for humanitarian law as it applies to children. The principle that no child under 15 take a direct part in hostilities or be recruited into the armed forces, and that all children affected by armed conflict benefit from protection and care.

Article 39

States Parties shall take all appropriate measures to promote physical and psychological recovery and social reintegration of a child victim of: any form of neglect, exploitation, or abuse; torture or any other form of cruel, inhuman or degrading treatment or punishment; or armed conflicts. Such recovery and reintegration shall take place in an environment which fosters the health, self-respect and dignity of the child.

Rehabilitative care

The State's obligation to ensure that child victims of armed conflicts, torture, neglect, maltreatment or exploitation receive appropriate treatment for their recovery and social reintegration.

Article 40

1. States Parties recognize the right of every child alleged as, accused of, or recognized as having infringed the penal law to be treated in a manner consistent with the promotion of the child's sense of dignity and worth, which reinforces the child's respect for the human rights and fundamental freedoms of others and which takes into account the child's age and the desirability of promoting the child's re-integration and the child's assuming a constructive role in society.

2. To this end, and having regard to the relevant provisions of international instruments, States Parties shall, in particular, ensure that:

a) No child shall be alleged as, be accused of, or recognized as having infringed the penal law by reason of acts or omissions which were not prohibited by national or international law at the time they were committed;

Administration of juvenile justice

The right of children alleged or recognized as having committed an offence to respect for their human rights and, in particular, to benefit from all aspects of the due process of law, including legal or other assistance in preparing and presenting their defence. The principle that recourse to judicial proceedings and institutional placements should be avoided wherever possible and appropriate.

b) Every child alleged as or accused of having infringed the penal law has at least the following guarantees:

i   to be presumed innocent until proven guilty according to law;

ii to be informed promptly and directly of the charges against him or her, and if appropriate through his or her parents or legal guardian, and to have legal or other appropriate assistance in the preparation and presentation of his or her defence;

iii to have the matter determined without delay by a competent, independent and impartial authority or judicial body in a fair hearing according to law, in the presence of legal or other appropriate assistance and, unless it is considered not to be in the best interest of the child, in particular, taking into account his or her age or situation, his or her parents or legal guardians:

iv not to be compelled to give testimony or to confess guilt; to examine or have examined adverse witnesses and to obtain the participation and examination of witnesses on his or her behalf under conditions of equality;

v   if considered to have infringed the penal law, to have this decision and any measures imposed in consequence thereof reviewed by a higher competent, independent and impartial authority or judicial body according to law;

vi to have the free assistance of an interpreter if the child cannot understand or speak the language used;

vii to have his or her privacy fully respected at all stages of the proceedings.

3. States Parties shall seek to promote the establishment of laws, procedures, authorities and institutions specifically applicable to children alleged as, accused of, or recognized as having infringed the penal law, and in particular:

a) the establishment of a minimum age below which children shall be presumed not to have the capacity to infringe the penal law;

b) whenever appropriate and desirable, measures for dealing with such children without resorting to judicial proceedings, providing that human rights and legal safeguards are fully respected.

4. A variety of dispositions, such as care, guidance and supervision orders; counselling; probation; foster care; education and vocational training programmes and other alternatives to institutional care shall be available to ensure that children are dealt with in a manner appropriate to their well-being and proportionate both to their circumstances and the offence.

Article 41

Nothing in this Convention shall affect any provisions that are more conducive to the realization of the rights of the child and that may be contained in:

a) the law of a State Party; or

b) international law in force for that State.

PART II

Article 42

States Parties undertake to make the principles and provisions of the Convention widely known, by appropriate and active means, to adults and children alike.

Article 43

1. For the purpose of examining the progress made by States Parties in achieving the realization of the obligations undertaken in the present Convention, there shall be established a Committee on the Rights of the Child, which shall carry out the functions hereinafter provided.

2. The Committee shall consist of 10 experts of high moral standing and recognized competence in the field covered by this Convention. The members of the Committee shall be elected by States Parties from among their nationals and shall serve in their personal capacity, consideration being given to equitable geographical distribution as well as to the principal legal systems.

3. The members of the Committee shall be elected by secret ballot from a list of persons nominated by States Parties. Each State Party may nominate one person from among its own nationals.

4. The initial election to the Committee shall be held no later than six months after the date of the entry into force of the present Convention and thereafter every second year. At least four months before the date of each election, the Secretary-General of the United Nations shall address a letter to States Parties inviting them to submit their nominations within two months. The Secretary-General shall subsequently prepare a list in alphabetical order of all persons thus nominated, indicating States Parties which have nominated them, and shall submit it to the States Parties to the present Convention.

5. The elections shall be held at meetings of States Parties convened by the Secretary-General at United Nations Headquarters. At those meetings, for which two-thirds of States Parties shall constitute a quorum, the persons elected to the Committee shall be those who obtain the largest number of votes and an absolute majority of the votes of the representatives of States Parties present and voting.

Respect for existing standards

The principle that if any standards set in national law or other applicable international instruments are higher than those of this Convention, it is the higher standard that applies.

Implementation and entry into force

The provisions of articles 42–54 notably foresee:

i) the State's obligation to make the rights contained in this Convention widely known to both adults and children.

ii) the setting up of a Committee on the Rights of the Child composed of ten experts, which will consider reports that States Parties to the Convention are to submit two years after ratification and every five years thereafter.

iii) States Parties are to make their reports widely available to the general public.

iv) The Committee may propose that special studies be undertaken on specific issues relating to the rights of the child, and may make its evaluations known to each State Party concerned as well as to the UN General Assembly.

v) In order to 'foster the effective implementation of the Convention and to encourage international co-operation', the specialized agencies of the UN (such as the ILO, WHO and UNESCO) and UNICEF would be able to attend the meetings of the Committee. Together with any other body recognised as 'Competent', including NGOs in consultative status with the UN and UN organs such as the UNHCR, they can submit pertinent information to the Committee and be asked to advise on the optimal implementation of the Convention.

6. The members of the Committee shall be elected for a term of four years. They shall be eligible for re-election if renominated. The term of five of the members elected at the first election shall expire at the end of two years; immediately after the first election the names of these five members shall be chosen by lot by the Chairman of the meeting.

7. If a member of the Committee dies or resigns or declares that for any other cause he or she can no longer perform the duties of the Committee, the State Party which nominated the member shall appoint another expert from among its nationals to serve for the remainder of the term, subject to the approval of the Committee.

8. The Committee shall establish its own rules of procedure.

9. The Committee shall elect its officers for a period of two years.

10. The meetings of the Committee shall normally be held at the United Nations Headquarters or at any other convenient place as determined by the Committee. The Committee shall normally meet annually. The duration of the meetings of the Committee shall be determined, and reviewed, if necessary, by a meeting of the States Parties to the present Convention, subject to the approval of the General Assembly.

11. The Secretary-General of the United Nations shall provide the necessary staff and facilities for the effective performance of the functions of the Committee under the present Convention.

12. With the approval of the General Assembly, the members of the Committee established under the present Convention shall receive emoluments from the United Nations resources on such terms and conditions as the Assembly may decide.

Article 44

1. States Parties undertake to submit to the Committee, through the Secretary-General of the United Nations, reports on the measures they have adopted which give effect to the rights recognized herein and on the progress made on the enjoyment of those rights:

a) within two years of the entry into force of the Convention for the State Party concerned,

b) thereafter every five years.

2. Reports made under this article shall indicate factors and difficulties, if any, affecting the degree of fulfilment of the obligations under the present Convention. Reports shall also contain sufficient information to provide the Committee with a comprehensive understanding of the implementation of the Convention in the country concerned.

3. A State Party which has submitted a comprehensive initial report to the Committee need not in its subsequent reports submitted in accordance with paragraph l(b) repeat basic information previously provided.

4. The Committee may request from States Parties further information relevant to the implementation of the Convention.

5. The Committee shall submit to the General Assembly of the United Nations through the Economic and Social Council, every two years, reports on its activities.

6. States Parties shall make their reports widely available to the public in their own countries.

Article 45

In order to foster the effective implementation of the Convention and to encourage international co-operation in the field covered by the Convention:

a) The specialized agencies, UNICEF and other United Nations organs shall be entitled to be represented at the consideration of the implementation of such provisions of the present Convention as fall within the scope of their mandate. The Committee may invite the specialized agencies, UNICEF and other competent bodies as it may consider appropriate to provide expert advice on the implementation of the Convention in areas falling within the scope of their respective mandates. The Committee may invite the specialized agencies, UNICEF and other United Nations organs to submit reports on the implementation of the Convention in areas falling within the scope of their activities.

b) The Committee shall transmit, as it may consider appropriate, to the specialized agencies, UNICEF and other competent bodies, any reports from States Parties that contain a request, or indicate a need, for technical advice or assistance along with the Committee's observations and suggestions, if any, on these requests or indications.

c) The Committee may recommend to the General Assembly to request the Secretary-General to undertake on its behalf studies on specific issues relating to the rights of the child.

d) The Committee may make suggestions and general recommendations based on information received pursuant to articles 44 and 45 of this Convention. Such suggestions and general recommendations shall be transmitted to any State Party concerned and reported to the General Assembly, together with comments, if any, from States Parties.

PART III

Article 46

The present Convention shall be open for signature by all States.

Article 47

The present Convention is subject to ratification. Instruments of ratification shall be deposited with the Secretary-General of the United Nations.

Article 48

The present Convention shall remain open for accession by any State. The instruments of accession shall be deposited with the Secretary-General of the United Nations.

Article 49

1. The present Convention shall enter into force on the thirtieth day following the date of deposit with the Secretary-General of the United Nations of the twentieth instrument of ratification or accession.

2. For each State ratifying or acceding to the Convention after the deposit of the twentieth instrument of ratification or accession, the Convention shall enter into force on the thirtieth day after the deposit by such State of its instrument of ratification or accession.

Article 50

1. Any State Party may propose an amendment and file it with the Secretary-General of the United Nations. The Secretary-General shall thereupon communicate the proposed amendment to States Parties with a request that they indicate whether they favour a conference of States Parties for the purpose of considering and voting upon the proposals. In the event that within four months from the date of such communication at least one-third of the States Parties favour such a conference, the Secretary-General shall convene the conference under the auspices of the United Nations. Any amendment adopted by a majority of States Parties present and voting at the conference shall be submitted to the General Assembly of the United Nations for approval.

2. An amendment adopted in accordance with paragraph (1) of this article shall enter into force when it has been approved by the General Assembly of the United Nations and accepted by a two-thirds majority of States Parties.

3. When an amendment enters into force, it shall be binding on those States Parties which have accepted it, other States Parties still being bound by the provisions of this Convention and any earlier amendments which they have accepted.

Article 51

1. The Secretary-General of the United Nations shall receive and circulate to all States the text of reservations made by States at the time of ratification or accession.

2. A reservation incompatible with the object and purpose of the present Convention shall not be permitted.

3. Reservations may be withdrawn at any time by notification to this effect addressed to the Secretary-General of the United Nations who shall then inform all States. Such notification shall take effect on the date on which it is received by the Secretary-General.

Article 52

A State Party may denounce this Convention by written notification to the Secretary-General of the United Nations. Denunciation becomes effective one year after the date of receipt of the notification by the Secretary-General.

Article 53

The Secretary-General of the United Nations is designated as the depositary of the present Convention.

Article 54

The original of the present Convention, of which the Arabic, Chinese, English, French, Russian and Spanish texts are equally authentic, shall be deposited with the Secretary-General of the United Nations.

In witness thereof the undersigned plenipotentiaries, being duly authorised thereto by their respective governments, have signed the present Convention.

APPENDIX 2

SUMMARY OF THE RECOMMENDATIONS OF THE REVIEW OF SCOTTISH CHILD CARE LAW (THE SCOTTISH OFFICE 1991)

(* = majority view only)

Improvements in general welfare services for children:

- a re-phrasing of the 'general welfare duty' in Section 12 of the Social Work (Scotland) Act 1968, to create a more positive promotion of children's welfare (1)

- a Code of Practice illustrating a range of support services in relation to duties under the 1968 Act, including services for young people aged 16-18 (2)

- regulations for respite care, to be part of Section 12 services (3)

- explicit reference in Section 10 of the 1968 Act, for local authorities to have regard to Section 12 when deciding grants to voluntary organisations (4)

- review of system for young people who offend aged 16-21 (87)

- examine formation and feasibility of Scottish Child Welfare Commission (88)

Improvements in inter-agency co-ordination and co-operation through:

- a Code of Practice for health, education and social work, in regards to children in long-stay care in health and education establishments (5)

- a duty on health or education establishments to notify social work departments, if a child has not had (or is not likely to have) parental contact for ≥ 3 months; social work must then investigate (6)

- duty on independent residential schools to safeguard and promote the welfare of children resident in schools; local authority duty to ensure welfare met, and power to review children's welfare (7-8)

- improved consideration of health and education needs of children in care (31-37): e.g. social work to identify, and seek to meet, the health and education needs of children in care; care reviews to include consideration of these

- children's hearings to have access to full range of local authority resources for children who reject normal schooling (54)

- revised connections between courts and children's hearings, when application for parental responsibilities order, freeing or adoption order and the child is on supervision requirement (72-74, 76)

- when matrimonial, adoption and guardianship proceedings, court can refer child to Reporter with grounds established (81)

Time limits

- time limits for adoption and freeing proceedings (92-94)

- tighten time-tables for care reviews (18)

- limit time between Reporter or referring agency knowing of facts and children's hearing, with qualifications (65-68)

- Place of Safety Orders (PSOs) must be implemented forthwith or discharged by Reporter (55)

Balancing parents' rights and local authorities' duties and powers towards children

- before a child is received into 'voluntary care', local authority must assess availability and appropriateness of support services (9)

- when child in care of local authority under supervision requirement, local authority full responsibility for decisions concerning child's medical care and treatment (38); when child at home on supervision requirement, primary responsibility with parents (39) and child not in local authority care (70★)

- child in place of safety to be in care of local authority (62); PSO empower local authority to arrange for child's medical examination or treatment (63), with conditions of medical examination/ treatment possible on place of safety warrant (64)

- local authority only gain parental responsibilities and rights through court, under specific criteria (40-42); court power to appoint curator ad litem or reporting officer (43-44)

- natural parent right to have views considered when children's hearing considering supervision requirement, once local authority has parental rights (75-76)

- parent/ carer must notify Reporter, if intends to remove child from Scotland, who is subject to supervision requirement (77); children's hearings power to continue existing supervision requirements outside Scotland and to constrain the removal of the child (78-79)

parental access:

- local authority must provide reasonable access to parents of child in voluntary care (10)

- if a child is subject to a supervision requirement, explicit legal presumption that parent have access to child (11); if difficulties or major changes in parental contact, local authorities must request Reporter to arrange children's hearing (12)

- when children's hearing are considering a place of safety warrant, empowered to include access conditions (13); when no access condition, legal presumption parents have reasonable access (14)

- court power to regulate parental access when local authority parental rights application, except when supervision requirement has conditions of access (45)

- parental right to attend care review of child, with some qualifications (20★); if parents not allowed to attend by local authority, parental right to put forward views in writing and local authority must report decisions in writing (21)

Protecting children's rights, including welfare

- children's hearings power to attach a condition to supervision requirement and place of safety warrant preventing disclosure of the child's residence (15)

- care review if child in care of local authority, due to a supervision requirement (16–17); child ≥ 12 years should have legal right to attend care review, with consideration of younger children offending (19); regulations on care reviews (22)

- local authority duty to advise and assist children in care, to prepare them for life after care (23); duty to advise and assist young person >16 years, who has spent 'significant part of life in care' since age 12—available to young person < 21 years (24); duty to have a range of after-care services (25)

- local authority must have due regard to a child's religious persuasion, racial origin and cultural background, as part of the welfare duty to children in care (27)

- improve and tighten inspections of residential child care establishments (46-48)

- Chairman of children's hearing power to exclude parent, to obtain child's views; substance of what was said must be conveyed to parent, unless detrimental to child's interests (82)

- safeguarders should be required to prepare a report; should be appointed by children's hearing (and not just Chairman); when appointed by court, should be required to attend start of proceedings but not required to prepare a report (85)

Other up-dates for children's hearings

- dispense with requirement for Reporter to take application to Sheriff, when understanding of the child is the only point at issue (49)

- clarify and modify referral grounds for children's hearings (50-53)

- Reporter must lay full statement of referral grounds before children's hearing, following a PSO (56), which will affect the practicality of a 'first lawful day hearing' within 7 days (57)

- rationalise place of safety and other warrants (58, 61); ensure parents successive rights to appeal to warrants (59), with Sheriff able to exercise such powers (60); rationalise present possibility of 2 supervision requirements, to one (69)

- children's hearings power to set supervision requirement review (83); Reporter can call for review of existing supervision requirement, when new grounds identified (84)

- child and parents/ guardian to know they have a right to see reports submitted to children's hearings (86)

Complaints procedures: to be established, publicised and regulated (28-30)

Other up-dates for adoption:

- mandatory adoption allowance schemes (89)

- modify step-parent adoption, so natural parent not have to adopt when new spouse is adopting (90)

- adoption law review to consider particular issues in relation to overseas adoption (91), and natural parents (95)

Appendix 3
Orkney Inquiry: Summary

Introduction

Background

In 1987, a woman on the island of South Ronaldsay reported her husband to the police; he was later convicted of physical and sexual abuse of his children and was jailed for seven years.

Three years later, seven children from this family were taken into care because of alleged sibling abuse. While they were in care, the children made disclosures which led social workers to believe that organised sexual abuse was occurring on the island; in particular, they made allegations about the abuse of nine children from four other families, and named the alleged perpetrators. Following an investigation conducted by the Orkney Social Work Department, the RSSPCC, and the police. Place of Safety Orders were obtained from a Sheriff and the nine children were removed from their homes in February 1991

The children were the subject of a reference to the Children's Hearing, but their parents denied the grounds for referral, and a proof to establish the grounds was arranged before the Sheriff. In April 1991 the Sheriff held that the proceedings were flawed because of procedural irregularities; the evidence in relation to the alleged abuse was never heard, and the children were returned to their families that same day.

In June 1991, Lord Clyde was appointed by the Secretary of State for Scotland to conduct an Inquiry into the actions of the agencies involved in the removal of the nine children. The Inquiry's terms of reference specifically excluded any investigation of the original allegations of abuse. The resulting *Report of the Inquiry into the Removal of Children from Orkney in February 1991* was published in October 1992, on the same day as the *Report of the Inquiry into Child Care Policies in Fife,* which examined child care policies in Fife including a number of related issues.

Findings

The main recommendations **include:**

Child protection

- Child law reform in general, and child protection in particular, should take account of the European Convention on Human Rights and the UN Convention on the Rights of the Child.

- Allegations made by a child regarding sexual abuse should be treated seriously, should not necessarily be accepted as true, but should be thoroughly examined and tested before any action is taken.

- Recommendations on investigation **include,** in relation to multiple sexual abuse, a high level of secrecy and careful planning; designation of senior members of staff of Police and Social Work Departments to co-ordinate joint work; and special arrangements to ensure co-operation between the different agencies involved in separate local authorities.

- Improved co-ordination of investigations between police and social work with joint training and joint guidelines as a means of securing this.

- All agencies involved with children should be alert to possible signs of sexual abuse; schools in particular should have close links with social work departments with training of designated teachers.

- Consideration to Sheriffs having the power to have a suspected abuser excluded from contact with the child.

- Consideration of alternatives to prosecution in appropriate cases, and alternatives to imprisonment at least in cases of intra-familial abuse.

- Guidelines should not be mandatory but guidance for normal procedure; new national guidance should cover inter-agency liaison and co-operation.

- Establishment of central resource to provide assistance, particularly to smaller authorities.

- More research into child sexual abuse , and in particular, cases of multiple abuse and provision of personal social services in the islands

The removal of children to places of safety

'Child Protection Orders' to empower removal of child where necessary for protection where no alternative exists and where required by 'urgency of the risk'.

- Detailed recommendations relating to the procedures for child protection orders **include** the orders being obtained where practicable from Sheriffs and not JPs; further training of JPs; qualification of the Reporter's existing power to have the child returned by the proviso that the child should not be exposed to the risk of significant harm.

- Recommendations relating to the enforcement of orders and interim protection orders **include** the welfare of the child remaining the prime consideration in timing the removal of the child; those involved in complex cases being given full written instructions; social workers and police officers removing children being given sufficient information to enable them to inform the child and parents about the place of safety and a spare copy of the Order and explanatory document being left with the parent.

Children in places of safety

Detailed recommendations covering management, facilities, foster carers, parents, medical examination and interviewing of the children **include** due consideration being given to the views of the child; pilot scheme to enhance the role of a 'safeguarder' before further consideration is given to possible development of the Child's Advocate. Extensive detailed recommendations in relation to interviewing **include** greater recognition of the complexity involved in interviewing children in relation to allegations of sexual abuse; and national guidelines for investigative interviews as part of the national guidance.

Children's Panel and the Reporter

- Consideration of review of the work of Children's Hearings in the area of child protection, including transfer to Sheriff of all matters relating to a child in a place of safety order.

- Recommendations in relation to procedure **include** allowing a parent, guardian or 'safeguarder' immediate recourse to the Sheriff on whether a child requires to be in a place of safety, and entitlement to apply to the Sheriff for recall of the order at any time within seven days of child's removal; allowing a child to have an immediate opportunity to have an Order varied or cancelled by the Sheriff;

- transfer of processing of child protection orders from the Children's Hearing to the Sheriff; consideration to further restrictions on press reporting of hearings.

- Recommendations on the role of the Reporter **include** recognition of independence of action of a Reporter in discussions with social work departments; a Reporter considering abandonment of a case passed to the Sheriff for proof should consult the social work department before action; consideration to preparation of guidance for Reporters to secure greater uniformity and practice across Scotland.

Agencies and the Community

- Child protection work should be seen as a specialist area with increased training and support.

- Introduction of three year qualifying course for social workers, development of more extensive post qualifying training to cover interviewing children in cases of suspected sexual abuse; more joint training between social work and other agencies including the police.

- More training for police participation in interviewing children.

- Improved public understanding of child protection; accessibility of social workers to the community and avoidance of technical jargon.

Government Response

Presenting the report to Parliament, the Secretary of State for Scotland indicated that the Government was "minded to accept the great majority of the recommendations and to take them forward in consultation with the agencies involved as a matter of priority" (Hansard 27.10.92).

The Scottish Office Social Work Services Group outlined future action as follows:

- joint investigation and interviewing, and a second on practice guidance on child protection for social workers.

- Revised inter-agency guidance and practice guidance.

- A programme of consultation on certain of the recommendations.

- Immediate requests to certain agencies to act on specific recommendations.

- Legislation, particularly concerning place of safety orders.

One of the major recommendations on social work qualifying training, that it be extended to three years, has initially been ruled out by the Government. Funding for specialist training of social workers in the islands is to be immediately increased.

Other Issues

Cleveland Report Findings

The Cleveland Report examined the arrangements for dealing with suspected cases of child sexual abuse in Cleveland in 1987. The Inquiry started in August 1987 and reported in June 1988. The recommendations include:

- Greater recognition and more accurate data on child sexual abuse.

- Taking seriously what the child has to say; taking the views and wishes of the child into account although 'these should not necessarily predominate'.

- Children should not be subjected to repeated medical examinations nor to repeated interviewing.

- Parents should be kept informed and where appropriate consulted; receive all important decisions in writing, be advised of rights of appeal and not left isolated and bewildered.

- Place of Safety orders should be sought for the minimum time necessary and there should be Code of Practice for administration by social workers of emergency orders.

- Structured arrangements for professional supervision and support of social workers.

- Area review committees/joint child abuse committees should review arrangements for training.

- Development of inter-agency cooperation.

- Establishment of specialist assessment teams to undertake full multidisciplinary assessment of child and family.

- Improved training including urgent need for immediate in-service training to professionals to bring them up to date on child sexual abuse.

- Need for inter-agency training.

- Other detailed recommendations covered place of safety orders, emergency protection orders, juvenile courts, guardians ad litem and the media.

UN Convention: relevant clauses

Although the inquiry was only concerned with the procedures and actions of the agencies involved, it had important implications for wider issues of children's rights. Relevant articles in the UN Convention on the Rights of the Child, include Articles 3 (all actions concerning a child to take into account the child's best interests), 12 (child's right to express opinions and participate in proceedings), 16 (protection from arbitrary interference with privacy) and 37(d) (the right to prompt assistance when a child is deprived of liberty).

European models

In mainland Europe there are different approaches to the professional response to child abuse, particularly sexual abuse. The impact of an inquisitorial, rather than an adversarial legal system, creates a different framework for the investigative process. The French 'Juge des enfants' receives referrals of concern directly, and referral is mandatory where anyone has knowledge of actual abuse to a child under the age of fifteen. The Juge causes inquiries to be made about any allegations and deals with the civil law responses. Criminal issues are dealt with by the criminal courts. The Netherlands, together with some areas in both Belgium and Germany, operate the Confidential Doctor system, whereby concerns about a child may be passed in confidence to the agency which investigates and co-ordinates a therapeutic response. Legal action would only be taken in cases where earlier efforts to achieve a response on a voluntary basis have failed. In considering the potential applicability of European models to the UK, it is important to bear in mind that child protection systems in other countries reflect different historical, political and religious traditions and must be viewed within their own context. For example the Netherlands' Confidential doctor service mirrors other aspects of Dutch life such as the emphasis on access to facilities and the dislike of bureaucratic control of individual action. In France, there is a much greater tolerance of bureaucratic control.

This Appendix is published as a factsheet available from Children in Scotland (1992)

♦

Appendix 4

Summary of the Provisions of the Children (Scotland) Act 1995

The Act is 134 pages long, includes 105 sections and 5 schedules. It has four parts.

Part I – Parents, children and guardians (Sections 1 – 15)

- introduces new statements of parental responsibilities and rights, including the right and responsibility to maintain contact if the child is not living with the parent;

- establishes the principle that when making an order relating to parental responsibilities or rights, a court must make the welfare of the child its paramount concern;

- introduces a new legal procedure for unmarried fathers to acquire parental responsibilities and rights with the agreement of the mothers;

- stipulates that children should, bearing in mind their age and maturity, be consulted by their parents or guardians on all major decisions affecting them

- replaces the terms 'custody' and 'access' with 'residence' and 'contact' for court orders: courts can refer children who are involved in parental responsibilities proceedings to children's hearings;

- introduces new provisions for guardianship and administration of children's property

Part II – Promotion of children's welfare by local authorities and by children's hearings etc.
(Sections 16 – 93)

- establishes the principle that local authorities, children's hearings and courts must have due regard for the views of the child when making decisions affecting that child, and that the child's welfare must be the paramount consideration in these decisions (these principles are overridden when there is a risk of 'serious harm' to the public)

- replaces the terms 'in care' for those children in the care of the local authority, with 'looked after'; 'voluntary care' is replaced by 'accommodation'; and 'compulsory measures of care' is replaced by 'compulsory measures of supervision'

- places a duty on local authorities to publish information about children's services, and to publish a children's services plan

- repeals the duty to promote the welfare of specific categories of children eligible for services under Section 12 of the Social Work (Scotland) 1968, replacing it with a new duty to provide services for 'children in need', and a power to provide early years services to all children;

- includes new terminology of 'children with and *affected by* disability' as a group for whom services must be provided by the local authority; such services must seek to minimise the effects of the disability and give children the opportunity to live 'as normal lives as possible'; also provides for new assessments for these children and their carers;

- allows a local authority to ask for help from another agency, and that agency must help if it is compatible with its mandate and other obligations;

- extends duty on local authorities to provide after-care support for young people up to the age of 19, with further power to help until 21 and beyond that age to finish a course of education; extends the age limit for the duty to provide accommodation by one year, to 18, with a further power to provide it until 21;

- broadens inspection of independent and residential schools, and strengthens requirements to inform local authorities of children in hospitals, nursing homes etc. who for 3 months or more have been without parental contact

- confers powers on local authorities, who may also register voluntary organisations' establishments, to provide 'short-term refuges' for those children who run away (a refuge may be a residential establishment controlled or managed by a local authority, or an otherwise approved household or establishment);

- provides for increased privacy in children's hearing proceedings and extends rights of appeal for children and their parents

- makes explicit the right of children and young people to attend their own hearing; obliges hearings and courts to consider the appointment of a safeguarder in most proceedings, and expands the grounds for appointment; and gives Sheriffs the right to substitute their own decision for that of the hearing, on appeal;

- introduces new arrangements for sheriffs to consider new evidence to review the grounds of referral to a children's hearing

- introduces revised child protection procedures including a new child protection order, child assessment order and exclusion (of alleged abuser) order; alters children's hearings' warrants, conditions and secure accommodation procedures;

- obliges local authorities to seek a court order to assume parental rights and responsibilities

- provides for legal aid for children in respect of new proceedings.

Part III – Adoption (Sections 94 – 98)

- strengthens key principles relating to children's rights in adoption proceedings

- stipulates that adoption agencies must consider alternatives to adoption;

- implements conclusions of the Adoption Law Review;

- removes requirement for birth parent to 'adopt' their own child when new partner wishes to adopt.

Part IV – General and Supplemental

- allows local authorities to hold inquiries into relevant children's services;

- establishes panel for curators ad litem, reporting officers and safeguarders;

- lists consequential and supplementary provisions

- gives a commitment to necessary regulations and guidance.

The Act's 5 schedules include important clauses relating to adoption, in particular post-adoption support, the regulation of adoption allowance schemes by the Secretary of State, time tables for adoption proceedings, lowering the age of adopted peoples' right to information from 17 to 16, requiring all adoption agencies to have complaints procedures, slight modification of exceptions to parental agreement, and new interfaces between children's hearings and adoption proceedings. They also address transnational provisions and savings, and minor amendments to this and other legislation.

INDEX

Note: page numbers in *italic* indicate figures. There may also be textual references on these pages.

Aberlour Child Care Trust 131
abuse 8, 26, 27
  cases in 1980s 15, 16, 39
  exclusion orders (EOs) 96, 146
  inter-agency collaboration 32
  and professionals 102
  see also child protection; Clyde Report;
    Orkney (Inquiry)
abusers
  exclusion of alleged 6, 38-9, 40, 41, 55-
    7, 90, 96, 124-5, 127, 146
  prosecution of alleged 146
accommodation 111
  bed and breakfast 101
  see also 'voluntary care'
Acting Reporter, Orkney case 18-19
adoption 8, 16, 28, 78, 148
  Adoption Review 26
  child welfare 14, 47, 88
  children's hearings 32
  children's rights 140-1
  curators ad litem 116
  post-adoption support 85
  religion/race/culture 119, 120
  time limits 38
  UK practices 118-19
adoption law 1, 2, *9*, 14, 23-4, 37, 98
Adoption (Scotland) Act 1978 14, 37
after-care 73, 78, 105, 147
Age of Legal Capacity (Scotland) Act 1991
  37, 90, 116
age of maturity 25
alcohol abuse 72
Another Kind of Home see Skinner Report
APPG *see* Scottish APPG; UK APPG
assessments 78, 81
  children in need 75-6, 77, 78
  see also Child Assessment Orders
Association of Child Care Officers 11
Association of Directors of Social Work
  (ADSW) 59

Audit Commission 104, 124, 133

bed and breakfast accommodation 101
Booth, Dame Margaret 122-3
British Agencies for Adoption and Fostering
  (BAAF) 16, 68, 128, 133
British Association of Social Workers in
  Scotland 55
Butler-Sloss, Lord Justice 116, 122

care orders 124, 126-7
care reviews 85, 117
carers 85
carer's assessment 75
Carers (Recognition and Services) Act 1995
  75
child abuse *see* abuse
'Child Advocate' 39
Child Assessment Orders (CAOs) 45, 69,
  92, 95, 125
child care law *see Review of Scottish Child
  Care Law*
child protection
  and children's hearings 27, 42-3, 44, 92-
    6, 102, 135, 144-7
  children's services plans 78
  children's views 118
  emergency protection orders (EPOs) 36,
    125
  and ethnic background 120
  and family support services 101, 102
  inter-agency collaboration 135
  local authority services 71
  local government reform 137
  media attention to 28
  partnership with parents 34-5, 36, 112-
    13, 138-9
  Social Work (Scotland) Act 1968 26, 31,
    34

child protection, *contd.*
  in UK 124-7
  see also abuse; abusers; Place of Safety
    Orders
Child Protection Committees 32
Child Protection Orders (CPOs) 40, 43, 45,
  68, 69, 92, *93*, 95, 96, 116, 124, 125, 144
child safety 80
Child Welfare Commission 38, 149
'Child Welfare Hearing' 89-90
ChildLine Scotland 41, 55
Children 1st 58, 59, 60
children: government structures for 149
Children Act 1908 10
Children Act 1975 1, 8, 14, 27, 35, 36, 88
Children Act 1989 2, 7, 51, 132
  child protection 113, 124, 125, 127, 146
  child religion/race/culture 119, 121
  child representation 115, 116
  child welfare 121, 122-3
  child/parental rights 144
  'children in need' 62, 63, 65, 71, 99,
    100-1
  corporal punishment 58
  family assessment 103
  guardians 114
  housing 105-6
  implementation 98, 127, 129-30
  inter-agency collaboration 83-4, 106,
    108
  making information available 110
  monitoring 128
  parental responsibilities 113
  Parliamentary process 48, 49
  partnership with parents 110
  review of child care services 73
  'voluntary care' 111
  young offenders 123-4
Children Act 1989 (Amendment)
  (Children's Service Planning) Order SI
  1995 106
Children Act Advisory Committee (CAAC)
  113
Children Act Report 1994 103
'children in need' 68, 70-8
  allocation of services 85, 97, 126
  children's services plans 79, 106
  definition 63, 65, 98, 104, 147, 148
  and ethnic communities 121
  housing needs 84
  local authorities 105
  as new concept 1, 6
  Northern Ireland 99, *100*, 103-4, 109
  Parliamentary process 62-6
  preventive work 132-4

Children Act Report 1994, *contd.*
  targeting of services 69
  throughout UK 99-104
Children in Need Working Group in Wales
  80
Children (NI) Order 1995 2, 7, 99, *100*,
  132
  child protection 124
  child religion/race/culture 119
  child welfare 121, 122
  'children in need' 103-4
  implementation 98, 128
  making information available 110
  parental responsibilities 113
  'voluntary care' 111
Children in Scotland viii, 50, 51, 53, 68,
  79, 136
Children and Young Persons Act 1969 124
Children and Young Persons (Scotland) Act
  1932 10
Children and Young Persons (Scotland) Act
  1937 57
Children's Commissioner 149
children's hearings 7, 26, 30, 78, 132
  and child protection 27, 42-3, 44, 92-6,
    102, 135, 144-7
  child representation 145
  children's rights 38, 39, 40-1, 87
  children's views 89
  home supervision contracts 138
  inter-agency collaboration 31, 32, 33,
    82, 97
  introduced 2-3, 8, 12-14
  'non-intervention' 85
  Orkney 18
  parental responsibilities 86
  and press reporting 40, 89
  safeguarders 90-1
  welfare v. justice 6, 41-6
  workload 29
  and young offenders 123, 124
  see also Children's Panels
Children's Panels 11, 12
  Fife policies 20, 21
  Kilbrandon Report 11
  parental involvement 33-4, 35
  Reporters to 4, 21-2
Children's Reporters *see* Reporters
children's rights 6, 8, 36-41, 68, 87-92, 97,
  98, 140-4, 149-50
  consent to medical examination/
    treatment 90, 117
  emergence of 1, 3, 47
  exceptions to 122
  in hearings 41-2, 44, 45

children's rights, *contd.*
  meeting across services 121-3
  and responsibilities 22-3
  to identity 119-21
  see also children's views/opinions; United
    Nations Convention
Children's Rights Development Unit
  (CRDU) 117-18
children's services plans 4, 7, 33, 68, 78-82,
  83, 85, 98, 106-10, 111, 135, 147
children's views/opinions 7, 25, 40, 74,
  139, 149-50
  across UK 114-19
  on care and adoption 36-7
  in court/children's hearings 89-90, 147
  qualified impact of 88-9
  on welfare 121-2
Chronically Sick and Disabled Persons Act
  1970 74, 84
Citizens Advice Bureaux 110
Citizen's Charter 3
Cleveland case 16, 39
Clyde Report 2, 8, *9*, 17-19, 146
  child protection 36, 43, 92
  children's rights 39-40
  exclusion of alleged abuser 41, 55
  safeguarders 90
  welfare and justice 43-5, 46
Colwell, Maria 36
community care 76-7, 84, 130, 134, 137,
  142
community-based assessments 81
complaints procedures 118
compulsory competitive tendering (CCT) 3
Consortium for the Children (Scotland) Bill
  53, 55, 56, 57, 58, 59, 60, 61, 63-4, 65,
  66, 67
'consultation' 83
'contract culture' 136-7
contracting out services 131
corporal punishment 6, 24, 25, 28, 57-62,
  141
CoSLA 9, 22
Court of Appeal 122
Court of Session 19, 95
Court Welfare Officers 115
courts
  child representation 115, 116
  children's rights 115, 117, 141
  interpretations of Act 147
  safeguarders 90-1
  and 'significant harm' 126
  social services departments 103
  and welfare 94
  young offenders 10-11, 14, 123

crime 14, 92, 123-4
  prosecutions of alleged abusers 146
curators ad litem 91, 115-16

day care 31, 48, 73, 79, 135, 147
decentralisation 4, 71, 135
Denmark: National Council on Children's
  Rights 149
disabilities 26, 30, 31, 32
  assessments 76
  and 'children in need' 65, 71, 72, 73-4,
    75, 77, 99, 133
  inter-agency collaboration 82, 84
  services for 78, 81, 97, 102-3
  voluntary agencies 137
Disability Discrimination Act 1995 72 &
  n.1, 74
Disabled Persons (Services, Consultation
  and Representation) Act 1986 74, 76, 84
divorce/separation 78, 86-7
Douglas-Hamilton, Lord James, MP 1, 56-
  7, 59, 60, 64, 65, 66, 79
drug/solvent abuse 101

education
  'children in need' 74, 133
  children's rights 40, 143
  devolved school management 6, 135
  independent schools 38, 143
  inter-agency collaboration 31, 32, 33,
    84, 104, 106, 108, 134, 135
  Northern Ireland 5-6
  parental rights 3, 144
  poor attainment in 101
  school exclusion 23, 101, 104, 132, 134,
    142
  special educational needs 75, 76, 77, 84
Education and Employment, Department of
  108
Education (Scotland) Act 1980 3, 74, 75,
  76, 84
Education (Scotland) Act 1996 84
emergency protection orders (EPOs) 36,
  125
employment and unemployment 135
'enabling authorities' 3, 4, 99
England
  child abuse cases 16, 27, 36, 39
  child care law 15
  Children Act 1975 36
  juvenile justice 14
  local government reorganisation 5, 6
  unmet need 77
  see also Children Act 1989

European Convention on Human Rights 37-8, 44, 56, 60, 67, 94, 144
European Court of Human Rights 2, 37, 46, 67, 144
   access to children in care 15
   corporal punishment 58, 62
European 'Structure Funds' 104
Ewing, Margaret, MP 50, 60
exclusion orders (EOs) 96, 146
Exeter, parental contact arrangements 114

Faithfull, Baroness 49-50, 60, 61
families 1, 2
   and religion/race/culture 120
   state intervention in 8, 14, 34
   support services 27, 101
Family Law Act 1996 124, 146
Family Law Report *see* Scottish Law Commission (SLC)
Fife Council
   child care policies 19-20, 29-30
   strategies 5, 134-5
   see also Kearney Report
Finlayson Report 8, *9*, 21-2, 46
fostering 14, 16, 68, 78, 128, 133
   and child religion/race/culture 119
   children's views on 117
   day care 135
   Orkney case 18
   and parents 86, 111, 112
Fraser of Carmyllie, Lord 51, 52, 61, 64-5, 86
Fyfe, Maria, MP 56, 58-9, 66

Gallie, Phil, MP 59, 60, 66
'general welfare duty' 29-31, 47, 62
Gillick v West Norfolk Health Authority (1986) 15, 117
Godman, Dr Norman, MP 50, 59
government, structures in 149
GP fundholders 135
GPs 110
grandparents 114
guardians as litem (GALs) 115, 116
guardianship of children 25, 35, 114

Health Boards 3, 4, 5, 23, 79, 82, 83, 103, 135
Health, Department of 106, 108, 109, 111, 115, 118, 126
health services
   inter-agency collaboration 31, 32, 33, 106, 108
   local needs 80
   targeting of 133-4

health visitors 102
Henderson of Brompton, Lord 61
holiday care 73
home supervision 34, 138, 145
homelessness 32, 78, 101, 102, 104, 105-6, 132, 134, 135
Hope, Lord 43, 61, 62, 94
House of Lords, care order application 126-7
housing 5, 74, 101
   inter-agency collaboration 32, 33, 82, 84, 133
   local needs 4, 80, 81-2
   provision for 105-6
Housing (Scotland) Act 1987 84

identity, children's rights to 119-21
illegitimacy 24, 25
implementation (of the Act) 127-8
independent schools 38, 143
India 149
information, making available 90, 110-11, 118, 147
information systems 80, 81
inter-agency collaboration 17, 31-3, 47, 82-5, 97, 139
   difficulties 130, 134-6, 148
   Skinner Report 23
   UK comparisons 104-6, 107-8
interim care orders (England and Wales) 124
International Fund for Ireland's Communities in Action Programme 104
International Year of the Child (1979) 49
Island local authorities 4, 14

joint assessment 75
'justice' *see* 'welfare versus justice'
Justices of the Peace (JPs) 34, 43, 45

Kearney Report 2, 8, *9*, 20-1, 22, 30, 40
   social workers' role 39, 137
   welfare and justice 43, 44-5, 46, 94
Kelbie, Sheriff 18-19
Kilbrandon Report *9*, 21, 27, 31
   children's hearings 8, 10-11, 12, 13
   justice and welfare 94
   partnership with parents 33
Kynoch, George, MP 50

Labour Party, European Convention on Human Rights 37
Lang, Rt. Hon. Ian 87
Law Commission, report on child custody, guardianship and wardship (1988) 15

Law Society's Children Panel 123
legal aid 90, 91, 145
leisure and recreation services 74
Lindsay, Earl of 92
local authorities
    and CCT 3-4
    child protection 95-6, 126
    child religion/race/culture 119, 121, 122
    child welfare 122
    'children in need' 70-4, 75, 77, 99, *100*,
        101-3, 105
    children's services plans 78-80, 82, 106,
        107
    choices in service delivery 147
    'contract culture' 131, 136
    decentralisation 4, 71, 135
    duties 31, 91
    duties and powers 68, 69, 97
    exclusion of alleged abuser 125
    implementation of Act 128
    information provision 90, 111, 147
    inter-agency collaboration 82-3, 84, 85,
        106, 134-5
    parental contact with children 111-12
    partnership with parents 85-6
    reform of 3, 4-5, 6, 14, 21, 50, 130, 131,
        137
    and Skinner Report 23
    social services provision 12
    young offenders 124
    see also social work departments
Local Enterprise Companies 135
Local Government etc. (Wales) Act 1994
    106
Local Government Information Unit 108
Local Government (Scotland) Act 1994 4-5,
    130
London Boroughs 103, 112
Lord Chancellor's Department 122

Macaulay of Bragar, Lord 61
McKelvey, William, MP 53
Major, John (Prime Minister) 52
Mar and Kellie, Earl of 64
Marshall, Kathleen 59
medical examination/treatment, child
    consent to 90, 117
Mental Health (Scotland) Act 1984 72
'minimum intervention' 85
Mitchell, Sheriff 94, 95
Moray Council, contracting out services
    131
Munich, 'children's advisers' 149

NACRO (National Association for Care
    and Resettlement of Offenders) 49
National Children's Bureau 106, 109
National Commission of Inquiry into the
    Prevention of Child Abuse (NIPC) 115
National Health Services and Community
    Care Act 1990 84
National Lottery 130-1
NCH Action for Children Scotland 131
Nicholls, Lord 126
'non-intervention' 85, 86, 87, 113
non-residential care 19-20
Northern Ireland
    adoption rules 118-19
    'children in need' 99, *100*, 103-4, 109
    children's services 5-6, 109
    see also Children (NI) Order 1995

Oldham Social Services Department 103
'one-stop assessment' 75-6
Orkney
    Council 4
    Inquiry 17-19, 20, 26, 39, 67, 116, 145,
        185-90
    Social Work Department (SWD) 17, 18
    see also Clyde Report

parents
    and adoption 14, 23-4
    child protection 112-13, 124
    and children's hearings 41-2, 144
    and children's rights 40-1
    children's rights to sue 90
    'custody' and 'access' 114
    information to 110-11
    partnership with 33-6, 85-7, 110-14,
        138-9
    responsibilities 1, 24-5, 26, 85-7
    responsibilities and rights 69, 113-14
    rights 32, 44, 91, 142-3, 145
    rights in education 3, 144
    rights to access children in care 15, 42
    separation/divorce 78, 86-7
    and 'voluntary care' 111-12
Parents' Charter for Scottish education 3
Parliament, process in 6, 7, 48-67, *54*
'Peace Programme' (Northern Ireland) 104
Place of Safety Orders (PSOs) 18, 34, 35,
    39, 42-3, 45, 69, 113, 144
police 33, 106, 135
press, and children's hearings 40, 89
Principal Reporter 4, 82
probation service 106

qualitative assessments 81

race/culture 1, 87, 141, 147
    and child welfare 38
    'children in need' 72-3, 99, 103, 120-1,
        133
    children's services plans 81
    rights to identity 119-20
    UK comparisons 122
    use of voluntary agencies 137
rate-capping 4
referrals: children's hearings 13, 18, 20, 21,
    30, 38, 42, 71, 93, 94
religion
    'children in need' 72, 97, 99, 133
    children's rights 1, 87, 119, 120, 121,
        122, 141, 147
    in Northern Ireland 6
Reporters 9, 11, 12, 13, 79
    administration of 4
    and child justice 94-5
    and Child Protection Orders (CPOs) 93
    Fife policies 20, 21, 30
    Place of Safety Orders (PSOs) 34
    role and function 21-2
    training and inspection 8, 21, 46
residential care 19, 27, 78, 104, 143
    children's views on 40, 117
    reports (1992) 2, 8-9, 22-3, 39
    see also 'voluntary care'
respite services 30, 103
Review of Scottish Child Care Law 1, 8, 9, 16-
    17, 27, 30-1, 39, 149, 181-4
    'general welfare duty' 30
    parental involvement 34-5
    parental rights 42
Robertson, George, MP 60, 61
Robertson, Raymond, MP 66
Royal Scottish Society for the Prevention
    of Cruelty to Children (RSSPCC) 18
    see also Children 1st

'safe refuges' 41, 69, 71, 78, 90, 127, 147
'safeguarders' 36, 38, 39, 40, 90-1, 115,
    116, 145
Saltoun, Lady 50
school exclusion 23, 101, 104, 132, 134,
    142
The Scotsman 52
Scottish APPG for Children 50, 51-2, 53,
    55, 66
Scottish Child Law Centre 53, 68, 90, 145
Scottish Children's Reporter Administration
    4

Scottish Grand Committee 51-2, 53, 58,
    66, 67
Scottish Labour Party 55, 58
Scottish Law Commission (SLC): Family
    Law Report 2, 9, 24-5, 35, 36, 57-62, 89,
    114, 121
Scottish Office 128, 129, 132
Scottish Rules Council 129
Sheriff Principal 95
Sheriffs
    child protection 41, 124, 125, 145
    Child Protection Orders (CPOs) 40, 45,
        92-6, 93
    children's hearing system 13
    exclusion of alleged abuser 40, 55
    Place of Safety Orders (PSOs) 34, 43
Sheriffs Substitute Association 11
Shetland 4
'Short Report' 15, 99
Skinner Report on residential care (SWSI
    1992) 2, 8-9, 9, 22-3
Slovenia, children's Parliament 149
social security 99-100, 148
social service departments (SSDs) 101, 102,
    103, 104, 105-6, 107-8
Social Services Inspectorate (SSI) 83, 102-3,
    106, 107, 108, 110, 111
Social Services (NI) Order 1993 5
social work
    criticisms of 1980s reports 15-16
    local government reorganisation 5
    role of social workers 137-8
    terminology 2 & n.1
social work departments
    children's hearing system 12, 13
    Fife SWD 19-21, 30, 39
    inter-agency collaboration 31-3
    local government reorganisation 14
    Orkney SWD 17, 18
    unified departments created 8
Social Work (Scotland) Act 1968 1, 6, 9,
    11-14, 16, 29, 30, 35, 62, 94, 132
    amendment: child representation 36
    child protection 26, 31, 34
    'children in need' 70
    children's services 78
    child's religious persuasion 87
    as foundation 8, 27
    intervention in families 34
    Parliamentary process 48
Social Work Services Group (SWSG) 16, 17
    adoption law 23-4
    'children in need' 70, 72, 73, 133
    Fife policies 20
    Reporters 21
    see also White Papers (Scotland's Children)

Social Work Services Inspectorate (SWSI) report on residential care *see* Skinner Report
South Ayrshire 17, 93
special educational needs 75, 76, 77, 84
'Specific Issues Order' 74
Stirling Council 5

targeting of services 6, 29-31, 47, 69, 98, 133-4
time delays, and child welfare 122-3
Tower Hamlets, London Borough of 103
trade unions 9, 22
truanting 32

UK APPG for Children 49-50
unitary local authorities 4, 5, 6
United Kingdom
  child involvement 149
  children's rights 37
  comparisons across 98-128
  and UN Convention 148
  see also Children Act 1989
United Nations Convention on the Rights of the Child 37-8, 39, 46, 140-3, 160-80
  child legal representation 41, 145
  children's views 57, 67, 142-3
  corporal punishment 60, 141
  ratification by UK 1, 37, 48-9, 148-9
  rights unacknowledged by 40
  welfare test 87-8
unmet needs 76-7, 81
Urban Aid 131

voluntary agencies 90, 106, 136-8
'voluntary care' 14, 30, 34-5, 37, 111-12
  see also residential care

voluntary organisations 12, 32-3, 82-3, 107, 130-1, 135

Wales 15, 16, 80, 106
  Children Act 1975 36
  juvenile justice 14
  local government 4, 5, 6
  social service departments (SSDs) 101, 102
  unmet need 77
  see also Children Act 1989
Walker, Bill, MP 59
Wallace, Jim, MP 50, 56
welfare test 87-8
'welfare versus justice' 6, 41-6, 92-7, 98, 123-4, 145
Western Isles 4
White Papers
  Scotland's Children 2, *9*, 25-6, 30, 31, 92
    children's hearings 45-7
    children's rights 40, 74
    exclusion of alleged abuser 55
    home supervision contracts 138
    inter-agency collaboration 32, 33, 84, 85
    Parliamentary process of Bill 50, 51, 58
    partnership with parents 35, 36
    safeguarders 90
  Social Services (Department of Health and Welsh Office) 109-10
  Social Work and the Community 9, 12, 13
  The Law on Child Care and Family Services 15
Who Cares? Scotland 22, 50, 55, 56, 57, 67, 143

Published by The Stationery Office Limited and available from:

The Stationery Office Bookshops
71 Lothian Road, Edinburgh EH3 9AZ
(counter service only)
59–60 Holborn Viaduct, London EC1A 2FD
(counter service and fax orders only)
Fax 0171-831 1326
68-69 Bull Street, Birmingham B4 6AD
0121-236 9696 Fax 0121-236 9699
33 Wine Street, Bristol BS1 2BQ
0117-926 4306 Fax 0117-929 4515
9-21 Princess Street, Manchester M60 8AS
0161-834 7201 Fax 0161-833 0634
16 Arthur Street, Belfast BT1 4GD
01232 238451 Fax 01232 235401
The Stationery Office Oriel Bookshop
The Friary, Cardiff CF1 4AA
01222 395548 Fax 01222 384347

The Stationery Office publications are also available from:

The Publications Centre
(mail, telephone and fax orders only)
PO Box 276, London SW8 5DT
General enquiries 0171-873 0011
Telephone orders 0171-873 9090
Fax orders 0171-873 8200

Accredited Agents
(see Yellow Pages)

and through good booksellers

Printed in Scotland for The Stationery Office Limited J24772, C10, CCN 003808 11/97